Mahatma Gandhi and Buddha's Path to Enlightenment

Other Theosophy Trust Books

The Voice of the Silence
by H.P. Blavatsky

The Yoga Sutras of Patanjali
by Raghavan Iyer

Meditation and Self-Study
Essays on the Spiritual Life
by Raghavan Iyer

The Origins of Self-Consciousness
in *The Secret Doctrine*
by H.P. Blavatsky

Wisdom in Action
Essays on the Spiritual Life
by Raghavan Iyer

The Dawning of Wisdom
Essays on Walking the Path
by Raghavan Iyer

Teachers of the Eternal Doctrine
From Tsong-Ka-Pa to Nostradamus
by Elton Hall

Symbols of the Eternal Doctrine
From Shamballa to Paradise
by Helen Valborg

The Key to Theosophy
An Exposition of the Ethics, Science, and Philosophy
by H. P. Blavatsky

Evolution and Intelligent Design
in *The Secret Doctrine*
by H.P. Blavatsky
Compiled by the Editorial Board of Theosophy Trust

Mahatma Gandhi and Buddha's Path to Enlightenment

BY RAGHAVAN IYER

COMPILED BY
THE EDITORIAL BOARD OF THEOSOPHY TRUST

THEOSOPHY TRUST BOOKS
WASHINGTON, D.C.

Mahatma Gandhi and Buddha's Path to Enlightenment

Copyright © November 17, 2014 by Theosophy Trust

All rights reserved. No part of this book may be used or reproduced by any means - graphic, electronic, or mechanical - including photocopying, recording, taping or by any information storage retrieval system without the written permission of the publisher, except in the case of brief quotations embodied in critical articles and reviews.

Theosophy Trust books may be ordered through Amazon.com, CreateSpace.com, and other retail outlets, or by visiting:

http://www.theosophytrust.org/online_books.php

ISBN-13: 978-0-9916182-2-4
ISBN-10: 0-9916182-2-X

Library of Congress Control Number 2014941137

Printed in the United States of America

DEDICATION

Dedicated to all who seek to purify themselves through that mental devotion and skill in action which are the hallmark of the Fraternity of *Buddhas* and *Bodhisattvas*.

Gandhi, like Gautama, did not try to escape the evident truth of human suffering through seeking mindless oblivion or neurotic distractions, nor did he choose to come to terms with it through compensatory spiritual ambition or conventional religious piety. Rejecting the route of cloistered monasticism, he pondered deeply and agonizingly upon the human condition, and sought to find the redemptive function and therapeutic meaning of human misery. Translating his painful insights into daily acts of *tapas* – self-chosen spiritual exercises and the repeated re-enactments of lifelong meditation in the midst of fervent social activity – he came to see the need for a continual rediscovery of the purpose of living by all those who reject the hypnosis of bourgeois society, with its sanctimonious hypocrisy and notorious 'double standards' for individual and public life.

The Gandhian Bridge Between Heaven and Earth
Hermes, January 1988
Raghavan Iyer

CONTENTS

INTRODUCTION i
TRUTH AND NON-VIOLENCE 1
THE GANDHIAN BRIDGE BETWEEN HEAVEN AND EARTH 16
GANDHIAN SOCIALISM: The Constructive Programme 28
GANDHIAN SOCIALISM Isms and Individuals 40
NON-VIOLENT RESISTANCE AND SOCIAL TRANSFORMATION: SATYAGRAHA 50
NON-VIOLENT RESISTANCE AND SOCIAL TRANSFORMATION: SWARAJ AND SARVODAYA 59
GANDHIAN TRUSTEESHIP IN THEORY AND PRACTICE The Art of Renunciation 68
GANDHIAN TRUSTEESHIP IN THEORY AND PRACTICE Regeneration and Rebirth 78
BUDDHI YOGA AND SVADHARMA 88
CIVILIZATION, POLITICS AND RELIGION 101
SAT AND SATTVA 113
TRUTH 125
LOVE 134
THE SEVEN DEADLY SINS I. The Historical Context 141
THE SEVEN DEADLY SINS II. Sin and Violence 152
THE SEVEN DEADLY SINS III. Non-Violence and Regeneration 162
THE SOUL OF TIBET 173

ENLIGHTENMENT 185

BUDDHA AND THE PATH TO ENLIGHTENMENT I.
Renunciation and Enlightenment 196

BUDDHA AND THE PATH TO ENLIGHTENMENT II.
The Message of Buddha 206

BUDDHA AND THE PATH TO ENLIGHTENMENT III.
The *Dharma* and the *Sangha* 218

BUDDHA AND THE PATH TO ENLIGHTENMENT IV.
The *Dhammapada* and the *Udanavarga* 235

THE DIAMOND SUTRA 246

THE FLUTE OF KRISHNA 252

THE FIRE OF SELFHOOD 259

THE SEVENTH IMPULSION: 1963–2000 272

THE VIGIL NIGHT OF HUMANITY 277

AQUARIAN CIVILIZATION 288

INDEX 303

INTRODUCTION

Students of Professor Raghavan Iyer – and there are many thousands scattered around the world – will need no further explanation regarding his *HERMES* essays on Mahatma Gandhi's thought and life other than noting that all of those remarkable essays are gathered together here in one place for the first time, along with his *HERMES* essays on *Buddha and the Path to Enlightenment*. As far we understand his intent, these articles were never meant to be an exhaustive explication of the thought of Gandhi, in the way in which it is treated in his *The Moral and Political Thought of Mahatma Gandhi* (MPTMG). Rather, the articles were meant to clarify the central concepts and ideals in Gandhi's thought and to deepen the understanding of students of Gandhi and the wider public about those concepts, which are the titles of the core articles in this work: *Truth and Non-Violence, Gandhian Socialism; Non-Violent Resistance and Social Transformation: Satyagraha, Swaraj and Sarvodaya; Gandhian Trusteeship in Theory and Practice; Buddhi Yoga and Svadharma; Civilization, Politics and Religion; Sat and Sattva; Truth; Love;* and *The Seven Deadly Sins*.

As the quotation near the front of this book makes clear, Mahatma Gandhi conducted a good deal of his adult life – his "experiments with truth" – very much in the tradition and the manner of Gautama Buddha. Gandhi took the foundation of Buddha's revelation – his First Noble Truth, that life is fraught with pain and suffering, from birth to death – and turned it inward in a unique and deeply creative manner. In his article, *The Gandhian Bridge Between Heaven and Earth* (in *Hermes*, January 1988) Prof. Iyer makes clear what should be an obvious connection to the student of Gandhi's life and thought, but is – remarkably – hardly noticed by many chroniclers of Gandhi. Even to the diligent student of Gandhi, this connection is difficult to grasp, as it is frequently understood only in an external sense. One can readily grasp that life brings suffering to every incarnated being, but it requires a profound revolution in consciousness to understand the necessity to actively choose suffering as a means of self-purification and the means by which an "enemy" might be purged of enmity, opposition, and violence.

This remarkable insight of Gandhi's seems to derive from his foundational concept of *svadharma*. "... there is for every human being a clear opportunity to accept or not accept that which one cannot alter. In that context, one may be said to choose one's *svadharma*." The idea that one can choose what one cannot alter is not fatalism. "Rather," in Prof. Iyer's words, "it is a critical assessment in consciousness of those elements in one's life which are innate. In the very act of understanding and in the attempt to give meaning to these initial parameters, one must develop and apply some understanding of the karmic field. Moreover, by understanding the karmic tendencies in one's own constitution and confronting one's likes and dislikes, one may come to sense something about one's lower nature and gain some understanding of one's possible behaviour in other lives." (*Buddhi Yoga and Svadharma*) Hence the role of choosing suffering plays an indispensable role in self-purification, as all such work revolves around ridding oneself of the *kleshas* (sources of affliction, delusion, and sorrow – ignorance, egoism, attachment, hate and the fear of death) that one has produced through ignorance in previous lives.

Gandhi exemplified the life of the *karma yogin*, one who works toward spiritual perfection in the precise performance of one's self-chosen duty, or *svadharma*. As a devoted student of the *Bhagavad-Gita*, Gandhi was aware of the fundamental importance of the right performance of duty in the battle portrayed in that text, that (in Prof. Iyer's words) "the whole of the *Gita* is a summons and challenge to engage in that righteous warfare which every human soul must undertake. In the eighteenth chapter of the *Gita*, Lord Krishna declares that if one will not voluntarily choose to engage in this righteous war, karmic necessity will compel one to do so. The wise are those who cooperate with cosmic necessity, with their own divine destiny, with their own sacrosanct duty or *svadharma*. The wisest are those who choose as firmly and as early as possible, making an irreversible and unconditional commitment, in the gracious manner and generous spirit of Lord Krishna. Without doubt or hesitation, they choose His path, His teaching and His prescribed mode of skill in action."

In these essays, Prof. Iyer returns again and again to a central theme found in many of his writings, that the recognition of those Beings who have far transcended the neophyte stages of *Buddhi Yoga* is a powerful purifier for the minds and hearts of the neophyte, that there are men and women who are perfected in the power of *Buddhi Yoga*, ceaselessly ideating and meditating, yoked to the good of the whole of Humanity. These beings comprise the sacred Fraternity of *Buddhas* and *Bodhisattvas*, who exemplify above all else perfection in mental devotion and skill in action. The sacrificial work of these beings makes it possible for those caught in the realm of *Samsara* to purify themselves. Like the Himalayas, they are immovable in relation to their devotion to the Self of All.

Editor, Theosophy Trust

NOTES: *MPTMG* was first published by Oxford University Press in 1973 and is still available from amazon.com.

All of the articles in this volume can be found at http://www.theosophytrust.org/ under the heading *The Lead Articles*.

TRUTH AND NON-VIOLENCE

The ethical potency of Gandhian thought was grounded in moral clarity and metaphysical simplicity. Without succumbing to either the illusion of infallibility or the delusion of indispensability, Gandhi sought to achieve a balance of intellect and intuition, warning his followers against both rationalization of weakness and erratic emotionalism. Again and again he found that the powerful combination of faith and experience, pure reason and daily application, was both self-transforming and infectious, and he felt that his own life vindicated its strength. Spurning all Manichaean tendencies as snares, he deepened his conviction that God is formless and utterly beyond formulation. Individual integration and self-transcendence, he thought, can be achieved through considering and consolidating the close connection between truth and non-violence, *satya* and *ahimsa*. His unassailable belief that the conceptual foundation of his ethics was strong and sound – though he would refine his insights whenever his daily experience required him to do so – enabled him to find flexibility amid constancy.

Gandhi was a practical idealist. Untrammeled by the dead weight of convention, he was equally unconcerned with formal consistency. As a *karma yogin*, he had neither the time nor the aptitude for constructing a systematic philosophy. Instead, he discerned archetypal patterns and eternal possibilities for growth in the shifting conditions of human interaction. "Men are good," he wrote, "but they are poor victims making themselves miserable under the false belief that they are doing good."[1] To overcome the false basis of thought and action, human beings must learn to question themselves and others, for, said Gandhi, "we are all bound to do what we feel is right". In translating his metaphysical assumptions into ethical principles, Gandhi always

---

[1] M.K. Gandhi, "Letter to A.H. West", *The Collected Works of Mahatma Gandhi*, K. Swaminathan, ed., Navajivan (Ahmedabad, 1958–1984), vol. 10, p. 127 (hereafter cited as *CWMG*); reprinted in *The Moral and Political Writings of Mahatma Gandhi*, Raghavan Iyer, ed., Clarendon (Oxford, 1986–1987), vol. 2, p.16 (hereafter cited as *MPWMG*).

pointed to the basic impulses that underlie all action. Holding that there is a universal human nature which mirrors the Divine and may best be characterized as pure potential, he found it natural to use his own life as a crucible in which to test his principles and precepts. He felt that the extreme burden of expectation which the masses thrust upon him expressed the yearning of men and women for a freedom and self-reliance they could sense but seldom experienced. Conscious of his own limitations, he in turn drew strength from the latent goodness of the untutored peasants he sought to help.

Gandhi held that intelligent submission to the laws of cosmic interdependence and natural harmony would result in enduring fulfilment of one's true being. "Has an ocean drop an individuality of its own as apart from the ocean? Then a liberated soul has an individuality of its own." For Gandhi, this hoary metaphor enshrined the key to the metaphysical problem of the individual and the whole, and to what Plato formulated as the problem of the One and the many: "I do believe that complete annihilation of one's self-individuality, sensuality, personality – whatever you call it, is an absolute condition of perfect joy and peace." [2] However bestial in origin, man is human because he is potentially and essentially divine. Any pattern of thought, direction of energy or line of action hostile to that primordial unity leads eventually to frustration and misery; those acts in tune with it will initiate a happy, if sometimes unanticipated, outcome. Thus the individual who would be truly human must reduce himself to a zero in the eyes of the world. Then he can mirror infinitude in his heart and in his life.

Any feasible conception of human nature, Gandhi felt, must allow for the heights as well as the depths of human attainment and longing. *Satya* and *ahimsa*, truth and non-violence, were the two ultimate and universal principles he used to clarify the chaos of sense-impressions and conflicting desires. Human beings are, at heart, amenable to moral persuasion. Any compelling moral appeal must, therefore, be addressed to the human soul, not to the assemblage of habits and traits that make up the separative personality. A constant awareness of the primacy and supremacy of Truth *(sat)* frees one from needless over-

---

[2] M.K. Gandhi, A Letter, *CWMG*, vol. 29, pp. 397–398; *MPWMG*, vol. 2, p. 20.

assertion or violent appropriation of any partial or particular truths. "My *anekantavada* [belief in the manyness of reality] is the result of the twin doctrine of *satya* and *ahimsa*." [3]

Gandhi castigated much in modern civilization because it withers human dignity and impedes moral growth. It establishes a social structure based on the law of the jungle, a tense and competitive rat race relieved only by spasms of furtive self-indulgence. If the salty drop cannot exist without the ocean, the ocean itself has no existence independent of its myriad drops. Using another metaphor, Gandhi wrote that "we are all sparks of the divine and, therefore, partake of its nature, and since there can be no such thing as self-indulgence with the divine, it must of necessity be foreign to human nature". [4] The process of igniting the spark must, therefore, begin within individual consciousness, then spread among the masses, before ultimately transforming the entire social order. To effect such a change, the questions which the mentally lazy and morally cowardly set aside as irrelevant must be honestly confronted. Inverted notions must be corrected. And fundamental issues – the scope of self-consciousness, the purpose of life, the role of the individual – must be considered and reconsidered.

For Gandhi, one central truth becomes the starting-point for all such enquiries. "The purpose of life is undoubtedly to know oneself. We cannot do it unless we learn to identify ourselves with all that lives. The sum total of that life is God." [5] Though individual perfection may be distant, human perfectibility is omnipresent. "To say that perfection is not attainable on this earth is to deny God.... Life to me would lose all its interest if I felt that I *could* not attain perfect love on earth." [6] The permanent possibility of perfection can be translated into a continuous expansion of love and truth as embodied in selfless service. Nonetheless, the gap between the elusive ideal and an existing reality

---

[3] M.K. Gandhi, "Three Vital Questions", *Young India,* Jan. 21, 1926; *MPWMG*, vol.2, p. 23.

[4] M.K. Gandhi, A Letter, *CWMG*, vol. 69, p. 231; *MPWMG*, vol. 2, pp. 27–28.

[5] M.K. Gandhi, A Letter, *CWMG*, vol. 50, p. 80; *MPWMG*, vol. 2, p. 28.

[6] M.K. Gandhi, "Letter to Esther Faering", *CWMG*, vol.14, p. 176; *MPWMG*, vol. 2, p. 36.

will inevitably distort one's understanding of individual perfection. Each individual must constantly rethink and renew his sense of the relation between ideal and reality. He must contemplate these matters with a faith that is beyond knowledge, but not incompatible with reason. "Faith is not a thing to grasp, it is a state to grow to",[7] and "the fact is that perfection is attained through service".[8] Firm faith prompts selfless service, as selfless service preserves firm faith. Such is the time-honoured pathway to individual perfection and universal enlightenment.

Faith is not itself to blame if some who profess religious faith prove corrupt. In men of great intellect, mental agility can sometimes obscure the intuitions of the heart. Only when the intellect is in harmony with the heart can it be rescued from the tyranny of egotism and enlisted in the service of humanity. But the process of purification is arduous indeed. For even if self-centeredness and hostility are transcended, irrational fears and doubts, tensions and pressures, may remain.

The moral culture of man must begin, then, not with an external improvement of morals, but with a basic transformation of the mind, a systematic training of the will. Only sustained *tapas* – self-suffering – is permanently purifying. Prolonged suffering is therapeutic only when undertaken for the sake of all and for Truth. "Progress is to be measured by the amount of suffering undergone by the sufferer."[9] Suffering for the truth facilitates self-knowledge; in addition, it may subtly heal the individual and those around him. Whilst Gandhi saw no reason to assume a linear historical process of collective ascent, his view of *tapas* as a foreshadowing of *moksha* or emancipation, and his conviction that the human spirit is one with the divine, fortified his optimism. "Only an atheist can be a pessimist."[10] By optimism, he meant not that everything will invariably augment the happiness of every person, but that all moral strivings will ultimately find their fruition.

---

[7] M.K. Gandhi, A Letter, *CWMG*, Vol. 61, p. 28; *MPWMG*, Vol. 2, p. 34.

[8] M.K. Gandhi, "Letter to K. Santanam", *CWMG*, vol. 30, p.180; *MPWMG*, vol. 2, p. 38.

[9] M.K. Gandhi, "The Law of Suffering", *Young India*, June 16, 1920; *MPWMG*, vol.2, p. 41.

[10] M.K. Gandhi, "Optimism", *Navajivan*, Oct. 23, 1921; *MPWMG*, vol. 2, p. 45.

Since individuals can intuit ethical principles when the veil of forgetfulness and fear is lifted, and since the patient application of principles is strengthened by self-correction, no one needs to be taught what is right. Nor does anyone need to be shown the practice of self-examination. Instead, everyone must be encouraged to exemplify what he or she knows to be right. True religion is identified by moral vigour and contagious example, not by theological sophistry or hortatory skill. Gandhi constantly shattered the hypnotic spell cast by sanctimonious beliefs in collusion with hypocritical practices. He knew that mere moralism cannot redeem a materialistic social structure estranged from the rhythms of Nature or an economic framework which fosters greed and exploitation. "Is it not most tragic", Gandhi lamented, "that things of the spirit, eternal verities, should be regarded as utopian by our youth, and transitory makeshifts alone appeal to them as practical?" [11] The penetrating clarity of W.M. Salter's *Ethical Religion* spoke to Gandhi's heart, and he paraphrased eight of its chapters in Gujarati. He strongly endorsed Salter's reasoned conviction that an ethical idea is useless unless put into practice, even though right action may not always be recognized or repaid. Fidelity to conscience, however, needs no public approval; it is its own reward.

However strong the moral impulse in men and women, living in the world seems to demand intolerable yet inescapable compromises. In response, Gandhi advised all social reformers to assume responsibilities willingly, accept the limitations they involve, and trust in Truth, which is God. "As the sea makes no distinction between good rivers and bad, but purifies all, so one person, whose heart is purified and enlarged with non-violence and truth, can contain everything in that heart and it will not overflow or lose its serenity." [12] Divine discontent and a natural longing for *moksha* or emancipation should not be distorted into selfish salvationism or crafty escapism. Liberation from the bonds of conditioned existence admits of no short-cut or escape-route, but comes unsought from assiduous perseverance in *dharma*, the path of duty. For Gandhi, *dharma* has no more to do with

---

[11] M.K. Gandhi, "Academic v. Practical", *Young India*, Nov. 14, 1929; *MPWMG*, vol. 2, p. 25.
[12] M.K. Gandhi, "Letter to Gangabehn Vaidya", *CWMG*, vol. 35, p. 220; *MPWMG*, vol. 2, p. 71.

ritual or convention than true religion has to do with church-going or temple-worship. *Dharma* is nothing less than progressive concern for *lokasangraha*, the welfare of the world. Just as self-realization depends upon self-conquest, so both must be cherished in terms of their contribution to the common good. *Dharma* is to be ceaselessly discovered. Its avenues are self-chosen.

Gandhi drew a firm distinction between ultimate values, which must be impervious to concessions or compromises, and concrete applications, which derive from patient efforts to discern meaning and truth within the flux of events. "You may have faith in the principles which I lay down," he wrote, "but the conclusions which I draw from certain facts cannot be a matter of faith." [13] This elusive ideal is interpreted differently by each individual. But it is always true that *dharma* lies, not in securing uniformity of conception, but in striving for the ideal without allowing its remoteness to tempt one into shrinking or twisting it. Under all circumstances, "the striving should be conscious, deliberate and hard." [14] Self-discipline is not a matter of technique; it must become a way of life. Moreover, the temptation to compromise grows stronger as it becomes subtler. "Man's ideal grows from day to day and that is why it ever recedes from him." [15] Since true knowledge and free action consist in conformity with an order which is prior to human action, Gandhi felt that man's moral stature depended on a constant readiness to hold certain values as sacred and absolute. At first, one must relinquish everything that distracts one from the universally valid ethical order. One must free oneself from passion and prejudice, from whatever bears the stamp of the conditioned personality and the circumscribed environment. To think and live universally – the height of true individuation – necessitates a purificatory discipline. Such discipline, at any level, can best be undertaken with the help of a binding oath.

Such a vow is not merely a promise to oneself to do the best one can,

---

[13] M.K. Gandhi, "Letter to Mathuradas", *CWMG*, vol. 38, pp. 216–217; *MPWMG*, vol. 2, p. 87.
[14] M.K. Gandhi, "Discussion with Teachers", *Harijan*, Sept. 5, 1936; *MPWMG*, vol.2, p. 91.
[15] M.K. Gandhi, "Letter to Gangabehn Vaidya", *CWMG*, vol. 63, p. 451; *MPWMG*, vol. 2, p. 88.

for any conditionality betrays a lack of self-confidence as well as a shallow conception of human potential. "If we resolve to do a thing, and are ready to sacrifice our lives in the process," wrote Gandhi, "we are said to have taken a vow." [16] The assumption of unconditional vows acknowledges lapses, but provides criteria and incentives for growth. It is far better to fail and to learn, Gandhi thought, than to live with so much moral ambiguity that growth becomes impossible. "A life without vows is like a ship without anchor or like an edifice that is built on slip-sand instead of a solid rock." [17] With the aid of vows, *tapas* becomes more catalytic than mere suffering. It is transformed into creative self-restraint and therapeutic self-sacrifice; it purifies consciousness and clarifies vision. Vows can help to induce self-knowledge and enhance self-transcendence. They can spur one to refine *dharma*, to discharge one's duties with skill and timeliness, and to hold true to a programme of progressive self-reform.

For Gandhi, the English term 'vow' carried with it all the meanings of the original Sanskrit terms *vrata* (a solemn resolve or a spiritual decision) and *yama* (a spiritual exercise or a self-imposed restraint). In its oldest meaning, *vrata* refers to a divine will or command, which establishes and preserves the order of the universe. Since this divine nature is inseparable from essential human nature, individuals can, through their vows, reflect cosmic order by deliberate and vigilant performance of *dharma*. Gandhi did not set limits to the degree of moral development and spiritual resolve of which any person is capable. Taking vows beyond one's capacity betrays thoughtlessness and lack of balance; the essential value of a vow lies in a calm determination to hold to it regardless of all difficulties. By holding the vow intact within one's heart, the energies of the soul may be released, transforming one's nature.

Conscience remains a potential force in every human being, but in all too many it remains half asleep. "Conscience has to be awakened" through the power of a vow. Emotions which are stimulated by

---

[16] M.K. Gandhi, "Importance of Vows", *Indian Opinion*, Oct. 8, 1913; *MPWMG*, vol.2, p. 92.
[17] M.K. Gandhi, "The Efficacy of Vows", *Young India*, Aug. 22, 1929; *MPWMG*, vol.2, p. 102.

unconscious social and environmental pressures cannot count as conscience. Indeed, a person who has not consciously sought to strengthen and sharpen conscience cannot be said to possess one." [18] "Youngsters as a rule must not pretend to have conscience. It is a quality or state acquired by laborious training. Wilfulness is not conscience.... Conscience can reside only in a delicately tuned breast." [19] Conscience is, moreover, the single strongest force against the degradation of human dignity; once man is stripped of conscience and reduced to a mechanical aggregate of perfunctory acts, he becomes an object rather than a subject, a passive instrument rather than an intrinsic end. By casting the cultivation of conscience in terms of vows, Gandhi sought to socialize the individual conscience rather than internalize the social conscience. At once compelling and self-validating, the awakened conscience is an inner voice, the voice of God or Truth. The veracity of such an inner voice can be confirmed only by direct experience resulting from training in *tapas*; indirect evidence, however, can be seen in the inner consistency and transparent integrity of a Socrates or Gandhi. A well-nurtured conscience results in heroism, humility and high saintliness. Such virtues are the ripe fruit of *tapascharya* a consecrated life of austere yet unanxious commitment.

Heroism is a quality of the heart, free of every trace of fear and anger, determined to exact instant atonement for every breach of honour. More than any rule-governed morality, heroism can enable a person to stand alone in times of trial and isolation. It can also establish a deep concord between like-minded men and women loyal to their conscience. But for Gandhi, the greatest obstacle to the incarnation of the heroic ideal in society is, paradoxically, the absence of humility. When human beings do not adequately recognize their fallibility, they will not make sufficient effort to arouse individual conscience. Foundering in a delusive sense of security, they are caught in a 'mobocratic' state of collective helplessness. Only after the heart is touched by the enormity of divine truth will the distance between the ideal and reality become painfully evident. And only then will genuine

---

[18] M.K. Gandhi, "Note to Gope Gurbuxani", *CWMG*, vol. 79, p. 206; *MPWMG*, vol.2, p. 128.
[19] M.K. Gandhi, "Under Conscience's Cover", *Young India*, Aug. 21, 1924; *MPWMG*, vol. 2, p. 125.

humility flow forth. Whilst heroism is cultivated skill in action *(karma yoga)*, humility is the virtue of effortlessness *(buddhi yoga)*.

> Humility cannot be an observance by itself. For it does not lend itself to being deliberately practised. It is, however, an indispensable test of *ahimsa*. In one who has *ahimsa* in him it becomes a part of his very nature.... Truth can be cultivated as well as love. But to cultivate humility is tantamount to cultivating hypocrisy. [20]

Gandhi's conception of human nature, social solidarity and historical promise compelled him to rethink constantly his ultimate principles. Throughout his life, he was convinced that God is Truth. But if *sat* or Truth is the essence of Deity, every relative truth is a reflection of God from some particular angle. Since every standpoint or perspective contains some kernel of truth, God is everywhere. In 1929 Gandhi subtly altered the emphasis by declaring not that "God is Truth", but that "Truth is God." This simple juxtaposition of equivalencies radically changed the questions Gandhi felt he had to ask and answer. One can always ask if a certain proposition is true, but one need not strain to prove the reality and pervasiveness of Truth. That one can ask the question, or even breathe, is proof enough. Further, Gandhi's formulation curbs the itch to anthropomorphize. It also clarifies the close relation between truth and love. If truth is corrupted, it ceases to be truth, even though corrupt love may still be love. When one obtains the assurance of truth, one's love is purged of consoling illusions. In metaphysical priority, one must say "Truth is God", then add "God is Love", and yet "the nearest approach to Truth is through love." [21] † Like Plato, Gandhi here distinguished between how one knows and how one learns. Fifteen years later he wrote: "I do not believe in a personal deity, but I believe in the Eternal Law of Truth and Love which I have translated as non-violence. This Law is not a dead thing like the law of

---

[20] M.K. Gandhi, "Letter to Narandas Gandhi", *CWMG*, vol. 44, p. 203; *MPWMG*, vol. 2, pp. 145–146.
[21] M.K. Gandhi, "Speech at Meeting in Lausanne", *CWMG*, vol. 48, p. 404; *MPWMG*, vol. 2, p. 165.

a king. It's a living thing – the Law and the Law-giver are one." [22]

Gandhi saw no sense in the claim that one must know all truths to adhere to Truth. One need merely follow the truth one knows, little or partial though it may be. The individual who would be faithful to what he knows and who aspires to greater wisdom will work to reduce himself to a cipher in his quest. For Gandhi, there can be no beauty and no art apart from truth. When one finds truth beautiful, one discovers true art. When one loves Truth, one expresses a true and unconditional love. The seeker must only be honest with himself and truthful to others. Where he cannot speak the truth without doing great harm, he may be silent, but Gandhi, like Kant, insisted he must never lie. The truth-seeker cannot be so concerned with his own safety or comfort that he abdicates from his larger duties. "He alone is a lover of truth who follows it in all conditions of life." [23] The virtues stressed by most religious and philosophical traditions cannot be dismissed by the genuine seeker of truth as alien or beyond his concern. He must, rather, synthesize these virtues in *ahimsa* or non-violence, the moving image and decisive test of truth. If all existence is a mirror of the divine, violence in any form is a blasphemous repudiation of Deity itself; if all souls are sparks of the divine, rooted in the transcendental Truth, all violence is a species of deicide.

Just as humility is the natural accompaniment of true heroism, *ahimsa* is the necessary correlate of fearlessness. In Gandhi's vision, the maintenance of moral stature and spiritual dignity must be based upon the practice of *ahimsa*. He conceived of *ahimsa* as an integral part of *yajna* or sacrifice, a concept rooted in the Indian conception of a beneficent cosmic order and a humane discipline requiring self-purification and self-examination. The moral force generated by *ahimsa* or non-violence was therefore held by Gandhi to be infinitely greater than any force founded upon selfishness. The essential power of non-violence was viewed alternatively by Gandhi as being 'soul-force' and 'truth-force'. The two terms are fundamentally equivalent, and differ only in their psychological or ontological emphasis. For Gandhi, *ahimsa*

---

[22] M.K. Gandhi, "Letter to Roy Walker", *CWMG*, vol. 77, p. 390; *MPWMG*, vol. 2, pp. 192–193.
[23] M.K. Gandhi, A Letter, *CWMG*, vol. 50, p. 76; *MPWMG*, vol. 2, p. 204.

represented not a denial of power but a renunciation of all forms of coercion and compulsion. He held in fact that *ahimsa* had a strength which no earthly power could continue to resist. Although Gandhi was noted for his advocacy of *ahimsa* in social and political arenas, its most fundamental and intimate use lay for him in the moral persuasion of free souls.

Just as Gandhi sometimes inflated the word *ahimsa* to encompass all virtues, he equally broadened the notion of *himsa* or violence to include all forms of deceit and injustice. *Himsa* proceeds from fear, which is the shadow of ignorant egotism. Its expulsion from the heart requires an act of faith which transcends the scope of analysis. Gandhi held, however, that just as intellect plays a large part in the worldly use of violence, so it plays an even larger part in the field of non-violence. The mind, guided by the heart, must purge all elements of egotism before it can embody *ahimsa*. Gandhi postulated that the willingness to kill exists in human beings in inverse proportion to their willingness to die. This must be understood in terms of *tanha* – the will to live – which is present to some degree in every human being and reinforces the concept of the separative ego. As that ego is illusory and transitory in nature, it has a necessary tendency to fear for its own future, and with that an inevitable propensity towards violence. Gandhi held that *ahimsa* could be taught and inculcated only by example, and never by force. Coercion, indeed, would itself contradict *ahimsa*. The roots of violence and *himsa* lie in the mind and heart, and therefore mere external restraint or abstention from violence cannot be considered true *ahimsa*. Gandhi chose the term *ahimsa* because *himsa* or violence is never wholly avoidable; the word *ahimsa* stresses that which is to be overcome. Whilst acknowledging that some violence can be found in every being, Gandhi could never concede that such violence was irreparable or irreducible. He held that those who begin by justifying force become addicted to it, while those who seek the practical reduction of *himsa* in their lives should be engaged in constant self-purification.

Ahimsa, in the widest sense, means a willingness to treat all beings as oneself. Thus *ahimsa* is the basis of *anasakti*, selfless action. It is equivalent to the realization of absolute Truth, and it is the goal towards which all true human beings move naturally, though unconsciously. *Ahimsa* cannot be realized alone; it has meaning only in the context of universal human interaction and uplift . Like truth, *ahimsa*, when genuine, carries conviction in every sphere. Unlike many forms of love, however, *ahimsa* is embodied by a truth-seeker not out of longing or lack, but out of a sense of universal obligation. It is only when one takes the vow of *ahimsa* that one has the capacity to assess apparent failures in terms of one's own moral inadequacies. *Ahimsa* means, at the very least, a refusal to do harm. "In its positive form, *ahimsa* means the largest love, the greatest charity." [24] * Gandhi's refusal to set different standards for saints and ordinary men, combined with his concern to give *ahimsa* a practical social function rather than a purely mystical use, led him to extend and employ the word in novel ways. The political strength which *ahimsa* can summon is greater and profounder than the impact of violence precisely because *ahimsa* is consubstantial with the immortal soul. Any programme of social or political reform, including civil disobedience, must, therefore, begin with the heroic individual, for only when such pioneers radiate the lustre of *ahimsa* will all humanity be uplift ed.

Anyone may practise non-violence in the absence of support and even in the face of hostility. Indeed, *ahimsa* in the midst of adversity becomes the sovereign means of self-purification and the truest road to self-knowledge. *Ahimsa* is the anti-entropic force in Nature and the indefeasible law of the human species. Just as unconditional commitment to Truth can lead to limited truth in action, so too the universal creed of *ahimsa* may yield an appropriate policy of non-violence. As a policy, non-violence is a mode of constructive political and social action, just as truth-seeking is the active aspect of Truth. Truth and non-violence are the integrated aspects of immutable soul-force. "Non-violence and truth together form, as it were, the right angle of all religions." [25]

One must be sure, however, not to believe conveniently in *ahimsa* as

---

[24] M.K. Gandhi, "On Ahimsa", *Modern Review*, Oct. 1916; *MPWMG*, vol. 2, p. 212.
[25] M.K. Gandhi, "Problems of Non-Violence", *Navajivan*, Aug. 9 1925; *MPWMG*, vol. 2, p. 218.

a policy, whilst doubting the creed. [26] Whether or not any specific policy is demonstrably effective, it is imperative to hold true to the creed. Gandhi distinguished, moreover, between policy and mere tactics. Some successful tactics might at times be inappropriate, but the policy itself continues to be apt. Gandhi marvelled at those who, conceding that his non-violent programme worked in the case of the British, insisted that it must inevitably fail against a Hitler or Mussolini. Such a view romanticized the benevolence of the British and altogether denied that tyrants are a part of the human species. Gandhi's own experience had shown him that the British could be utterly ruthless or devious, even though his firm faith forbade him from excluding anyone from the possibility of growth, change of heart and recognition of necessity. Something more reasonable than subtle racism would be required to challenge the universal relevance of *ahimsa*.

It is in the application of *ahimsa* to the issues of war and peace, however, that Gandhi's teachings can be seen to be uncompromising. Non-violence does not signify the unwillingness to fight against an enemy. But, he argued, the enemy is always ignorance and the evil which men do: it is not in human beings themselves. Even though he loathed war and violence in all its forms, Gandhi could not be classified as an orthodox pacifist. Indeed, he held that the courage and heroism often displayed by war-struck individuals reflected well upon their moral character, even if war itself was a dark moral blot on those who encouraged or allowed it to happen. For himself, he rejected indirect participation in war, and refused to let others fight his battles for him. "If I have only a choice between paying for the army of soldiers to kill my neighbours or to be a soldier myself, I would, as I must, consistently with my creed, enlist as a soldier in the hope of controlling the forces of violence and even of converting my comrades." [27]

Training for war demoralized and brutalized people, Gandhi

---

[26] See Raghavan Iyer, *The Moral and Political Thought of Mahatma Gandhi*, Oxford University Press (New York, 1973, 1978); second edition: Concord Grove Press (Santa Barbara, 1983), ch. 8.

[27] M.K. Gandhi, "Difficulty of Practice", *Young India*, Jan. 30, 1930; *MPWMG*, vol. 2, p. 394.

believed, and its after-effects brought nations down to abysmal levels of dissolution and discontent. He therefore strove to show how non-violence was the cleanest weapon against terrorism and torture. He asserted that the man who holds to a high sense of dignity and brotherhood, even to the point of death, confounds aggression and may even shame his attackers. Whilst insisting that non-violence was the only means for bringing to an end the familiar vicious cycles of revenge, he recognized that this required expert timing. Poor timing could lead through foolhardiness to a form of suicide or martyrdom, and Gandhi held that there was a higher truth in living for non-violence than in inadvertently dying in its name. Witnessing the course of warfare from the Boer War through the Second World War, he only strengthened his conviction in regard to the basic creed of non-violence. Indeed, when he heard of the bombing of Hiroshima, he declared, "Unless now the world adopts non-violence, it will spell certain suicide for mankind." [28] In a non-violent state, it should finally be possible to raise a non-violent army, which could resist armed invasion without recourse to arms. However distant such a prospect, Gandhi refused to relinquish it, for he knew that violent triumphs guarantee nothing but the brutalization of human beings and the perpetuation of further violence.

The individual who would strive to be fully human – to embody *satya* and *ahimsa* to the fullest possible extent – should not rely on others to display a moral courage which is the mature product of an inward transformation. Nonetheless, like-minded seekers and strivers can offer each other moral support and mutual encouragement. If the political life of any nation is to be spiritualized, the process must begin in intentional communities. Gandhi's *ashrams* were such pioneering attempts – small communities committed to embodying the principles they upheld. Chief amongst these principles were the vows of *satya* and *ahimsa*. Self-restraint and purification involved mental, verbal and physical continence, control of the palate, and the vows of non-possession and fearlessness. Also essential were non-thieving, in the broadest sense of the concept, and the vow of *swadeshi*, self-reliance.

---

[28] M.K. Gandhi, "Talk with an English Journalist", *Harijan*, Sept. 29, 1946; *MPWMG*, vol. 2, p. 455.

The strength of the *ashram* lay not so much in the establishment of detailed rules for living as in the conscious effort to exemplify a shared perspective and to conduct "experiments with truth".

The *ashram* may be seen as a sphere of fellowship in which one can test oneself, taking truth one step beyond oneself. *Anasakti* could be nurtured, errors corrected, solutions tried, *tapas* magnified. The fortunate could discover that "the secret of happy life lies in renunciation". [29] For Gandhi, the *ashram* was a microcosm which might come to mirror the full potential of the macrocosm, a minute drop that reflects the shimmering sea. The progressive renunciation of puny selfhood could, he felt, open minds and hearts to the Self of all humanity. Embracing the globe, Gandhi's hopes were addressed not only to his own generation but also to all posterity.

> It remains for those therefore who like myself hold this view of renunciation to discover for themselves how far the principle of *ahimsa* is compatible with life in the body and how it can be applied to acts of everyday life. The very virtue of a *dharma* is that it is universal, that its practice is not the monopoly of the few, but must be the privilege of all. And it is my firm belief that the scope of truth and *ahimsa* is world-wide. That is why I find an ineffable joy in dedicating my life to researches in truth and *ahimsa* and I invite others to share it with me by doing likewise. [30]

Hermes, March 1988

---

[29] M.K. Gandhi, "Living up to 125", *Harijan*, Feb. 24, 1946; *MPWMG*, vol. 2, p. 637.
[30] M.K. Gandhi, "Jain Ahimsa", *Young India*, Oct. 25, 1928; *MPWMG*, vol. 2, p. 224.

THE GANDHIAN BRIDGE BETWEEN HEAVEN AND EARTH

The Angels keep thou ancient places;
Turn but a stone, and start a wing!
'Tis ye, 'tis your estrangèd faces,
That miss the many-splendoured thing.
But (when so sad thou canst not sadder)
Cry; – and upon thy so sore loss
Shall shine the traffic of Jacob's ladder
Pitched betwixt Heaven and Charing Cross.
                              Francis Thompson

My heart has become capable of every form;
It is a pasture for gazelles and a convent for Christian monks,
And a temple for idols and the pilgrim's Ka'ba
And the tables for the Torah and the book of the Quran.
I follow the religion of Love: whatever way
Love's camels take, that is my religion and my faith.
                              Ibn al-'Arabi

Selfless service is the secret of life.
                              Mahatma Gandhi

Mahatma Gandhi held that all human beings are always responsible to themselves, the entire Family of Man and to God, or Truth (*SAT*) for their continual use of all the goods, gifts and talents that fall within their domain. This is necessarily true because of his basic assumption that Nature and Man are alike upheld, suffused and regenerated by the Divine. There is a luminous spark of divine intelligence in the action of each atom and in the eyes of every man, woman and child upon this earth. This is the enduring basis of effective self-regeneration at all levels – individual, social, national and global. We fully incarnate our latent divinity when we deliberately and joyously put our abilities and assets to practical use for the sake of the good of all. In this tangible sense, the finest exemplars of global trusteeship are those who treat all possessions as though they are sacred or priceless, beyond any worldly or monetary scale of valuation.

Thus, it is only through daily moral choices and the meritorious and sagacious employment of our limited resources that we sustain our inherited or acquired entitlements. For this very reason, the divisive notion and dangerous illusion of exclusive ownership is systematically misleading and, at worst, a specious and subtle form of violence. It connotes assertive rights or claims, and even privileged access, that far exceed the legitimate bounds of actual human need – even though protected by statutory law or social custom. It also obscures the generous bounty of Nature and the potential fecundity of human resourcefulness and innovation, which together can readily provide enough for all denizens of the earth, if only each person would hold in trust whatever he has to meet his essential needs, without profligate excess or any form of exploitation. This is the basic presupposition behind *sarvodaya*, non-violent socialism at its best, which is as old as the spiritual communism taught by Buddha and Christ.

Ancient Indian thought viewed the entire cosmos and all human souls as continually sustained by the principle of harmony (*rita*), the principle of sacrifice (*yajna*), and the principle of universal interdependence, solidarity and concord. This is enshrined in the Golden Rule, which is found in all the major religions of mankind and is mirrored in the codes and norms of all cultures at different stages of development. The Vedic chants portrayed heaven and earth as indissolubly linked through the mighty sacrificial ladder of being, which is found in the Pythagorean philosophy and memorably conveyed in Shakespeare's *Troilus and Cressida*. Similarly, Jacob's celestial ladder of angels between heaven and earth signifies the indispensable linkage or Leibnizian continuity between the universal and the particular, the unconditional and the contextually concrete, the divine and the human, the Logos and the cosmos, the macrocosm and the microcosm. Jacob sensed, in his celebrated dream, that this vital connection provides a shining thread of hope for souls in distress. He also saw that it provides a helpful clue to action by binding together profound contemplation and the apt choice of available means, not because he claimed any supernatural wisdom or superhuman power, but only because he was content to remain an ardent seeker and a constant learner.

Philo Judaeus saw in Jacob a transparently good man who had gained the talismanic insight that everyone learns best by emulating noble exemplars instead of merely repeating the words of the wise without even trying to enact what they teach. Philo, who also saw the true statesman as a disguised soothsayer in the sense that he could interpret the deepest dreams of ordinary men and women, their irrepressible longings for the greater good, stated in his *De Congressu Eruditionis Gratia*:

> It is characteristic of the learner that he listens to a voice and to words, for by these alone is he taught, but he who acquires the good through practice and not through teaching pays attention not to what is said but to those who say it, and imitates their life in its succession of blameless actions. Thus it is said in the case of Jacob, when he is sent to marry one of his kin, 'Jacob hearkened to his father and mother, and journeyed to Mesopotamia' (*Genesis* 28:7), not to their voice or words, for the practicer must be the imitator of a life, not the hearer of words, since the latter is characteristic of one who is being instructed, the former of one who struggles through to the end.[1]

Jacob was perhaps a *karma yogin* (or its rabbinical equivalent), who conscientiously sought to translate what he knew into the concrete discipline of moral conduct. He deeply cherished his vision of the celestial bridge between *theoria* and *praxis*, the invisible arch (or ark of salvation) linking the rarefied empyrean of scriptural ethics and the actual pathway each human being must trace and tread in his life on earth. To Jacob it was given to discern the divine ladder upon which the angels tread (depicted like a spinal column in the Kabbalistic Tree of Life), and to salute the old men who dream dreams as well as the young men who see visions (Joel 2:28). This is poignantly suggestive of the profound statement of Herzen, which contemporary detractors of *perestroika* and *glasnost* ignore at their peril, that political leaders do not change events in the world by rational demonstrations or by syllogisms, but rather by "dreaming the dreams of men". No doubt,

---

[1] Philo of Alexandria (Philo Judaeus), *The Contemplative Life, The Giants and Selections*, David Winston, trans., Paulist Press (New York, 1981), p. 215.

this is easier said than done, but it would be an elitist form of defeatism to abandon the attempt in a world bedevilled by obsolete isms and irrational ideologies, yet trembling on the brink of nuclear annihilation and global chaos. As Mikhail Gorbachev frankly admitted:

> The restructuring doesn't come easily for us. We critically assess each step we are making, test ourselves by practical results, and keenly realize that what looks acceptable and sufficient today may be obsolete tomorrow....
>
> There is a great thirst for mutual understanding and mutual communication in the world. It is felt among politicians, it is gaining momentum among the intelligentsia, representatives of culture, and the public at large....
>
> The restructuring is a must for a world overflowing with nuclear weapons; for a world ridden with serious economic and ecological problems; for a world laden with poverty, backwardness and disease; for a human race now facing the urgent need of ensuring its own survival.
>
> We are all students, and our teacher is life and time.... We want people of every country to enjoy prosperity, welfare and happiness. The road to this lies through proceeding to a nuclear-free, non-violent world.

Whilst Gandhi was doubtless closer in spirit to Jacob and Philo than to Herzen and Lenin, he would have concurred in the sentiments behind *perestroika* and *glasnost*.[2]

Mohandas Karamchand Gandhi saw himself essentially as a *karma yogin*, who, without claiming any special or supernatural wisdom, was unusually receptive in his readiness to honour remarkable men such as Naoroji, Gokhale and Rajchandra as rare models of probity worthy of emulation. He showed consistent fidelity to the paradigm of the self-governed Sage[3] portrayed in eighteen *shlokas* which were daily chanted at his *ashram*. He took this classical model as the basis for assiduous self-study, ever seeking to correct himself whenever he saw that he

---

[2] Mikhail Gorbachev, *Perestroika*, Harper and Row (New York, 1987), pp. 253–54.
[3] *The Bhagavad Gita*, Raghavan Iyer, ed., Concord Grove Press (Santa Barbara, 1985), pp. 84–90.

had erred, especially when he made what he called, with playful hyperbole, "Himalayan blunders". He strenuously maintained the hard-won awareness that sensitive leaders must always share the trials and travails of the human condition, that ubiquitous suffering is the common predicament of humanity, whilst all earthly pleasures and intellectual joys are ephemeral and deceptive.

Gandhi, like Gautama, did not try to escape the evident truth of human suffering through seeking mindless oblivion or neurotic distractions, nor did he choose to come to terms with it through compensatory spiritual ambition or conventional religious piety. Rejecting the route of cloistered monasticism, he pondered deeply and agonizingly upon the human condition, and sought to find the redemptive function and therapeutic meaning of human misery. Translating his painful insights into daily acts of *tapas* – self-chosen spiritual exercises and the repeated re-enactments of lifelong meditation in the midst of fervent social activity – he came to see the need for a continual rediscovery of the purpose of living by all those who reject the hypnosis of bourgeois society, with its sanctimonious hypocrisy and notorious 'double standards' for individual and public life.

Gautama Buddha had taught his disciples in the *Sangha* that *bodhichitta*, the seed of enlightenment, may be found in the cleansed heart and controlled mind, and that it may be quickened by diligent practice of meditative altruism and honest self-examination of one's unconscious tendencies and hidden motives. As stressed in the later *Mahayana* schools of India, China and Tibet, *bodhichitta* can serve, like the Upanishadic *antaskarana* or mediating principle of intellection, as a reliable bridge between fleeting sense-experience and enduring spiritual aspiration, as an aid and stimulus to the ascent of consciousness to its highest possible elevation and even to the plane of *svasamvedana*, universal self-consciousness in the midst of *shunyata*, the voidness released through persistent philosophical negation.

Spiritual striving towards enlightenment can help to raise a ladder of contemplation along which the seeker may ascend and descend, participating in the worlds of eternity and time, perfecting one's sense of timing in the sphere of action. In most people, alas, the seed is not allowed to sprout or grow owing to chaotic and contradictory aims and desires, tinged by vain longings and delusive expectations, fantasies and fears, blocking any vibrant encounter with the realities of this world as well as any possibility of envisioning Jacob's ladder, "pitched betwixt Heaven and Charing Cross". Gandhi's own spiritual conviction grew, with the ripening of age, that social reformers and non-violent revolutionaries must repeatedly cleanse their sight and remove all self-serving illusions by placing themselves squarely within the concrete context of mass suffering.

Gandhi knew that his ideas and ideals were difficult to instantiate precisely because of their inherent simplicity. He recognized, therefore, that he could only clarify and illustrate them to all who sought his counsel. Those others would, through *tapas*, have to assimilate and apply them for themselves. But the hero and villain jostle in every soul. Morally sensitive individuals must learn to detect self-deception with firmness and forbearance, mellowness and maturity. They must come to know the obscuration of light within before they can ferret out evil at its roots. Eventually, "a man with intense spirituality may without speech or gesture touch the hearts of millions who have never seen him and whom he has never seen".[4] Through meditation, man can attain a noetic plane on which thought becomes the primary and most potent mode of action. Gandhi unwaveringly affirmed that living this conviction would bring sacrificial suffering, as well as an inner joy which cannot be conveyed in words.

On his seventy-eighth birthday in 1947, when well-wishers showered him with lavish and affectionate greetings, Gandhi thought only of the violence and suffering of his recently independent and hastily partitioned motherland:

> I am not vain enough to think that the divine purpose can only be fulfilled through me. It is as likely as not that a fitter instrument will be used to carry it out and that I was good enough to represent a weak nation, not a strong one. May it not be that a man purer, more courageous, more far-seeing, is wanted for the final purpose? Mine must be a state of complete resignation to the

---

[4] M.K. Gandhi in Young India, Mar. 22, 1928.

Divine Will.... If I had the impertinence openly to declare my wish to live 125 years, I must have the humility, under changed circumstances, openly to shed that wish.... In that state, I invoke the aid of the all-embracing Power to take me away from this 'vale of tears' rather than make me a helpless witness of the butchery by man become savage, whether he dares to call himself a Mussalman or Hindu or what not. Yet I cry, 'Not my will but Thine alone shall prevail.'[5]

Gandhi was sometimes apt to speak of God in the language of Christian mystics, despite his explicit commitment to a more philosophical view of Deity, as given in the most advanced Hindu schools of thought and practice. He wavered at times between the standpoints and terminologies of contemplative monists and ecstatic dualists, but he never abandoned his early axiom that Truth is God, which he preferred to the statement that God is Truth, and he also held that Truth is the root of pure love and unconditional compassion.[6] His lifelong faith in God as Truth (*SAT*) implied a concrete, if inviolable, confidence in the spiritual and ethical potential of all humanity, far surpassing the historicist and immanentist beliefs of reductionist sociological doctrines and rival political ideologies. He could, he felt, honestly call himself a socialist or a communist, although he explicitly repudiated their materialistic assumptions, violent methods, utilitarian programmes and totalistic claims. He spoke of socialism of the heart and invoked the Ishopanishadic injunction to renounce and enjoy the world, which nourished his own reformist aspirations, revolutionary zeal, and Tolstoyan conviction that the Kingdom of God is attainable on earth and is, in any event, a feasible, life-sustaining ideal. He knew, especially in his last decade, moods of pessimism and even moments of despair, when his inner voice would not speak, which lent a poignant and heroic quality to his life reminiscent of the passion of Jesus Christ, the psychological martyrdom of saints, and the early

---

[5] M.K. Gandhi in D.G. Tendulkar, *Mahatma: Life of Mohandas Karamchand Gandhi*, V.K. Jhaveri and D.G. Tendulkar (Bombay, 1951-1954), vol. 8, p. 144; reprinted in *The Moral and Political Writings of Mahatma Gandhi*, Raghavan Iyer, ed., Clarendon (Oxford, 1986–1987), vol. 1, pp. 10–11 (hereafter cited as *MPWMG*).

[6] M.K. Gandhi, "Speech at Meeting in Lausanne", Mahadev Desai's Diary (MSS); *MPWMG*, vol. 2, pp. 164–66.

strivings of the wandering monk, Siddhartha Kapilavastu, who became the enlightened Buddha. But he returned always to the conviction that it is presumptuous to deny human perfectibility or the possibility of human progress, let alone to take refuge in the fashionable armchair doctrine that *Ramarajya* is irrelevant to *Kali Yuga*, that the Kingdom of God is wholly unattainable in the world of time.

He held firmly to the view which Vinoba Bhave, his leading disciple, made his life-motto, that the social reformer and spiritual anchorite must be committed to the gospel of the *Gita* and to a life of ceaseless, selfless service of the weak and the wretched of the earth. He must choose to become a *satyayugakari*, an exemplar and witness of *Ramarajya* even in the midst of *Kali Yuga*, the Age of Iron. He could thus serve as a heroic pioneer and a patient builder, contributing bricks to the invisible, ideational endeavour to rebuild Solomon's Temple, to re-establish the reign of Truth and Love even in the small circles of human fellowship. As a *karma yogin*, he could yoke a microcosmic approach to social experimentation with a macro-cosmic vision of universal peace, human solidarity and a global "civilization of the heart". This requires a staunch refusal to think in terms of nations, tribes, castes and classes, or the tedious distinctions made by the insecure in terms of race and creed, sex and status. What is needed at all times is a purgation of the *psyche*, a restoration of purity of the heart, and a release of the spiritual will in simple acts consecrated to the good of all. This was strongly stressed by Soren Kierkegaard and Simone Weil. It was powerfully exemplified by many a legendary hero and heroine of the Indian epics and *Puranas*, extolled in song and story to this day among millions of impoverished but indefatigable peasants in thousands of Indian villages, and also known to the homeless and the dispossessed exiles and tramps in crowded cities and decaying townships.

Towards the close of his extraordinarily eventful life, so crowded with petitioners and visitors of every sort from all over the globe and from the farthest corners of rural India as well as from the towering Himalayas, he reaffirmed his inward vision of the "Himalayas of the plains" and the inextinguishable integrity of socialist *sannyasa* and Bodhisattvic compassion. He ever recalled the formative early influences in his life – the *Vaishnava* ideal of Narasinh Mehta, *The Key to*

Theosophy of Helena Petrovna Blavatsky, and the telling instructions of Bishop Butler, William Salter and Henry Drummond. He evidently knew the vivid encomiums of Drummond to Jesus as the Man of Sorrows, though he never explicitly cited the most memorable of such statements:

> Christ sets His followers no tasks. He appoints no hours. He allots no sphere. He Himself simply went about and did good. He did not stop life to do some special thing which should be called religious. His life was His religion. Each day as it came brought round in the ordinary course its natural ministry. Each village along the highway had someone waiting to be helped. His pulpit was the hillside, His congregation a woman at a well. The poor, wherever He met them, were His clients; the sick, as often as He found them, His opportunity. His work was everywhere; His workshop was the world.[7]

In his *ashrams* and during the periods of abstention from politics, which were longer and more frequent than many imagined, Gandhi was fortunate to experience the secret joy of living in the *atman*, which he early saw in Rajchandra, the jeweller and *theodidact*. Gandhi's demanding conception of his *svadharma*, his self-chosen obligations, repeatedly thrust him back into the arenas of political conflict and conciliation, as well as into the wider forums of the Constructive Programme, social reform and nation-wide rural reconstruction. Even here his quintessential philosophy of *anasakti yoga*, the gospel of selfless, disinterested action taught by Krishna in the *Gita*, came to his aid in distilling non-violent socialism to its irreducible core, as construed by Henry Drummond:

> The most obvious lesson in Christ's teaching is that there is no happiness in having and getting anything, but only in giving.... And half the world is on the wrong scent in the pursuit of happiness. They think it consists in having and getting, and in being served by others. It consists in giving and serving others. He that would be great among you, said Christ, let him serve. He that

---

[7] Henry Drummond, "The Ministry of Christ", in *The Jewel in the Lotus*, Raghavan Iyer, ed., Concord Grove Press (Santa Barbara, 1983), p. 201.

would be happy, let him remember that there is but one way – it is more blessed, it is more happy, to give than to receive.[8]

This is the secret of *sarvodaya*, the doctrine of non-violent socialism which Gandhi fused with his alkahest of global trusteeship and his lifelong experience of the reality and continual relevance of radical self-regeneration through selfless service. Krishna's sovereign remedy of *Buddhi Yoga*, the *yoga* of divine discernment, points to the crucial connection between *viveka*, discrimination, and *vairagya*, detachment, between self-chosen duty and voluntary sacrifice, *dharma* and *yajna*, individual self-conquest and the welfare of the world, *lokasangraha*. Even a little of this practice, as taught in the *Gita* and as realized by Gandhi, is invaluable:

> In this path of yoga no effort is ever lost, and no harm is ever done. Even a little of this discipline delivers one from great danger.[9]

In the words of Dnyaneshwar, the foremost saint and poet of Maharashtra, "just as the flame of a lamp, though it looks small, affords extensive light, so this higher wisdom, even in small measure, is deeply precious".

This is the ideal of the suffering servant of Isaiah, the means of entry into the wider human family as shown by Ibn al-'Arabi in his haunting poems, the evocative vision of the monkish revolutionaries known to the Russian Populists, the basis of inspiration of many a Christian socialist and even the Christian Communists of the thirties, the demanding conception of Philo, who concluded from his observation of the Therapeutae and other small communes that "every day is a festival",[10] let alone the ancient Hindu ideal of the true Mahatma or self-governed Sage, the *Jivanmukta* or spiritually free man, for whom each day is like unto a new incarnation, and each incarnation like unto a *manvantara*, the vast epoch of cosmic manifestation.

Gandhi prophesied that for thirty years after his death, his ideas would be largely forgotten, but that, generations later, the *tapas* of millions

---

[8] Henry Drummond, "*Happiness*", *ibid.*, p. 71.
[9] *The Bhagavad Gita*, Raghavan Iyer, ed., p. 79.
[10] Philo of Alexandria, *The Contemplative Life*, p. 200.

would bear fruit, and that out of his ashes "a thousand Gandhis will arise".[11] Even though this is still an elusive hope, it is enormously encouraging that courageous pioneers have emerged from the host of the disillusioned who find the world of today too ghastly to contemplate, a world of mindless mass consumerism induced by the rising curve of shallow expectations, a world in which there is a widespread alienation of lonely individuals from disintegrating societies, of conscience from the intellect, of angry rebels from the agonies of the compassionate heart, of impotent politicians from the global imperatives of radical change and genuine coexistence among all nations and peoples, creeds and ideologies. Ragnarok, the end of the gods and of the world, is the sole alternative in Nordic mythology to the rainbow bridge between heaven and earth, Bifrost, at which crossing many may camp at the boundary of a new land, a new frontier, a new settlement. Whether or not a New Jerusalem is attainable on earth in the lifetime of the humanity of the present, there is much wisdom in Gandhi's own well-tested message in times of trial.

In "One Step Enough for Me" he said:

> When, thousands of years ago, the battle of Kurukshetra was fought, the doubts which occurred to Arjuna were answered by Shri Krishna in the *Gita*; but that battle of Kurukshetra is going on, will go on, forever within us; the Prince of Yogis, Lord Krishna, the universal *Atman* dwelling in the hearts of us all, will always be there to guide Arjuna, the human soul, and our Godward impulses represented by the Pandavas will always triumph over the demoniac impulses represented by the Kauravas. Till, however, victory is won, we should have faith and let the battle go on, and be patient meanwhile.[12]

Those who cannot share this testament of faith, rooted in the spiritual convictions of antiquity concerning the periodic descent of *Avatars* or Divine Redeemers, the immortality of the soul and the inexorable law of Karma, the law of ethical causation and moral

---

[11] M.K. Gandhi, "Message to Students", *Harijan*, Jan. 16, 1937; *MPWMG*, vol. 1, p. 35.
[12] M.K. Gandhi, "*One Step Enough for Me*", Speech at Wardham Ashram, Navajivan, Dec. 27, 1925; *MPWMG*, vol. 1, p. 21.

retribution, may yet actively respond to "the still, sad music of humanity". After all, even agnostics and atheists, socialists, humanists and communists, may share a living faith in the future of civilization and hold a truly open view of human nature, social solidarity and global progress. All alike may well ponder upon Mahatma Gandhi's life-message. Towards the end of his pilgrimage on earth he delivered a deeply moving and testable challenge to theophilanthropists everywhere:

> I will give you a talisman. Whenever you are in doubt, or when the self becomes too much with you, apply the following test. Recall the face of the poorest and weakest man whom you may have seen, and ask yourself if the step you contemplate is going to be of any use to him. Will he gain anything by it? Will it restore him to a control over his own life and destiny? In other words, will it lead to *swaraj* [self-rule] for the hungry and spiritually starving millions? Then you will find your doubts and yourself melting away.[13]

Hermes, January 1988

---

[13] M.K. Gandhi in D.G. Tendulkar, *Mahatma*, vol. 8, p. 89; *MPWMG*, vol. 3, p. 609.

GANDHIAN SOCIALISM:
The Constructive Programme

Mahatma Gandhi's genius as a social reformer lay in his intuitive ability to fuse timeless principles with evolving strategies. This is best seen in the vast array of activities he initiated under the single umbrella of the Constructive Programme. From the twenties until his death in 1948, Gandhi gradually shifted the emphasis of his political endeavours from non-violent resistance to constructive schemes for the social good. For him, non-violent resistance (*satyagraha*) and the Constructive Programme – a concrete embodiment of *sarvodaya* – were logical corollaries of the same philosophical perspective. Non-violent resistance, however, aimed to set right entrenched abuses or to abolish some patently unfair law or practice. But persisting non-cooperation with perceived evils cannot by itself create a socialist society. Gandhi's position was not wholly like Thoreau's and he could readily concede the importance, stressed by T.H. Green, of invoking the public interest (*sarvodaya*). He could also concur that the dictates of individual conscience, if genuine, would culminate in social action that would arouse and appeal to the conscience of others. But he could not make the enlightened individual's duty to follow his conscience dependent upon social recognition or public approbation.

Gandhi's continual concern was always with duties rather than with rights; in fact, there is no concept of 'rights' as such in Indian political thought. Further, his lifelong emphasis on *ahimsa* as the sole means to be used in the vindication of *satya* required him to hold that the courageous resistance to injustice, properly conducted, could not lead to general anarchy. Thus Gandhi differed from Thoreau chiefly in that his language and his emphasis were less anarchistic, but he distinctly differed from T.H. Green (whom he never read) in his own moral conception and political justification of the right of resistance to the

State. [1] Cessation of persistent wrongdoing is a necessary prerequisite for, but is hardly identical with, positive social welfare. The Constructive Programme did not rule out non-violent resistance or non-cooperation, but it simply focussed upon constructive ways of rebuilding a demoralized society. It sought to transform a servile nation habituated to sectional loyalties and social apathy into a fearless community of mutual service and sacrifice, in which every responsible individual readily identified with others, especially the poor and the meek.

By instilling a lofty conception of labour, Mahatma Gandhi sought to uplift the whole of society, whilst encouraging self-sufficiency in each sector and region. If civil disobedience and non-violent resistance could arouse the conscience of others, the Constructive Programme could channel that awakened sensitivity in beneficial ways. Within the Indian context, this meant nurturing communal unity, abolishing untouchability, fostering adult education and systematic improvement of villages. It meant uplifting the peasants and developing non-violent labour unions, working towards economic and social equality, promoting cottage and small-scale industries as a means for decentralizing economic production and distribution, and eradicating a wide variety of social evils. The Constructive Programme drew its hidden inspiration from the hoary concept of trusteeship which could sustain both a narrower economic interpretation and a broader social application. If labour is as much social capital as metal, everyone capable of working should consider himself or herself an ethical trustee, even if one's own sphere of effective action is no larger than the village or the home.

Since each facet of the Constructive Programme is related directly to trusteeship, the various programmes are coherently if loosely associated with one another. Such an overarching conception allows for efficient coordination of different endeavours, whilst permitting each line of action to develop on its own and at its own pace. At the same time, since the whole Constructive Programme is based on

---

[1] Raghavan Iyer, *The Moral and Political Thought of Mahatma Gandhi*, Oxford University Press (New York, 1973). Second edition: Concord Grove Press (Santa Barbara, 1983), pp. 268-269.

trusteeship as a shared ideal, it can proceed even when there is varying resistance to the effective realization of the ideal. The scope and simplicity of the Constructive Programme was a source of annoyance to those socialists who tended to look for detailed plans and quantifiable criteria of accomplishment. Gandhi, however, thought that its unique virtue lay in its generality, both because it avoided the psychological defeatism which readily emerges when rigid objectives are not met, and because it gave ample recognition to the intangible and unquantifiable elements of human progress.

When an inflexible calendar for social reform is established, the repeated failure to meet its publicized deadlines tends to nurture the suppressed tendency to show violence of various sorts as the only decisive means to secure the desired ends. The Constructive Programme, with its almost unlimited plasticity, embodies the realistic perspective required for social revolution as well as specific criteria by which to measure what is in fact possible. By fusing means and ends in the Constructive Programme – so that the means cannot contain any element which would be unacceptable in the ends – one could guarantee that the ends would be right when realized. This familiar problem is poorly handled by State socialists and communists who find themselves 'extending' the timetable of the revolution to explain the failure of ends. At the same time, the continual adherence to morally acceptable means would increasingly make clear just what ends were actually attainable in any given time and place. Rather than imposing preconceived ends upon a people incapable of or unwilling to accept them, Gandhi sought to uphold the highest ideals while making full use of what was actually possible in respect to specific situations. The intense wish to ameliorate depressing conditions was not in itself sufficient to effect a real change for the better. He wrote to a village worker in 1925:

> It is only recently that we thought of going into the villages. At first, we wanted things from the village people. It is only now that we are going to the villages in order to give the people something. How can we expect to win their confidence in such a short time?... We have to win back our honoured place among the village people, and will get nothing through impatience. Some persons serve their own interests under the guise of service. What other

means do the village people have, except experience, to distinguish between such persons and genuine workers? Public workers, therefore, must cultivate patience, forbearance, selflessness and such other virtues. The masses can have no other knowledge but experience to guide them. [2]

Gandhi remained sceptical of imposing any social reformation from the top, and he parted company with ideological and State socialists on this crucial point. To them, his bold attempts at non-violent resistance at least had the merit of being national in scope even when local in origin, but the Constructive Programme seemed to them like pouring water through a sieve into local villages and small community groups. Gandhi respected innate intelligence and acquired scholarship, but he felt that urban intellectuals could be useful as creative leaders in social reform only when they identified with and merged themselves with the rural masses. They could not, as Marx thought, conveniently fire the proletariat from revolutionary cloisters and then be drawn along by the mass fervour they had helped to kindle. Rather, they could light the fire of non-violent revolution only by living in villages and working conscientiously to improve the lot of the peasantry. Replying to a critic who maintained a Marxian perspective on the strategic role of intellectuals in the social revolution, Gandhi said:

> Whereas you have before your mind's eye that microscopic minority, the educated Indian, I have before my mind's eye the lowliest illiterate Indian living outside the railway beat. Important as the former class undoubtedly is, it has no importance in my estimation except in terms of the latter and for the sake of the latter. The educated class can justify its existence only if it is willing to sacrifice itself for the mass.[3]

Revolution has to be from the bottom up, if it is to be non-violent, successful and permanent. Neither panaceas in the form of ingenious reorganization of fixed components in the social structure nor the wholesale reassignment of unaltered roles can make any significant difference to the human condition. If dissatisfied intellectuals

---

[2] "Who Is to Blame?", *Navajivan*, June 28, 1925.
[3] "Letter to Captain J.W. Petavel", SN 12648, Sabarmati Sangrahalaya, Ahmedabad.

genuinely wished to help, they must not preach to the multitudes and encourage incendiary reactions while they themselves remain aloof from the muddy arena of conflict. Instead, they must merge with the masses of the disinherited and demonstrate collective uplift through their own heroic labours. Thus Gandhi divorced sattvic or noetic politics from the turba of ideological froth. Fusing the political art with the gospel of service to the community, he restored to politics its classical concern with the Good, the *Agathon*. He was firmly convinced that the persuasion of helping hands would generate a more lasting, if more gradual, revolution than ideological pronouncements could possibly achieve.

> The harder the task, the fewer willing workers will there be.... But understanding workers, when they observe the paucity of volunteers, will become more devoted to their work and make greater sacrifices. If they do so, the number of workers will increase again. There is no exception to this law. [4]

If Gandhi had little faith in the presumed capacity of modern institutions to ameliorate unacceptable social and economic conditions, he was also fully aware that arduous work in villages would not miraculously transform most political workers. Just as he had employed the enigmatic methods of *satyagraha* on a national scale, so too he found that they could be utilized on a micro-level to preserve cohesiveness and direction amongst voluntary workers in the Constructive Programme. When critics wrote to him of the manifold ways in which dedicated workers seemed to succumb to the enticements of power, he advised appropriate forms of non-cooperation. But, he warned,

> During my long experience, I also noticed that those who complain of others being ambitious of holding power are no less ambitious themselves, and when it is a question of distinquishing between half a dozen and six, it becomes a thankless task.[5]

---

[4] "Letter to Dahmibehn Patel", GN 9206, Gandhi Memorial Museum and Library, New Delhi.
[5] "Speech at Prayer Meeting", *Harijan*, March 2, 1947.

Workers in villages would not miraculously escape the pervasive ills which infect the noisy advocates of State socialism, but cultivating social reform at the local level could afford the best conceivable opportunities for holding them in check and even eradicating them. At least, the tendency to leap to hastily drawn conclusions regarding what could and could not be accomplished would be moderated. Proclivities arising from the weaker side of human nature could be mitigated. Tangible improvements should not be overlooked because the 'big picture' failed to enthuse volunteers, whilst the intangible transformation of human consciousness must not be missed out owing to the excessive psychological generalizations of large theories. Workers should refine and renew their activities, not on the basis of abstract models but out of their well-earned experience. In 1947 Gandhi spoke plainly to a large gathering of socialists on the eve of Indian independence.

> No doubt the transfer of power will remove many obstacles. But we shall have to do solid work among the people. Since you look upon me as an adviser and seek my advice of your own free will, I have only one advice to give, and that is that, if you wish to establish socialism, there is only one way in which it can be done: go and live among the poor in the villages, live as they live, be one with the village people, work for eight hours daily, use only village-made goods and articles even in your personal lives, remove illiteracy among the village people, eradicate untouchability and uplift the women. I will even go so far as to suggest that you should establish such a living bond with the village people that, if anyone amongst you is unmarried and wishes to marry, he or she should choose a partner from among the village girls or boys. If anyone else seeks your advice on this subject, give him or her, too, the same advice. Make your life an ideal one in this way; when the people see your transparent lives every minute of the day as clearly as we see pictures on a screen, their influence will be felt throughout the country and reform its life. [6]

This is a bold vision, but one which Gandhi believed could be

---

[6] "Talk with Socialists", *Bihar Pachhi Dilhl*, pp. 14-19.

embodied with increasing approximation and one which would remain an index of progress in social reform.

Except for strict adherence to non-violence as a principle and a policy at all times, Gandhi did not dispute the socialist and communist ideals of a society in which basic economic, social and political equity supported a fundamental equality amongst all citizens. He doubted that the centralized State could serve these ends unless it had actually arisen from a people already dedicated to them. Like Marx, he thought that a people so dedicated would not need the State in its contemporary form, since much of its socio-political apparatus would have become irrelevant. The social transformation of a nation could not be achieved in purely social terms, if for no other reason than that social action and political authority cannot be wholly disentangled. Gandhi was deeply convinced that political power could be brought to bear on institutionalized practices which subvert social and economic ends, but just as his radical ideas of social and economic reform require that these arenas be purified and understood in a new light, politics too must be purified and understood anew. When criticized for his political action, he once responded, "Is not politics too a part of *dharma*!", [7] but he thought of political power – like all power – as a means and not an end.

> Political power, in my opinion, cannot be our ultimate aim. It is one of the means used by men for their all-round advancement. The power to control national life through national representatives is called political power. Representatives will become unnecessary if the national life becomes so perfect as to be self-controlled. It will then be a state of enlightened anarchy in which each person will become his own ruler.... In an ideal State there will be no political institution and therefore no political power. That is why Thoreau has said in his classic statement that that government is the best which governs the least. [8]

Recognizing that "enlightened anarchy" was an ideal, Mahatma Gandhi nonetheless believed that only the loftiest ideal could effectively motivate the advancement of a people. Gandhi was closer to

---

[7] "A Letter", *Bihar Pachhi Dilhi*, p. 350.
[8] "Enlightened Anarchy – A Political Ideal", *Sarvodaya*, January 1939.

Marx than to Weber in his insistence upon an open-textured vision of human nature, a fundamental standpoint which allowed him to point to social perfectibility without the arbitrary restraint of predetermined time limits on its realization. In practice, he was always ready to settle for much less at any given time, provided it did not foreclose further progress nor actually negate the ideal. Gandhi's entertaining dialogues with socialists and communists, as well as his ready application of their basic vocabulary to much of his political work, reveal a deep insight into the methodology of social transformation. In addition to the need for a bold vision, which all social reformers accept, and the principle and policy of non-violence, which many socialists and all traditional communists would reject, Gandhi discerned a number of requirements for permanent social reform which cannot be ignored without peril by reformers of any persuasion.

First of all, Gandhi comprehended that the key to lasting social transformation lay in securing constructive change in the social and economic infrastructure of a nation. He knew that governments and policies pass and are forgotten, whilst the roots of the social structure remain firm if nurtured in the villages and amongst the people. For Gandhi, India had to revitalize these roots precisely because myriad villages were allowed to decline steadily from the seventeenth century under colonial rule. Drained of their traditional resources, they were promised very little of the fascinating and deceptive goods of 'modern civilization' and given much less. What others bemoaned as a horrendous lack Gandhi saw as a distinct advantage. The villages had been more abandoned than altered, and so he saw the possibility of revitalizing them along constructive lines even while encouraging social democracy and self reliance, ideas that depend upon character, not capital.

Secondly, a critical factor in radically renewing the entire infrastructure, but also valuable at every level, was the necessity for both individual and collective *yajna* or sacrifice. No nation can expect to reconstitute itself on an equitable basis without its people giving up at least those things necessarily dependent on inequities. Yet, merely to divest portions of the population of cherished privileges or properties is to provoke class war. Therefore, Gandhi saw that the potent ideal of voluntary sacrifice for a larger common good had to become mandatory common sense within the social system and of exemplary nobility in the eyes of peers. If trusteeship is to bring about social reform without bitter conflict, a broad conception of stewardship must command the allegiance of leaders and the people alike. Socialist and communist systems have already demonstrated the awesome capacity of the masses to sacrifice in vain for a vague ideological promise of a glorious future. Gandhi uncompromisingly insisted that those who would be responsible leaders of a socialist society must lead the way in making tangible sacrifices. Failure to do this voided all claims to wisdom, insight and credibility. Sacrificing freely amidst the people demonstrated minimal and authentic understanding of equity and equality, and every honest effort could foster a contagious change in all arenas of society.

Thirdly, and closely related to the need for the sacrificial spirit, was Gandhi's own continual realization in his intensely active political life that reformers need the very reforms they sought for others. For Gandhi, there were not two species of human being – those who needed reform in a socio-economic context and those who advocated reform and yet had marvellously remained untouched by the societies in which they lived. If modern civilization is a disease – as Gandhi believed – all are more or less infected by the virus. Though he acknowledged the rich resources of some individuals in wisdom and knowledge, and even in experience, he held to the uncompromising equality of all in the need to transform thinking, motivation and modes of action. Though this powerful realization came from a penetrating insight into the complexities of human nature and social structures, Gandhi expressed it in Euclidean terms: the ideal society is not a closed circle, but an open one in which all its citizens work towards extending the horizons of human perfectibility, knowing that they can always do much better, whilst no one is in a position seriously to claim that he can in no way do better.

Fourthly, whilst Gandhi cherished the grand vision of social possibility offered by optimistic socialists and communists, and indeed expressed a distinct vision of his own that they found daring in its long-term faith in the human race, he could not concede the practicability of magisterial demands for total reformation *all at once*. Gandhi's embryonic plan for social transformation is properly called revolutionary not in respect to time but rather to its texture. The revolution he projected must be total but gradual. It is essential to nurture the revolution by degrees, however vast the whole picture might be. Gandhi felt that many self-styled revolutionaries were not really committed to a transformation they would not live to see. The willingness to labour patiently for incremental gains towards an end which one would not live to share was for Gandhi part of the sacrifice required of all, especially those who would lead.

Fifthly, the Constructive Programme was designed not only to disseminate Gandhi's basic principles but also to ensure that a variety of shifting opportunities could be taken to secure modest successes wherever possible. A mere succession of violent thrusts at the existing social structure is not acceptable. Gandhi preferred modest gains, each of which stood a reasonable chance of enduring. Leaving the dramatic action of demolishing the old social structure to those who preferred what he saw as misguided activity, he sought to build a new edifice brick by brick. The Constructive Programme could slowly build upon every success whilst leaving the future open to bold experimentation, in which there are invariably errors, without threatening to lose the gains already made.

Gilbert Murray, who was an early admirer of Gandhi and also grasped the significance of *satyagraha* as early as 1914, thought it necessary in 1928 to attack the Tolstoyan doctrine of non-resistance to evil as anarchic and subversive.

> It is all very well... to ridicule the law and peace and conventional morality when you are not in danger of being left with no law and no peace and the standards of behaviour broken. But we of the present generation have walked too deep in the valley of the shadow.... Our ship has got to be saved; saved with all its faults of construction and all its injustices, because only while it is safe shall we be able to correct the things that are wrong, reform the structure, improve the conditions of the cabin-boy, and bring ease to the starved and broken-legged cattle who

are moaning in the hold.... Let us think first of the great society of which we are members and to which we owe our loyalty. [9]

This noble and wise exhortation is specially applicable to the Ship of State in India today, in which it is more essential to teach the Gandhian concepts of *swadeshi* and *sarvodaya* than the methods of mass *satyagraha*. At the same time, we can think of pressing situations in India and elsewhere in which, even today, the revolutionary doctrine of *satyagraha* has its continuing relevance.

Many Indian socialists were fervently attracted to Gandhi's political, social and economic aspirations, but they were periodically frustrated by his specific policies, which they saw as strangely anomalous in the twentieth century. Yet, he was a deeply committed socialist and even a communist at heart. His appeal to past experience as well as his openness to thorough social experimentation outstripped the impetuosity of many whose wills were neither so strong nor so one-pointed. He combined rock-like convictions with a resilience and willingness to learn that gave credibility and credence to his terse utterance nearly six months before he died as a martyred Mahatma:

> My life is my message. [10]

Gandhi's faith in Truth *(Sat)* implied a concrete, if unconditional, confidence in every human being far surpassing the negative and suspicious notions of systems and ideologies. He could honestly call himself a 'socialist' and a 'communist' though he rejected many of their modern assumptions, methods and perspectives, if only because he truly lived out their deepest moral aspirations in his daily life. Towards the end of his life-odyssey, he enshrined the essence of those dateless and deathless aspirations and strivings in a striking and unanswerable challenge to all sincere Theophilanthropists:

> I will give you a talisman. Whenever you are in doubt, or when the self becomes too much with you, apply the following test.

---

[9] Raghavan Iyer, *The Moral and Political Thought of Mahatma Gandhi*, p. 337. The quotation is from Gilbert Murray, *The Ordeal of This Generation*, Allen and Unwin (Winchester, Mass., 1929), p. 210.
[10] "Message to Shanti Sensa Dal", *The Hindustan Standard*, September 7, 1947.

Recall the face of the poorest and weakest man whom you may have seen, and ask yourself if the step you contemplate is going to be of any use to him. Will he gain anything by it? Will it restore him to a control over his own life and destiny? In other words, will it lead to *swaraj* for the hungry and spiritually starving millions? Then you will find your doubts and yourself melting away. [11]

Hermes, October 1985

---

[11] "A Note", *Mahatma*, vol. VIII, p. 89.

GANDHIAN SOCIALISM
Isms and Individuals

If socialism means turning enemies into friends, I should be considered a genuine socialist.

Mahatma Gandhi

Mahatma Gandhi had a remarkable capacity to absorb potent ideas and radical proposals in original combinations that transformed them into refined instruments for the progressive realization of his own fundamental commitments. A *Karma Yogin* of deep reflection and fearless resolve, his wide if unsystematic reading was subordinated to a ceaseless winnowing on the basis of insights and values tested in his own life and in the bold social reforms he sought to initiate in South Africa and India. He willingly called himself a "socialist" and a "communist" in appropriate contexts, but his convictions were distilled from the moral stamina of the Indian masses and the spiritual heritage of humanity rather than from the secular theorists and sectarian ideologies of the past century and a half. His classical socialism was metaphysically prior to the ideological State socialism of the twentieth century, and his non-violent communism was ethically superior to the qualified Marxism of contemporary Communist nation-states. Since social and political institutions possess neither cognitive flexibility nor fidelity to conscience, Gandhi was wholly convinced that all social systems essentially depend upon and cannot rise beyond the enlightened individuals, however few, who participate in them. Neither political organizations nor social philosophies can be stronger in practice than their finest incumbents and fervent advocates.

Systems which truly seek to elevate the prevailing condition of humanity can succeed only to the limited extent that their avid supporters meet the minimal ethical and intellectual requirements which nurture and sustain freedom. Gandhi's seminal concepts of satya and ahimsa lay at the inmost heart of his evolving social and political philosophy. He patiently nurtured his own philanthropic vision of the radical transformation of the existing social order and political system, but he was even more ardently concerned to test his own revolutionary approach to political action and social change within the pressing limits of the prevailing conditions of Indian politics and society. Immediate resistance to injustice and coercion as well as a long-term programme of social and political reconstruction must alike be legitimated in terms of the twin absolutes of truth and non-violence. "His concept of *satya,* with *ahimsa* as the means, determined his doctrine of *satyagraha* or active resistance to authority, while the concept of *ahimsa,* with satya as the common end, enabled him to formulate his doctrine of *sarvodaya* or non-violent socialism." [1] Gandhi repudiated both State and reformist socialism because the first attempted to impose socialism from the top, whilst the second tolerated and sometimes even condoned violence as an inescapable means to attain its ends. His own conviction that any sharp distinction between means and ends was theoretically dubious and practically unhelpful confirmed his belief that violence, in any form and for any end, had to be rejected in principle and in practice.

Mahatma Gandhi found Marxist communism unacceptable both as a political philosophy and as a basic principle of social organization. He was not burdened by the social and philosophical inheritance that weighed heavily upon Karl Marx, and to the degree that he understood Marxist principles and rationalizations, he rejected many of them, especially utilitarian conceptions of social amelioration arising from capitalist economics. Marx was indeed a moralist rather than a moral philosopher. The *Communist Manifesto* is the hypnotic portrait of a bourgeois civilization and an industrial system iniquitous in its basic structure, standing condemned in the eyes of the compassionate spectator while also awaiting inevitable destruction by the dedicated revolutionary. Traditional moral philosophy in Western Europe has been a daring enquiry into the elusive nature of the good, a rather rigorous intellectual discipline that thrives upon methodological doubt and a philosophical suspension of commitment. In this sense, Marx

---

[1] See Raghavan Iyer, *The Moral and Political Thought of Mahatma Gandhi*, Oxford University Press (New York, 1973, 1978); Second edition: Concord Grove Press (Santa Barbara, 1983), p. 252.

was hardly a didactic moral philosopher. Like Gandhi, he readily reversed the traditional primacy of the *vita contemplativa* over the *vita activa* to such an extent that he dismissed contemplation without action as sterile, though he himself, unlike Gandhi, was a tortured *philosophe* and a solemn propagandist rather than a Promethean actor on the world's stage. Marxism shares with Augustinianism an awesome totality of scope, a hubristic attempt to provide an all-inclusive view of reality.

Marx's macro-conception of society as a flawed system in desperate conflict, "*a split self writ large*", is indeed metaphysical rather than scientific. The Hermetic-Hegelian axiom that man is the microcosm of the macrocosm is dramatically employed to draw individuals out, not from their spiritual restlessness, but from their social complacency. Marx's historicism and reductionism prevented him from pursuing his early philosophy to its logical conclusion and from asking fundamental questions about the ends of life and the deepest human urges that were frustrated under the competitive, acquisitive craze of the capitalist system. This prevented him from considering whether the ethical regeneration of man would automatically take place with a total change of system from capitalism to communism. His millennial dream was a powerful myth centered on the distant future, without any tangible basis in the historical reality he was so concerned to reveal. "Perfectionism and idealization, moralism and violence, ideologies and 'isms', are all the strange bed-fellows and destructive enemies of a living ideal of human perfectibility." [2]

Though sporadically aware of socialist and communist movements and governments across the globe, Gandhi's concrete experience of them was largely in the context of Indian coteries and political parties. When in 1924 baseless rumours circulated that he would be invited to visit Soviet Russia, he wrote that he had no intention of going there because his own work in India was still in an experimental stage and foreign excursions would be premature. Until his efforts succeeded in India, he saw no reason to move beyond that sphere of *dharma*. Though

---

[2] See Raghavan Iyer, *Parapolitics – Toward the City of Man*, Oxford University Press (New York, 1979). Second edition: Concord Grove Press (Santa Barbara, 1985), p. 17.

he did not claim to understand fully Bolshevism as a political philosophy, he was clear and decisive in his reaction to it.

> I am yet ignorant of what exactly Bolshevism is. I have not been able to study it. I do not know whether it is for the good of Russia in the long run. But I do know that in so far as it is based on violence and denial of God, it repels me. I do not believe in short-violent-cuts to success. The Bolshevik friends who are bestowing their attention on me should realize that however much I may sympathize with and admire worthy motives, I am an uncompromising opponent of violent methods even to serve the noblest of causes. [3]

Four years later he was asked whether the social economics of Bolshevism constituted an appropriate model for India. Replying that the abolition of the institution of private property was an economic application of the ethical principle of *aparigraha* or non-possession, [4] he insisted that it had to be undertaken voluntarily as a result of moral choice. Reiterating his rejection of violence to achieve even the most laudatory ends, he also pointed to the nobility of many Bolsheviks.

> .... there is no questioning the fact that the Bolshevik ideal has behind it the purest sacrifice of countless men and women who have given up their all for its sake, and an ideal that is sanctified by the sacrifices of such master spirits as Lenin cannot go in vain: the noble example of their renunciation will be emblazoned forever and quicken and purify the ideal as time passes. [5]

Since Gandhi traced ignorant wrongdoing by individuals to repressive systems and erroneous views, he rejected any social philosophy or political methodology that condoned violent retaliation against an individual or class of people. Systems may have to be dismantled and views transformed, but individuals who identify with them have to be morally persuaded by appeals to conscience rather than by coercion, including the disguised coercion of claims of national interest and historical inevitability. Communism as an ideology was

---

[3] "My Path", *Young India*, December 11, 1924.
[4] "The Students" Interrogatives", *Young India*, November 15, 1928.
[5] "My Notes", *Navajivan*, October 21, 1928; *Young India*, November 15, 1928.

repugnant to Gandhi, though he readily sympathized with its declared ideals and ultimate ends. "For experience convinces me that permanent good can never be the outcome of untruth and violence. Even if my belief is a fond delusion, it will be admitted that it is a fascinating delusion." [6]

When he encountered the shibboleths of socialism and communism among discontented intellectuals, some of whom were associated with the Indian National Congress, he was, generally speaking, unimpressed. In addition to his philosophical objections to any overt sanction of violence, he viewed the specious doctrine that nothing positive could be achieved without first gaining the power of the State as little more than a convenient excuse for avoiding useful work at hand – self-transformation through deliberate commitment to chosen values and the ungrudging willingness to sacrifice one's own social advantages for the sake of others, especially the disfranchised poor. He found socialists and communists alike wrangling interminably over details, engaged in endless political squabbles and petty grievances, and generally more prone to speechify than to work actively for others. Late in life, Gandhi generously appealed to communist workers to follow the essential principles they espoused, to abandon the fatalistic belief that India could be saved by external sources, and to take *satyagraha* seriously.

> Your principles are fine indeed. But you do not seem to follow them in practice, for you do not seem to know the difference between truth and falsehood or justice and injustice. What is more saddening about you is that, instead of having faith in India and drawing inspiration from its unrivalled culture, you wish to introduce Russian civilization here as if Russia was your motherland. I disapprove of relying on any outside power, however much that may materially benefit us, for I believe in the principle that your eating is not going to satisfy my hunger, that I can satisfy my hunger only by eating myself.... You also use the word *"satyagrahi"* as part of your jargon. But anybody who uses this word should realize that by doing so he accepts a great responsibility. A *satyagrahi* should rely wholly on truth. He cannot

---

[6] "My Path", *loc. cit.*

then afford to be ambiguous in his attitudes. He cannot jump on to a bandwagon. In brief, he cannot depart from his principles in the smallest degree. A *satyagrahi* cares for nothing but truth. He will give no pain or do no injustice whatever to anybody either in thought, word or deed. And he must always have perfect clarity in his thoughts. [7]

These fundamental criticisms of communism and socialism were largely similar because Gandhi discerned little difference in their actual weaknesses. This was partly because he saw little theoretical distinction between true communism and real socialism.

My communism is not very different from socialism. It is a harmonious blending of the two. Communism, as I have understood it, is a natural corollary of socialism. [8]

Nonetheless, though he sometimes called the same principles "communist" or "socialist" depending on the context, he made subtle distinctions in practice. Unlike his non-violent socialism, Gandhi did not try to translate his spiritual communism into a national movement. He tended to restrict his communism to the self-consciously constituted *ashram* or community wherein it was devoid of ideological content and was sustained upon the basis of voluntary vows of truthfulness, non-possession, non-stealing, sexual restraint and non-violence. Each of these pledges was given a precise, if broad, application and enshrined as an ideal, at once practicable and elusive even for the most committed adherents. The *ashram* was the vital centre of his communist experiments, several of which are candidly described in *Ashram Observances in Action*.

Gandhi rejected violence in any form, and though his periodic criticisms of capitalism, socialism and communism varied, they were all rooted in the sacrosanct principle that ends cannot be divorced from means and that violent means could never produce non-violent ends. Though sophisticated forms of capitalism may renounce raw violence as a basic tool of government, they readily employ the entire gamut of

---

[7] "Talk with Communist Workers", *Bihar Pachhi Dilhi,* June 8, 1947, pp. 202-204.
[8] "Interview to Louis Fischer", *Harijan,* August 4, 1946.

legalized coercion to protect private ownership and thereby maintain material and social inequities. In addition, crude applications of utilitarian principles easily become the basis of indirect coercion of the minority by the majority. Yet whether the State uses its resources coercively to safeguard private property or appropriates property to itself through violent means, the fundamental principle of non-violence is violated.

> .... from what I know of Bolshevism it not only does not preclude the use of force but expropriation of private property and maintaining the collective State ownership of the same. And if that is so I have no hesitation in saying that the Bolshevik regime in its present form cannot last for long. [9]

His essential views remained unchanged throughout the next twenty years. With the independence of India, however, the Indian communist movement emerged as a distinct political force, and Gandhi was impelled to express himself in stronger terms.

> Hardly one man in a thousand can be found who practices communism in everyday life. Communists have come to consider it their supreme duty, their supreme service, to create disaffection, to generate discontent and to organize strikes. They do not see whom this discontent, these strikes, will ultimately harm. Half knowledge is one of the worst evils. The best is either full knowledge or ignorance. We are thus caught in isms and take pride in them and consider it a fashion to belong to this or that ism. [10]

He could never look to the State, however conceived and constituted, as an instrument for imposing communist or socialist ideals. Rather, the State should exist solely to carry out the will of the people, and the masses should be enlightened – not dictated to – by the responsible leadership of the morally educated and politically committed.

---

[9] "My Notes", *loc. cit.*
[10] "Talk with Communists", *Dilhiman Gandhiji*, I, pp. 142-143.

> The socialists and communists say, they can do nothing to bring about economic equality today. They will just carry on propaganda in its favour and to that end they believe in generating and accentuating hatred. They say, when they get control over the State, they will enforce equality. Under my plan, the State will be there to carry out the will of the people, not to dictate to them or force them to do its will. I shall bring about economic equality through non-violence, by converting the people to my point of view by harnessing the forces of love as against hatred. I will not wait till I have converted the whole society to my view but will straightaway make a beginning with myself. [11]

Gandhi could not endorse any apocalyptic theory of revolution from the top down, even one in which the intelligentsia would be used to make the proletariat politically self-conscious. His political and social reformation had to emerge from the awakened masses, and any assistance by intellectual classes could be effective only if they lived amidst the poor, identified with them and worked alongside them. Preaching to workers was too easily the first step towards forming a new class of exploiters which replaced the ruling elite without radically altering the inherently unjust and inequitable social structure. A revolution from the bottom upwards – because all who desired to share in it had to start anew at the bottom by renouncing every vestige of class and privilege – could not only produce a genuinely socialist society but also avoid the brutal class war which many feared, some actually desired and armchair ideologists saw as inevitable. Class war was wholly unacceptable on the principle of non-violence, and it was unnecessary and even irrelevant in a large-scale social revolution from the bottom upwards. Gandhi could not countenance the possibility of class war even on theoretical grounds because it violated his unshakeable conviction that ends never rise morally above their means. He rejected it in daily practice owing to the triple criteria of his holistic socialism and communism. *First of all*, social reform must include everyone, oppressor as well as oppressed, capitalist as well as exploited. *Secondly*, such inclusion must be voluntary and not coerced.

---

[11] "Answers to Questions at Constructive Workers" Conference, Madras", *Harijan*, March 31, 1931; *The Hindu*, January 26, 1946.

And *thirdly*, it must clearly distinguish between the inequities that will necessarily remain even in the best societies while utterly abolishing eradicable inequalities.

> Inequalities in intelligence and even opportunity will last till the end of time. A man living on the banks of a river has any day more opportunity of growing crops than one living in an arid desert. But if inequalities stare us in the face the essential equality too is not to be missed. Every man has an equal right to the necessaries of life even as birds and beasts have. And since every right carries with it a corresponding duty and the corresponding remedy for resisting any attack upon it, it is merely a matter of finding out the corresponding duties and remedies to vindicate the elementary fundamental equality. The corresponding duty is to labour with my limbs and the corresponding remedy is to non-cooperate with him who deprives me of the fruits of my labour. And if I would recognize the fundamental equality, as I must, of the capitalist and the laborer, I must not aim at his destruction. [12]

There was no moral defeatism in the recognition of existing inequalities, so long as one did not resign oneself to glaring inequities, which could be readily ameliorated. Lest this crucial point be blurred, he warned in 1946:

> Let no one try to justify the glaring difference between the classes and the masses, the prince and the pauper, by saying that the former need more. That will be idle sophistry and a travesty of my argument. The contrast between the rich and the poor today is a painful sight. The poor villagers are exploited by the foreign Government and also by their own countrymen – the city-dwellers. [13]

Socio-economic reform necessitates a radical change in perspective on the part of organized workers and propertied owners alike. If the latter had to see economic ownership in a new light, so too the industrial workers had to realize their inalienable power, which was not the blind force of destruction but the latent strength of creativity.

---

[12] "Questions and Answers", *Young India,* March 26, 1931.
[13] "Answers to Questions at Constructive workers" Conference, Madras", *loc. cit.*

> By the non-violent method we seek not to destroy the capitalist, we seek to destroy capitalism. We invite the capitalist to regard himself as trustee for those on whom he depends for the making, the retention and the increase of his capital. Nor need the worker wait for his conversion. If capital is power, so is work. Either power can be used destructively or creatively. Either is dependent on the other. Immediately the worker realizes his strength, he is in a position to become a co-sharer with the capitalist instead of remaining his slave. If he aims at becoming the sole owner, he will most likely be killing the hen that lays golden eggs. [14]

If class revolution fails to alter the prevailing state of society, however much it may elevate the formerly oppressed and denigrate the overthrown masters, non-violent conversion will fail to sustain a viable political and economic system without a *modus operandi* which merges the requirements of social reform with those of economic improvement. This core method was, for Gandhi, the ethical idea of trusteeship, a powerful concept which, if put into practice, could obviate potential class conflict, link fundamental social reform with economic stability, and utilize every existing talent and capacity. Its intrinsic power to include all classes and make them contribute constructively to an emerging social order attracted Gandhi, who was strongly convinced that its honest and consistent application could demonstrate the practicability of the principle of non-violent social reformation.

Hermes, September 1985

---

[14] "Questions and Answers", *loc. cit.*

NON-VIOLENT RESISTANCE AND SOCIAL TRANSFORMATION: SATYAGRAHA

Satyagraha and *sarvodaya* were Mahatma Gandhi's most significant and revolutionary contributions to contemporary political thought. The fundamental concepts of *satya* and *ahimsa*, truth and non-violence, can be found in the world's major religious and philosophical traditions; Gandhi's originality lay in the way he fused them in both theory and practice. His doctrines of *satyagraha* or non-violent resistance and *sarvodaya* or universal welfare were at once the logical corollaries of his fundamental premises about human perfectibility, and the mature fruit of his repeated experiments with political action and social reform. If absolute values can never be upheld on utilitarian grounds, adherence to them can nonetheless lead to desirable results which may be extolled in the language of expediency. Whilst speaking of *satya* in the language of faith, even in terms of total conviction, Gandhi often advocated *ahimsa* as a creed, regardless of results, though capable at times of producing concrete advantages.

Since the doctrine of *satyagraha* is a comprehensive social and political application of *satya* and *ahimsa*, it inevitably reflects the deontic logic of those metaphysical conceptions. On the one hand, *satyagraha* is an ethical imperative: one cannot justifiably claim to adhere to *ahimsa* and *a fortiori* to *satya* without making appropriate efforts to apply *satyagraha* to social conflicts. In this sense, *satyagraha* connotes 'truth-force', the luminous power of truth directed towards the promotion of social welfare. At the same time, however, because it confronts injustice and its attendant hostility through an effective appeal to conscience, *satyagraha* is a policy for action and a stimulus for social reform. In this sense, it is 'non-violent resistance'. These two dimensions of *satyagraha* are indivisible aspects of a single standpoint, for truth-force is a ceaseless witness to justice in its transcendental and immanent implications, and it must resist injustice whenever and wherever it occurs. Just as light by its presence delimits darkness and makes it evident, so the *satyagrahi* by his suffering exposes injustice around him. And just as light dispels shadows, yet destroys nothing, so the *satyagrahi* dissolves injustice without harming its agents.

Although Gandhi employed the phrase 'passive resistance' during his earliest campaigns in South Africa, he was dissatisfied with it. The moral strength that is inherent in the immortal soul, which is essentially rooted in the Divine *(sat)*, spontaneously released by an awakened conscience and directed by reason to reveal a persistent social grievance, is in no sense passive. The term 'passive' implies impotence of spiritual will and political initiative. Passive resistance was often the last resort of those who had no power whatsoever. The combination of political weakness with psychological resentment implied in the phrase 'passive resistance' was basically incompatible with Gandhi's abiding convictions. People are politically weak, he held, not because they lack weapons or votes, but because they lack ethical direction. Weapons and votes can never compensate for moral confusion. Gandhi could sympathize with the earnest revolutionary committed to the abolition of an exploitative social system, but he saw no merit in mere destruction. Nor was he concerned to replace one set of misguided rulers and coercive instruments with a rival group of power-seekers. If voluntary social workers could achieve strength through fidelity to *satya* and *ahimsa*, while innovating constructive experiments with social transformation, they would gain sufficient authority from popular support to challenge the entrenched powers.

For Gandhi, short-term reforms bring about changes which do not necessarily elevate the ethical tone of individuals or institutions and are, therefore, doomed to fail. *Satyagraha*, as a method of social change, attempts to raise the welfare of all and to initiate a radical alteration in people and governments. It must be judged without narrow temporal constraints. It is better to establish the foundation for a genuine and lasting good that may not be apparent for decades than to produce some dramatic change that will be eroded or subverted within a few years. Gandhi was therefore much less concerned with the quantity of people involved in *satyagraha* than with their quality: he even went so far as to claim that if the masses became *satyagrahis* in British India, *swaraj* or self-rule would be attained in one year. And he was convinced that if a single individual could become an exemplary *satyagrahi,* subtle changes would ultimately result and be more far-reaching than massive demonstrations based on impetuous enthusiasm and latent violence. Unlike the enduring alchemy of *satya* and *ahimsa,* the outcome of hypocrisy and violence is demoralizing and short-lived.

Gandhi firmly believed that *satyagraha* was the most powerful conceivable force for social weal. It was therefore also the most hazardous, to be used only with wise deliberation. Recognizing this need for caution, and holding that numbers are not in themselves significant, he came to stress the strict preconditions that must govern non-violent resistance.[1] Thus he called off *satyagraha* campaigns even when successful in effect because they were impure in intention. He was also unwilling to take advantage of his antagonists in times of difficulty. *Satyagraha* cannot be grasped in utilitarian terms. But when rightly understood and properly executed, its effects are both predictable and precise. Duration alone remains the crucial variable; the length of time required for victory depends upon the number and quality of *satyagrahis* involved. For Gandhi, failure is the fault not of *satyagraha,* which is invincible, but of an impure motive or an inauthentic application.

Since "the exercise of the purest soul-force, in its perfect form, brings about instantaneous relief",[2] a *satyagrahi* needs to assimilate fully the prerequisites for its practice and develop the moral courage and political will to fulfil them. The *satyagrahi* does not see himself as starting from a position of inferiority or bondage; his stance is that of a free man. "A *satyagrahi* enjoys a degree of freedom not possible for others, for he becomes a truly fearless person." [3] His fearlessness is unqualified because it has crushed the root of all irrational anxieties,

---

[1] For a detailed consideration, see Raghavan Iyer, *The Moral and Political Thought of Mahatma Gandhi* (hereafter cited as *MPTMG),* Oxford University Press (New York, 1973, 1978); second edition, Concord Grove Press (Santa Barbara, 1983), ch. 11.

[2] M.K. Gandhi, "The Theory and Practice of Passive Resistance", *Indian Opinion,* Golden Number, December 1, 1914; reprinted in *MPWMG,* Raghavan Iyer, ed., Clarendon (Oxford, 1986-1987), vol. 3, p. 22.

[3] M.K. Gandhi, "Secret of *Satyagraha" Indian Opinion,* Feb. 22, 1908; *MPWMG,* vol. 3, p. 31.

the deep-seated fear of death. The *satyagrahi's* readiness to die – though like Socrates, he in no way desires to die – prepares him to face deprivation and suffering. Whether rich or poor, he is indifferent to wealth, since his loyalty to truth forbids any form of idolatry. Similarly, he revalues family attachments so that bonds of affection do not overshadow his commitment to truth. In renouncing tyranny he refuses to be tyrannized, and refrains from judging success and failure by the fickle declarations of others. Yet, though the freedom gained by enacting true *satyagraha* assures sublime contentment, it is by no means easily won. "Men of great physical strength are rare. Rarer still must be those who derive their strength from truth." [4]

The inherently individual and internal roots of *satyagraha* led Gandhi to elaborate the image of the ideal *satyagrahi* and to derive from this model the characteristics of broader *satyagraha* movements. A person grounded in *satyagraha* will in any campaign master the details of moral protocol. Harsh words are inadmissible, as is rudeness. When *satyagrahis* oppose a specifiable set of injustices, they must resist the "intoxication of power" and not confuse it with moral authority. They must help officials perform those duties which are free from the taint of injustice. They must never revile even their antagonists and critics, and they must not accept ready compliance. They should request, or expect, only minimal assistance, and in return they should use their free time to assist the local community in ameliorating social conditions. Even while *satyagrahis* seek to demonstrate to the government that civil resistance arises out of respect for law and for persons and constitutes no threat to public order, they must win the goodwill of the general population by working to give more than they receive. *Satyagraha* as an ideal may seem almost impossibly difficult to implement, yet it is, in fact, a familiar practice in family life. Members within a family often cheerfully endure untidy and even unjust situations. Through voluntary suffering the insensitive and the selfish may, surprisingly, be converted.

---

[4] M.K. Gandhi, "Who Can Offer *Satyagraha?*" *Indian Opinion,* May 29, 1909; *MPWMG,* vol. 3, p. 39.

Gandhi recognized that the credibility of resistance based on declared moral principles is maintained only so long as conduct, unconditionally if imperfectly, adheres to those principles. Any gap between intention and conduct leaves the civil resister open to charges of duplicity or hypocrisy. For civil resistance to merit the title, the *satyagrahi* can feel no anger and no violence towards his oppressor, however much he may be assaulted. His refusal to resist arrest testifies to his loyalty to law, just as his civil disobedience bears witness to injustice. While uncompromisingly condemning injustice, he will never presume to judge the doer, for he knows that oppressor and oppressed alike are victims of an unjust system. Thus non-retaliation is the guiding principle of civil resistance. Gandhi justified non-violent resistance by appealing to an alchemical analogy:

> My non-resistance is active resistance in a different plane. Non-resistance to evil does not mean absence of any resistance whatsoever but it means not resisting evil with evil but with good. Resistance, therefore, is transferred to a higher and absolutely effective plane. [5]

Differences of context might require differences of expression of *satyagraha*, but they could in no way justify the adoption of procedures and principles opposed to truth and non- violence. Since the theoretical basis of *satyagraha* is universal in its application, no limits can be set in advance to its efficacy. Mature judgements are always needed to determine who is the right person in the right place to do the right thing. Though all human beings could learn *satyagraha*, its actual exercise in domestic or public arenas was, Gandhi knew, strictly limited by the adequate preparation and training of aspiring *satyagrahis*. To involve masses of individuals in fiery ordeals for which they are not prepared internally is only to tempt them to violence or *duragraha*, and thus to betray the cause of truth.

Gandhi's unremitting concern with the purity and precision of every act of civil resistance occasionally frustrated his followers, for he would halt a campaign if he perceived the potential for violence. If the

---

[5] M.K. Gandhi, Letter to Wilhelm Wartenberg, *The Collected Works of Mahatma Gandhi*, K. Swaminathan, ed., Navajivan (Ahmedabad, 1958-1984), vol. 30, p. 513; MPWMG, Vol. 3, p. 69.

satyagrahis free to act because he is fearless, those against whom civil resistance is undertaken must be free to respond. If *satyagraha* inspires fear, its victims will react strongly to perceived threats. Only a government or institution which sees no cause for fear will respond with civility. Gandhi therefore recognized the need to remove fear from all kinds of interaction, and, since civil resisters were forcing an issue, the onus of dispelling fear lay with them. But the *satyagrahi* can hardly disabuse his opponent of fear, until he has purged himself of it. Gandhi felt that the surest way to banish fear was to demonstrate a greater willingness to suffer than to cause suffering. Coercion in all its forms – psychological as well as physical – had to be eliminated from the *satyagrahi's* strategy.

Civil disobedience includes many forms of non-compliance, but its most significant application is the deliberate defiance, on moral grounds, of particular laws. For Gandhi, "civil disobedience is the inherent right of a citizen. He dare not give it up without ceasing to be a man." [6] This basic right of the citizen is co-extensive with the duty of an individual to resist complicity in injustice and untruth, however sanctioned by public institutions. Gandhi held that the State, unlike a human being, is soulless and unguided by conscience. At best, it represents the efforts of legal authorities to establish external compliance within a complex network of social relations. States can claim no more finality or infallibility than any individual can.

Owing to the potent forces surrounding a public defiance of the law, Gandhi held that even individual civil disobedience in the public interest could be undertaken only after extensive preparation and as a last resort. As for mass civil disobedience, it could not, he thought, be an authentic form of *satyagraha* if it was engineered by only a handful of leaders. It must, rather, arise as a natural response to widespread moral distress. Even then, civil disobedience may give way to criminal disobedience and violence. Civil disobedience was for Gandhi not an exhilarating or emotive response to injustice, but a solemn undertaking only to be attempted with calm deliberation and a clear resolve to benefit others.

---

[6] M.K. Gandhi, "The Immediate Issue", *Young India,* Jan. 5, 1922; *MPWMG,* vol. 3, p. 99.

The exercise of *satyagraha* through non-cooperation, while still requiring careful preparation, could be best practised by the masses. Non-cooperation involves the withdrawal by individuals of allegiance and support from various public institutions. This may involve such measures as repudiating titles and privileges, withdrawing children from schools sponsored by governmental agencies, declining to participate in legislatures, and substituting private arbitration of civil disputes for public legal proceedings. None of these responses involves the defiance or breaking of a specific law. For where civil disobedience implies a direct confrontation with State authority, non-cooperation involves a voluntary effort to purify the soul by disassociating it from evil. Since Gandhi equated the element of self-purification in non-cooperation with the preservation of self-respect, he held that there was nothing negative about non-cooperation. Beyond its external capacity to bring government and institutions to a halt, it was, he believed, a therapeutic means for the release of truth-force that can reform and regenerate social institutions.

Gandhi envisaged the Constructive Programme as the indispensable positive component in the systematic practice of *satyagraha*. The Constructive Programme is the long-term prerequisite of a system of non-violent self-rule, without which political power or formal independence would prove to be a sham. The Constructive Programme included individual and collective efforts on behalf of unity between diverse religious communities, the removal of social abuses such as untouchability, programmes of rural education and reconstruction, the decentralization of production and distribution, schemes for the improvement of health, sanitation and diet, the promotion of local handicrafts, and, in general, concerted work by all to promote the common good.

> Thirty-four years of continuous experience in experimenting in truth and non-violence have convinced me that non-violence cannot be sustained unless it is linked to conscious body-labour and finds expression in our daily contact with our neighbours. This is the Constructive Programme. [7]

---

[7] M.K. Gandhi, "*Ahimsa* in Practice", *Harijan*, Jan. 27, 1940; *MPWMG*, vol. 3, p. 219.

Gandhi held that the Constructive Programme could not only generate a vast reservoir of non-violent energy, but could also serve as the basis of moral authority and even political power. He thought that much of the energy expended on behalf of external political ends was in fact wasted, and would be far better used by earnest *satyagrahis* in the immense project of social reform and public service. Whilst civil disobedience and other forms of resistance could advance social amelioration, they could not establish the firm foundation for a general and continuous improvement of society or for the full realization of economic, social and moral freedom. While acknowledging the possibility of a division of labour for the sake of efficiency, Gandhi rejected any sharp separation between so-called political programmes and the Constructive Programme. It is, he thought, the judicious combination of constructive work and effective resistance that makes *satyagraha* radically subversive of all forms of elitist politics. He urged volunteers in the Constructive Programme to occupy themselves with that neglected work which brings neither fame nor power. Those resisters who courted imprisonment he valued less highly than those who simply surrendered themselves to constructive work. All political work fell for him within the Constructive Programme and its merit could be judged only in terms of lasting social transformation.

Freedom for Gandhi was neither a condition granted by some social contract nor a gratuitous privilege; freedom was grounded in the moral autonomy of the individual and was thus inalienable. Furthermore, freedom he saw as a social necessity which cannot be severed from its roots in the individual *psyche*; only a society based on some minimal degree of awakened individual conscience can sustain itself for long. Freedom as an inherent characteristic of human nature is true *swaraj* or self-rule. The social and institutional dimensions of *swaraj* are enormously dependent upon the individual dimension. Thus, while *swaraj* is open equally to individuals and to groups, its first step lies in individual consciousness. National self-rule has the same exacting requirements for its nurture and sustenance as individual self-rule. "The outward freedom therefore that we shall attain will only be in exact proportion to the inward freedom to which we may have grown at a given moment." [8] In the intermediate structures between the village and all humanity, Gandhi perceived a variety of possible patterns of voluntary association. He could not, however, view the nation-state as a necessary member of the series. While nation-states have come to claim sovereignty and a special status, they are in no way sacrosanct.

At any level of collective action, the degree of freedom realized is a function both of confident self-rule and non-violent cooperation with other communities and associations. Gandhi held that there was a subtle interconnection between the *swaraj* or self-government realized by any political community and the *swaraj* of the individuals who emerge as moral leaders and social reformers. Since individual human beings alone are moral agents capable of exercising truth-force, all notions of collective *swaraj* are derivative and reflect the sum totals of individual growth. Collective authorities and agencies can neither confer *swaraj* upon awakened individuals, nor withhold it from them. Nor can they legitimately claim to dictate its meaning and content. Yet social and political institutions can create a climate within which individuals may promote their own realization of *swaraj*.

Hermes, April 1988

---

[8] M.K. Gandhi, "Notes", *Young India*, Nov. 1, 1928; *MPWMG*, vol. 3, p. 227.

NON-VIOLENT RESISTANCE AND SOCIAL TRANSFORMATION: SWARAJ AND SARVODAYA

Swaraj in its fullest sense is perfect freedom from all bondage and, for Gandhi, it could be equated with *moksha* or liberation. But, like that knowledge which can be gained even as one becomes increasingly aware of the scope of one's ignorance, *swaraj* is attainable by degrees so long as its achievements are measured honestly against ideals. This is possible because *swaraj* on the individual level involves perforce self-awareness and conscious choice. Only fearlessness permits the *satyagrahi* to substitute intelligent and responsible choice for the illusion of choosing, to become actor rather than reactor. "*Swaraj*", Gandhi once wrote, "is the abandonment of the fear of death." [1] *Swaraj* is vitally connected with the capacity for dispassionate self-assessment, ceaseless self-purification, continuous self-restraint, progressive self-realization, and growing *swadeshi* or self-reliance. Gandhi's metaphysical presuppositions, together with his long experience amongst unlettered peasants, convinced him that moral advancement and social rejuvenation were interdependent, and that individual and national evolution could be furthered simultaneously.

Owing to the necessary connection between individual and national *swaraj*, self-rule is incompatible with every form of exploitation. For Gandhi, common sense dictated that "when you demand *swaraj*, you do not want *swaraj* for yourself alone, but for your neighbour, too".[2] *Swaraj* which is the hallmark of the free individual is the basis for communitarian *swaraj*, which in turn lays the foundation for national *swaraj*, which could, in its turn, in a world dedicated to *satya* and

---

[1] M.K. Gandhi, "The Fear of Death", *Young India*, Oct. 13, 1921; reprinted in *The Moral and Political Writings of Mahatma Gandhi*, Raghavan Iyer, ed., Clarendon (Oxford, 1986-1987), vol. 3, p. 235 (hereafter cited as *MPWMG*).

[2] M.K. Gandhi, "Speech at Meeting of Village Workers, Nagpur", *Harijan*, Mar. 1, 1935; *MPWMG*, vol. 3, p. 262.

ahimsa, become the basis of global *swaraj*, a universal *Ramarajya* or Golden Age. Whilst there is a logical order of priority within the process of attaining *swaraj*, the inherent exploitation of dependence within a pyramidal hierarchy can be countered by the increased interdependence generated through *swadeshi*. Since self-rule suggests self-reliance, each unit in this expanding circle must stand on its own moral worth and lend strength to the others. The vampirical spectre of centralized government must give way to a decentralized confederation of village republics.

> In this structure composed of innumerable villages, there will be ever-widening, never-ascending circles. Life will not be a pyramid with the apex sustained by the bottom. But it will be an oceanic circle whose centre will be the individual always ready to perish for the village, the latter ready to perish for the circle of villages, till at last the whole becomes one life composed of individuals, never aggressive in their arrogance but ever humble, sharing the majesty of the oceanic circle of which they are integral units.
>
> Therefore the outermost circumference will not wield power to crush the inner circle but will give strength to all within and derive its own strength from it. I may be taunted with the retort that this is all Utopian and, therefore, not worth a single thought. If Euclid's point, though incapable of being drawn by human agency, has an imperishable value, my picture has its own for mankind to live. Let India live for this true picture, though never realizable in its completeness.[3]

Gandhi viewed the struggle for independence, or national *swaraj*, from the broader perspective of ideal *swaraj*. He was hardly interested in independence for its own sake. Only through national self-rule, he believed, India could become an active champion of international cooperation and global interdependence. Enslaving millions, the British Raj had prevented them from making a vital contribution to the universal *swaraj* of humanity. Gandhi flatly rejected any continuance of alien rule on the ground that it was demoralizing to the ruled. The oppressed had to endure indirect complicity with imperial iniquity,

---

[3] M.K.. Gandhi, "Independence", *Harijan*, July 28, 1946; *MPWMG*, vol. 3, p. 232.

whilst seeing their own legitimate aspirations persistently frustrated. At the same time, however, Gandhi could not set great store by political independence alone; authentic *swaraj*, he felt, could originate only at the individual and village level. Just as individual *swaraj* involves a constant process of self-purification, so national *swaraj* requires national self-purification - the removal of social abuses, the elimination of economic exploitation, the transcendence of religious differences, the inauguration of spiritual rebirth, the radical reconstruction of internal structures, and the comprehensive reform of an entire social system. Whilst castigating imperial rule, Gandhi also identified the weaknesses that Indians themselves would have to overcome in order to realize true *swaraj*.

Swadeshi, self-reliance, was for Gandhi an integral component of *swaraj*. Just as *satya* and *ahimsa* can be taken as absolute values, although *ahimsa* is logically dependent upon *satya*, so *swadeshi* follows logically from *swaraj*, *Swaraj* can be derived from *satya* (for self-rule is the expression of the intrinsic truth of the individual) and *swadeshi* can be derived from *ahimsa* (for complete non-violence requires full self-reliance). As a validating principle *swaraj* is prior to *swadeshi*, though in daily practice *swadeshi* provides the measure of realized *swaraj*. If *swaraj* is the individual and national goal, *swadeshi* is collective strength. By 'self-reliance', Gandhi did not intend to suggest any romantic notion of 'rugged individualism', but rather an active force only partially captured in phrases like 'self-help' and 'self-dependence'. He preferred the English term 'self-reliance' because it suggests an effort to do what one can for oneself, whilst leaving plenty of room for mutual assistance. Ultimately, Gandhi could see no real distinction between ethical self-transformation and working for the welfare of all.

The freedom of the *satyagrahi* is reflected in the collapse of an exaggerated contrast between selfishness and altruism, which is based upon *attavada*, "the dire heresy of separateness". In the selfless service (*anasakti yoga*) enjoined by the *Bhagavad Gita*, serving the needs of others is commensurate with nurturing the essential nature of the self. This religious standpoint can be translated into an economic programme: produce as much as possible for local consumption, and barter the rest for necessities. Gandhi was willing to go as far as needed to obtain essential goods, but no farther than was strictly required. Consumer economics not only encouraged mass poverty; it was also a social disease. Thus *swadeshi* could be rendered 'patriotism' in a political, and '*dharma*' in a moral, context. Fusing these contexts, Gandhi revealed new dimensions in both. "*Swadeshi* is service, and if we understand its nature we shall simultaneously benefit ourselves, our families, our country and the world." [4] In the protracted struggle for *swaraj*, Gandhi continually sought to give emphasis to the principle of *swadeshi* through his insistence upon the Constructive Programme, the revitalization of *panchayats*, the development of indigenous institutions of new education or *nai talim*, and the emergence of village industries through the use of the spinning wheel or *charkha*. Though willing to defend each of these programmes on its own merits, he consistently held that Indian *swaraj* could have no lasting foundation without the systematic application of *swadeshi*.

As with the principle of non-violence, each proposed application of *swadeshi* should be examined in relation to the principle of *satya* or truth. Such judgements are amenable to self-correction as long as one is ready to engage in daily self-examination and mental purgation. Specific means of attaining *swadeshi* must likewise be assessed in terms of their fidelity to the ideal of *swaraj*, authentic freedom. The pursuit of *swaraj* through *swadeshi*, like the pursuit of *satya* through *ahimsa*, is a matter of individual judgement based upon appeals to conscience and experience. The attainment of *swaraj* through *swadeshi* cannot come about if some areas of life are considered irrelevant. Gandhi rejected the division of life into separate and discrete compartments, and continually sought open-textured approaches that honoured the interdependence of different modes and means to a single long-term goal.

Gandhi's concept of *satya*, with *ahimsa* as the means, gave rise to his complex doctrine of *satyagraha*; his concept of *ahimsa*, with *satya* as the common goal, enabled him to develop the doctrine of *sarvodaya* or non-violent socialism. Self-dependence, when rightly understood and embodied, becomes the crucial lever for non-violent social transformation. "Self-dependence is a necessary ideal so long as and to

---

[4] M.K. Gandhi, "Swadeshi v. Foreign", *Navajivan*, June 19, 1927; *MPWMG*, vol. 3, p. 365.

the extent that it is an aid to one's self-respect and spiritual discipline." [5] It is not an end in itself, for those who become responsible through moral and spiritual renewal become the quickeners who can awaken a new impulse in the hidden depths of social life. Though he had no detailed plan for social transformation, Gandhi cherished the ideal of *Ramarajya* at the heart of his political vision, and firmly believed that *ahimsa* would eventually win global acceptance as a universal criterion of civilized life. This conviction, coupled with his faith in the magical power of millions striving in a common cause, gave him a clear, if intuitive, sense of direction.

Sarvodaya was predicated upon the diffusion of power, yoked to a firm recognition of the moral priority of social virtue over sectional interest. Competition must make way for concord. To be effective, this shift in social and political perspective must be understood as a spiritual requirement in a civilized world, a revolutionary enterprise which would eventually benefit all humanity. As a macrocosm of the individual seeker, society as a whole must come to renounce everything not supported by the concept of mutual responsibility. In practical terms, therefore, pioneering witnesses to truth and non-violence are obliged to teach through example the necessity of shifting the axis of social life from an aggressive emphasis on rights to an active concern with obligations. They must exemplify a spirit of fellowship that has nothing to do with levelling up or down, since each person's *dharma* is unique to himself. They must also renounce the material and psychological exploitation that causes poverty. The votaries of *sarvodaya* need not repudiate the innovativeness of the technological age, but they must shun soulless mechanization and trivial gadgetry.

The production, preservation and distribution of goods may be likened to the circulation of blood in the body. Generally, "the concentration of blood at one spot is harmful to the body and, similarly, concentration of wealth at one place proves to be the nation's undoing". [6] Employing this organic metaphor, Gandhi envisaged a radical reformulation of the elusive conception of collective welfare.

---

[5] M.K. Gandhi, "Our Helplessness", *Young India*, Mar. 21, 1929; *MPWMG*, vol. 3, p. 228.
[6] M.K. Gandhi, "Sarvodaya", *Indian Opinion*, June 20, 1908; *MPWMG*, vol. 3, p. 421.

Unlike utilitarians, he was unwilling to accept the principle of the greatest good of the greatest number. Instead he pleaded for a more synergistic conception of collective welfare, wherein the suffering of the least and the lowest inevitably interacts with the supposed well-being of the most prosperous so as to negate completely the alleged social value of such prosperity. He saw collective social welfare as a chain no stronger than its weakest link. At the same time, he held that the contributions of individuals to social welfare were not restricted in principle by their intellectual, economic, social or political status, although, to be sure, the possession of enough resources could help individuals move beyond greed and engage in service. Gandhi favoured the development of a true science of economics, based upon the principle of *sarvodaya* and directed towards an intelligent regulation of the flow of wealth. He defined the health of this flow in terms of justice, and proposed as a criterion for justice in economic exchange the principle that "a just wage for a worker will be that which will secure him the same labour, when he needs it, as he has put in for us today". [7]

Rejecting every form of exploitation and viewing all human beings as equal sacrificers for the welfare of all, Gandhi sought to lay the basis for a redistribution of wealth that would be consistent with the sacrificial moral order (*rita*) of the cosmos. However inequitable the distribution of material and mental resources among human beings, he believed that men and women could act as trustees, rather than as owners, of their resources, and could thus consider themselves as the partners of all their fellows in society. He had no objection to a large measure of society's wealth flowing through the hands of individuals, but he warned that this involved a moral temptation and a spiritual trial which would require a deliberate vow of non-possession and a self-conscious adoption of the principle of trusteeship. He advised every individual to weigh his circumstances in the court of conscience according to the criteria of truth and non-violence and the obligations of *sarvodaya*. Such a radical redefinition of both the means and the ends of production could serve as the basis of a fundamental reform of society.

---

[7] M.K. Gandhi, "Sarvodaya", *Indian Opinion*, July 4, 1908; *MPWMG*, vol. 3, p. 426.

Through a revolutionary change in attitudes towards consumption, wealth and work, the votary of *sarvodaya* could reverse the rising tide of personal expectations and mitigate the misery of poverty. Gandhi did not believe that the intelligentsia and their theories were capable of raising the lot of the toiling masses; all too often, indeed, the lives of privileged classes and even armchair revolutionaries were based upon cultivated hypocrisy. Gandhi therefore advised political workers to immerse themselves in the Constructive Programme, to engage in "bread labour", and to sacrifice their comforts wholeheartedly in the service of *daridranarayan*, God in the form of the poor.

If only individuals would incarnate the principles of *sarvodaya*, he knew they would find innumerable opportunities for service in the performance of *svadharma*. Anyone may nurture the spirit of *yajna* or sacrifice in his own immediate sphere of obligation. For Gandhi, the path of universal service involves a non-violent socialism devoid of scapegoats and rooted in a sense of mutual trust between all classes of society. *Sarvodaya* or non-violent socialism requires neither inevitable class war nor violent expropriation of property in the name of social welfare. Capitalism, socialism and communism, insisted Gandhi, are alike pervaded by violence and based upon a rigid assumption of human selfishness. He could commend the Marxian ideal of non-possession of property, but he could not accept Marx's narrow interpretations of human life and history. Nor was he willing to accept the proposition that a few revolutionary cadres could enduringly and beneficently transform the social order by politicizing the masses and polarizing them against any set of designated oppressors.

Instead of doctrinal isms or dogmas about historical inevitability, Gandhi addressed himself to the individual integration of precept and practice. He spoke of socialism of the heart and the soul. And he was inwardly sure that the capacity of individuals to contribute to social amelioration is a direct function of their spiritual strength and moral authority, achieved through sacrificial action (*anasakti yoga*).

> Even as members of the individual body are equal, so are the members of society. That is socialism. In it the prince and the peasant, the wealthy and the poor, the employer and the employee are all on the same level. In terms of religion there is no

duality in socialism. It is all unity. . . . This socialism is as pure as crystal. It, therefore, requires crystal-like means to achieve it. Impure means result in an impure end.[8]

Gandhi was deeply concerned with the entrenched tendency of State power to degenerate into active violence, but he was equally concerned lest human beings repudiate their humanity and lose their souls through abdicating individual moral responsibility for the sake of the Leviathan. The onus of responsibility for human life and universal welfare lies with the conscience of individuals, and it is a dangerous delusion to suppose that a human being can relinquish any portion of this responsibility in the name of social contract or legal sovereignty, tacit consent or rule of law. Nor can any moral agent give unconditional consent, for any reason, to the general body of laws, pronouncements and programmes of any political institution. The freedom of the individual to serve universal welfare (*sarvodaya*) must be perpetually preserved in principle against all the claims of State authority. Only thus may society be forever assured of the regenerating influence of truth-force. The ultimate political ideal for Gandhi was

> a state of enlightened anarchy in which each person will become his own ruler. He will conduct himself in such a way that his behaviour will not hamper the well-being of his neighbours. In an ideal State there will be no political institution and therefore no political power.[9]

Though such a stateless society seems a remote ideal in a world of institutionalized violence, authentic progress along these lines depends upon the private and potent resolves of men and women of courageous compassion and calm determination who search within themselves for the seeds of wisdom and strength.

> Euclid has defined a straight line as having no breadth, but no one has yet succeeded in drawing such a line and no one ever

---

[8] M.K. Gandhi, "Who Is A Socialist?", *Harijan*, July 13, 1947; *MPWMG*, vol. 3, pp. 591-592.

[9] M.K. Gandhi, "Enlightened Anarchy - A Political Ideal", *Sarvodaya*, Jan. 1939; *MPWMG*, vol. 3, p. 602.

will. Still we can progress in geometry only by postulating such a line. This is true of every ideal. . . . The only way is for those who believe in it to set the example.[10]

To acknowledge the continual relevance of pioneers such as Gandhi is to awaken the potential for growth in oneself. Once the inward source of strength is touched, the long journey of individual and social regeneration may begin. Faith can repeatedly triumph over fear, never more so than in times of trial.

Hermes, May 1988

---

[10] M.K. Gandhi, "Congress Ministries and Ahimsa", *Harijan*, Sept. 15, 1946; *MPWMG*, vol. 3, p, 606.

GANDHIAN TRUSTEESHIP IN THEORY AND PRACTICE
The Art of Renunciation

The act of renunciation of everything is not a mere physical renunciation, but represents a second or new birth. It is a deliberate act, not done in ignorance. It is, therefore, a regeneration.

Mahatma Gandhi[1]

For India, the most critical issue involves the current rethinking of Mahatma Gandhi's philosophy. Gandhi said that soon after his death India would bypass and betray his ideas, but that thirty years later India would be compelled to restore them. Events have begun to validate his prophecy, and the trend will accelerate.... When India fully accepts that it cannot conceivably emulate Japan without harnessing its own indigenous values and providing new motivations, and when out of necessity its leadership recognizes that it can no longer inflate the token symbols of Gandhi or the facile slogans of socialism, she will be forced to ask more fundamental questions. Only then can the real social revolution emerge, which could have a strong radical base and also borrow from ancient traditions as well as modern movements. While it would be difficult to predict the changes themselves, they will require serious reassessment of Gandhi's questions relating to the quantum of goods needed for a meaningful and fulfilling way of life.

Parapolitics – Toward the City of Man

Mahatma Gandhi held that all human beings are implicitly responsible to God, the Family of Man and to themselves for their use and treatment of all goods, gifts and talents that fall within their domain. This is so because Nature and Man are alike upheld, suffused and regenerated by the Divine. There is a luminous spark of divine intelligence in the motion of the atom and in the eyes of every man and woman on earth. We incarnate our divinity when we deliberately and

---

[1] M.K. Gandhi, "The Golden Key", *Harijan*, January 30, 1937.

joyously nurture our abilities and assets for the sake of the larger good. In this sense, the finest exemplars of trusteeship are those who treat all possessions as though they were sacred or deeply precious beyond any worldly scale of valuation. Thus, it is only through daily moral choice and the meritorious use of resources that we sustain our inherited or acquired entitlements. For this reason, the very idea of ownership is misleading and, at root, a form of violence. It implies rights and privileges over Man and Nature that go beyond the bounds of human need – although not necessarily beyond the limits of human law and social custom. It obscures the generous bounty of Nature, which provides enough for all if each holds in trust only what he needs, without excess or exploitation.

Gandhi sensed that all our resources and possessions, at any level, are not merely fragments of the Divine but are also inherently mortal and mutable. The Divine in its active aspect is ceaselessly creative and ever fluid in form. By analogy, human needs and material circumstances alter even while cultural patterns and social customs purport to maintain temporal continuity through established traditions. Ownership, from this standpoint, is truly a costly and illusory attempt to ensure permanency and succession. It gives birth to unwarranted attachments and insupportable expectations. The selfish grasping for possessions of any kind not only violates the deeper purposes of our human odyssey but eventually breeds possessiveness and greed, exploitation and revenge. This appalling moral malaise leads to inordinate self-assertion and self-projection which can only yield distrust, sorrow and "loss of all". But when we attain the sacred mental posture of the trustee who regards all possessions as held in trust for the good of all, we can progressively approach the high spiritual state of mental renunciation. We can, in the Upanishadic phrase, "renounce and enjoy". It is only when we voluntarily relinquish our unnatural claims and consecrate ourselves to a higher purpose that we can freely enjoy what we have. Thus, self-satisfaction is a natural outcome of a generous perspective and a greater purity of heart. It is truly a function of the harmonious cultivation of our spiritual, mental and material resources. In Gandhian terms, guilt-free enjoyment is inseparable from ethical probity. The real issue, then, is not how much or how little we possess in the way of property or talent, but the reasons and motives behind their allocations and uses.

Gandhi approached the concept of trusteeship at four different levels. First of all, trusteeship, as the sole universalizable means of continuously redistributing wealth, could be seen as a corollary of the principle of non-violence and simultaneously assure the generation and intelligent use of wealth.

> No other theory is compatible with non-violence. In the non-violent method the wrongdoer compasses his own end, if he does not undo the wrong. For, either through Non-violent Non-cooperation he is made to see his error, or he finds himself completely isolated.

Even if wealth could be coercively redistributed, the resulting greed and inexperience on the part of many and the resentment on the part of the dispossessed would lead to economic instability and rapid decline. More likely than not, it would lead to class war, anomic violence and widespread self-alienation. Trusteeship, however, encourages owners to see themselves as vigilant trustees of their accumulated wealth for the larger community without threatening them.

Secondly, Gandhi's practical psychological intuition allowed him to see that fear would prevent other means of economic distribution from succeeding in the long run. A fundamental change in the concepts of activity and courage is needed to overcome passivity and cowardice. Courage must be detached from violence, and creativity must be dislodged from the self-protective formulations of entrenched elites. This involves rooting new notions of noetic activity which are creative, playful and tolerant, and new notions of moral courage which are heroic, magnanimous and civil, in a search for universal self-transcendence. An individual must feel, both abstractly and concretely, a secure sense of joyous *eros* in fellowship, and a positive sense of solidarity with hapless human beings everywhere. He must feel at one with the victims of incomplete revolutions, with the understandably impatient and occasionally mistaken pioneers of great revolutions, and even more with those willing to defy every presumptuous criterion and form of authority which trespasses upon individuality.

The fearful man tyrannizes others: forced redistribution would bring fearful responses from owners, who would see their lives and futures threatened, and fearful masses would deal with excess wealth incompetently. For Gandhi, the ever-present possibility of social change must be approached from a position of truth and courage, whereas fear is weakness which leads to violence. Strength should not be mistaken for the modalities of violence, which are instruments of fear and always lead to varying degrees of self-destruction. Since strength rests on human dignity and respect, workers must approach exploitative capitalists from a position of self-respect based on the capital of labour, for "labour is as much capital as metal". To abolish fear and even failure itself requires a fundamental change in the social structure. The feasibility of this social transformation does not lie in denying the judgements of others, but rather in regarding them as partially relevant though in no sense compelling. Individuals can commit themselves to increasing their own capacity for self-transcendence of external criteria of differentiation, and thereby attain liberation from the self-perpetuating iniquities and horrors of the System.

> Therefore, workers, instead of regarding themselves as enemies of the rich, or regarding the rich as their natural enemies, should hold their labour in trust for those who are in need of it. This they can do only when, instead of feeling so utterly helpless as they do, they realize their importance in human economy and shed their fear or distrust of the rich. Fear and distrust are twin sisters born of weakness. When labour realizes its strength it won't need to use any force against moneyed people. It will simply command their attention and respect.† [2]

Gandhi discerned the critical role acceptability plays in legitimating a social order, and distinguished between a people's tacit acceptance and active dislike of an economic regime. So long as any society finds its socio-economic system acceptable, that system will stand even if a militant minority detests it. But should a significant number of individuals find it unacceptable, it is shaken to its foundations, regardless of the complacency of privileged élites.

---

[2] M.K. Gandhi, "Letter to B. Srirangasayi", *The Hindu*, October 11, 1934.

Thirdly, Gandhi contended that the idea of trusteeship could be put into practice non-violently, because it could be instituted by degrees. When asked if such 'trustees'–individuals who possessed wealth and yet saw themselves as stewards for society–could be found in India in his day, he rejected the question as strictly irrelevant to the theory, which can only be evaluated by extensive testing over time.

> At this point I may be asked as to how many trustees of this type one can really find. As a matter of fact, such a question should not arise at all. It is not directly related to our theory. There may be just one such trustee or there may be none at all. Why should we worry about it? We should have faith that we can, without violence or with so little violence that it can hardly be called violence, create such a feeling among the rich. We should act in that faith. That is sufficient for us. We should demonstrate through our endeavour that we can end economic disparity with the help of non-violence. Only those who have no faith in non-violence can ask how many trustees of this kind can be found.* [3]

Gandhi knew that he sought the widespread realization of a forgotten ideal, but he repudiated the conventional notion that an experiment is unworthy to be tried simply because it stems from an exacting ideal. Even if one argued that trusteeship was doomed to failure, it ran no greater risk than the conventional social proposals of the day. Committed to principles but flexible in policies, Gandhi saw no reason to neglect ideals and to institute social reforms from a defeatist standpoint. Such an approach only guaranteed that structural faults would be built into the new social order. Rather, he emphasized, it is better to move towards the ideal and make appropriate adjustments necessitated by the specific failures encountered in attempting to reach it. In doing so, principles would remain uncompromised and the possibility of improvement would always remain, whereas in a system which assumes cupidity and corruption in human nature, nothing encourages their eradication.

---

[3] M.K. Gandhi, "Answers to Questions at Gandhi Seva Sangh Meeting, Brindaban–II", *Gandhi Seva Sanghke Panchama Varshik Adhiveshan* (Brindaban, Bihar) *ka Vivaran*, pp. 50–59. Cf. "Gandhi Seva Sangh – IV: More Communings", by M.D., *Harijan*, June 3, 1939.

Gandhi not only had faith that it was possible for human beings to become trustees of their resources for the sake of all, but also that many in fact were already and had always been trustees. They are the preservers of culture and tradition, who show their ethical stance through countless daily acts of graciousness and concern for others. To treat man as man requires not so much the acceptance of the equal potentialities of all men, let alone the infinite potentialities of all men, but rather the acceptance of the unknown potentialities of all human beings. Given scarce resources and the limits of productivity and of taxable income, there are definitely limits to what the State can do, but is there any reason why voluntary associations should not be entrusted with the task of extending the avenues of opportunity available to the disinherited? The socialist could argue that by an indefinite extension of opportunities (not always requiring State action) and by changing not only the structure but the entire ethos and moral tone of society, new social values could slowly emerge and usher in an era in which men show mutual respect which is not based on skills and promotions, rank and status.

The minimal goal of basic economic equity is easily stated, yet it is the fundamental first stage for the uplift of the whole.

> Everybody should be able to get sufficient work to make the two ends meet. And, this ideal can be universally realized only if the means of production of elementary necessaries of life remain under the control of the masses. These should be freely available to all as God's air and water are, or ought to be; they should not be made a vehicle of traffic for the exploitation of others. Their monopolization by any country, nation or groups of persons would be unjust. The neglect of this simple principle is the cause of the destitution that we witness to-day, not only in this unhappy land, but other parts of the world, too.[4]

The principle of trusteeship in its application to the equitable distribution of wealth, as well as to the non-violent socialist

---

[4] M.K. Gandhi, "Economic Constitution of India", *Young India*, November 15, 1928.

reformation it underpins, is practicable because it does not require everyone to undertake it all at once. Unlike most socialists who reason that they must seize the power of the State before instituting effective reforms, Gandhi held that enlightened individuals could initiate the process of divesting themselves of what is unnecessary while becoming true trustees of their own possessions.

> It is perfectly possible for an individual to adopt this way of life without having to wait for others to do so. And if an individual can observe a certain rule of conduct, it follows that a group of individuals can do likewise. It is necessary for me to emphasize the fact that no one need wait for anyone else in order to adopt a right course. Men generally hesitate to make a beginning, if they feel that the objective cannot be had in its entirety. Such an attitude of mind is in reality a bar to progress.[5]

Once the barrier in consciousness is broken, the principle of trusteeship can be made to work by letting go of the demand for a mechanically equal distribution, something Gandhi doubted could ever be realized. Instead, he held to the revolutionary ideal of *equitable* distribution, which would not only be possible but necessary in the non-violent socialist State.

Should attempts to encourage the abandonment of exploitation through misappropriation of the means of production fail, trusteeship could be made to work through non-violent non-cooperation, wherein workers realize the capital worth and collective strength of their labour. Should it succeed, ideas which arise out of narrow acquisitive thinking would vanish because they were rooted in unacceptable and illusory assumptions.

> If the trusteeship idea catches, philanthropy, as we know it, will disappear.... A trustee has no heir but the public.[6]

Gradually, statutory trusteeship could be introduced in which the duties of the trustee and the public could be formalized. The trustee may serve so long as the people find his services beneficial. He may

---

[5] M.K. Gandhi, "Equal Distribution", *Harijan*, August 25, 1940.
[6] M.K. Gandhi, "A Question", *Harijan*, April 12, 1942.

even designate his successor, but the people must confirm it. Should the State become involved, the trustee's power of appointment and the State's power of review will strike a balance in which the welfare of the people will be safeguarded.

Fourthly and finally, Gandhi believed that social conditions were ripe for imaginative applications of the principle of trusteeship. The collapse of Western imperialism, the spiritual and social poverty of fascism and totalitarianism, the psychological failure of capitalism, the moral bankruptcy of state socialism and the ideological inflexibility of communism all indicate an ineluctable if gradual movement towards a reconstitution of the social order which will compel some form of redistribution.

The limits to growth make themselves felt through the undermining of social virtues like trust and truthfulness, restraint and mutual acceptance, as well as a sense of fraternal obligation, all of which are essential to individual initiative in a contractual economic system. If such virtues are treated as public goods necessary to universal welfare, then unrestricted individualism faces noticeable limits, lest the social justification and viability of the whole system be destroyed.

C.B. MacPherson went so far as to predict that the time will come when it will no longer be feasible to put acquisition ahead of spiritual values, and that national power will become a function not of market power but of moral stature. Although we have to confront scarcity, the emphasis on Hobbesian self-preservation alone is adequate.

> The rich should ponder well as to what is their duty today. They who employ mercenaries to guard their wealth may find those very guardians turning on them. The moneyed classes have got to learn how to fight either with arms or with the weapons of non-violence.... I see coming the day of the rule of the poor, whether that rule be through force of arms or of non-violence.[7]

Even though the war against poverty will take a long time to win, it is necessary for the State to adopt various measures to reduce the sharp economic inequalities that undermine the working of mass democracy, and to strengthen the organizing power of peasants,

---

[7] M.K. Gandhi, "Advice to the Rich", *Harijan*, February 1, 1942.

artisans, and industrial and clerical workers. In addition to fiscal and monetary measures to reduce income ceilings, it would be desirable to assist wealthy landlords and industrialists in parting with portions of their wealth, property and earnings as public contributions towards specific local schemes and plans. The more the redistributive process can be extended beyond legal compulsion and political action, the more democracy is strengthened at the social level. The more the State can bring together representatives of richer and poorer groups, stronger and weaker sections of society, in planning local programs, the better it will be for all.

At this point the socialist's faith as well as his integrity are tested, and so are his ultimate premises. Does he believe in perfectibility or in original sin? If, like Condorcet, he believes that the historical process and the progress of humanity involve an increasing equality among nations, equality within nations and the perfectibility of man, how much emphasis does it put on human growth and perfectibility rather than on inherent flaws and weaknesses? If committed socialists are not imbued with atavistic or original sin, if they hold to a truly open view of human nature, then they could adopt a different parapolitical standpoint.[8] They could say that it is because they believe in the unknown possibilities of every human being that they are concerned to extend the idea of human excellence to a point where external social distinctions do not matter, but where trusteeship is honoured wherever it is witnessed in human beings.

Owing to his unshakeable conviction that violence can never produce permanent results, only Gandhi's modesty prevented him from asserting that his ethical solution would come to be seen as the only feasible alternative to wholesale misery and destruction, if not now, then in the foreseeable future. He deliberately avoided elaborating a complete system of statutory or voluntary trusteeship out of the conviction that structural and organizational details necessarily varied with the social and political context and with the personnel, whilst the essential core of the ideal was universally applicable. Thus

---

[8] Raghavan Iyer, *Parapolitics–Toward the City of Man*, Chapter 5, Oxford University Press (New York, 1979). Second edition: Concord Grove Press (Santa Barbara, 1985), p. 89.

he could gain a serious hearing from those who would be most affected by the implementation of his proposals without threatening them.

> I am not ashamed to own that many capitalists are friendly towards me and do not fear me. They know that I desire to end capitalism almost, if not quite, as much as the most advanced Socialist or even Communist. But our methods differ, our languages differ. My theory of 'trusteeship' is no make-shift, certainly no camouflage. I am confident that it will survive all theories.[9]

Hermes, July 1985

---

[9] M.K. Gandhi, "Theory of 'Trusteeship'", loc. cit.

GANDHIAN TRUSTEESHIP IN THEORY AND PRACTICE
Regeneration and Rebirth

Ideals must work in practice, otherwise they are not potent.

Mahatma Gandhi

Looking at Gandhian trusteeship more closely, we might ask what it actually means to be a trustee. A trustee is one who self-consciously assumes responsibility for upholding, protecting and putting to good use whatever he possesses, acquires or earns. For an individual to be a trustee in any meaningful sense implies that he is self-governing and morally sensitive. He is acutely aware of the unmet needs of others and, simultaneously, is capable of controlling and transmuting his own appropriating tendencies. He is deeply committed to cultivating his most generous feelings and altruistic hopes for others while consciously and patiently freeing himself from all recognized exploitative attitudes and relationships. He strives to become self-regulating, reliable and sacrificial. But he must become so in a courageous and intelligent way. He must learn to think and feel altruistically. He must learn by degrees the heart's etiquette – to speak, touch and act with the utmost purity and solicitousness. He must become, by virtue of self-training, very attentive to every resource at his disposal – both inner and outer. It is precisely because he sees his abilities and possessions as belonging to God, mankind or to future generations that he is eager to use them to the maximum. His posture towards his overall resources is therefore not one of a lazy or selfish indifference. He is not concerned with hoarding nor is he fearful of multiplying his gifts, talents and possessions. Like the good servant in the *New Testament*, he wishes to increase his meagre "talents", but not for his own sake, nor merely for his own family.

The best trustee is indeed someone who has attained an inward moral balance. He is serenely detached, magnanimous and imaginative. But his detachment is never cold or narrow. It is an expression of his unshakeable confidence in the ontological plenty of Nature and the inexhaustible resourcefulness of Man. His steadfastness and trustworthiness are principally due to this broader focus of concentration. Likewise, his motive is benevolent and self-sustaining because it is not mixed with the turgid waters of personal aggrandizement. Instead, he expresses a quality of love and appreciation for what he has that enhances its moral and practical value for others. He might even possess little, but his sense of when, where and how to use what he has increases its potential good a hundredfold.

If this conveys the invisible grandeur of the Gandhian trustee, then what steps can we take to become more like such sage-like trustees and less like small-minded appropriators? Gandhi might well suggest that our first steps should be the fruit of honest self-examination. Grandiose gestures about giving up external possessions and impulsive statements about our good intentions have little practical impact on our character. The initial step should be at the level of thought. We should think clearly and deeply about the principles of trust and trusteeship. What does trusteeship mean as an idea and as an ideal? What are its practical implications? And what would we have to give up for it to become a potent *mantram* in our lives? This form of reflection and self-questioning initiates a period of "mental gestation". It allows us to strengthen our understanding, dispel illusions and light the subtle fire of altruism.

Once we have grasped the principle of trusteeship at a rudimentary level – and recognized its radical implications for our personal lives and impersonal relationships – then we could commit ourselves wholeheartedly to the moral heroism of non-possession. Thus moral commitment would be fused with clarity of thought and psychological honesty. Clarity in relation to the ideal of non-possession is vital, as is firmness of resolve. Mentally, we must see where we are going – even though it be only the next step – and we must be unconditional if we hope to approximate the end in view. Otherwise, we will neither overcome nor transform the possessive attitudes that self-examination reveals. This is a fundamental theme in Gandhian thought. We must be courageous and unflinching in our efforts to fulfil our self-adopted vows. Only an unqualified resolve can generate the curve of growth necessary to negate and transcend our appropriating tendencies.

If wholeheartedness or total renunciation is the ideal, we might ask ourselves, do little renunciations count? Yes, so long as they are unconditional. If, for example, I promise myself to return all that I borrow, then this promise is binding in relation to my children, to people I like, to people I dislike and to those who rarely return what I lend them. This illustrates the principle that non-possession (*aparigraha*) presupposes a change of heart, not merely a change of intellectual viewpoint. To be genuine, the change of heart must come about nonviolently through the *tapas* of a self-imposed discipline. This is why Gandhi encourages us to integrate unconditional commitment with both philosophical thought and mature self-honesty.

A second step towards instilling the spirit of trusteeship is taken when we simplify our wants. This is a pivotal point in Gandhi's concept of non-possession. If we want to make the most deliberate and compassionate use of our individual talents, gifts, faculties and skills, then we need to simplify our desires and wants. Gandhi insisted upon this minimal moral asceticism for the trustee because he saw that unrestrained wants waste our internal capital and channel our resources into selfish uses. Inordinate wants obscure perceptions both of basic needs and deeper human aspirations. They diminish our sense of dignity as self-governing agents and corrode our credibility with others. Furthermore, when the multiplication of possessive desires proceeds far enough, it leads to self-destruction. This is compellingly depicted in Tolstoy's short story "How Much Land Does a Man Need?", in which a petty landowner is undone by his unchecked desire for land and wealth. He is initially simple and good, but his wish to improve his lot in life is progressively corrupted by a swelling ambition to own and possess more. In the end, Tolstoy answers the question raised in the story's title by wryly stating that the only land we truly need is a grave six feet long by three feet wide.

We might ask ourselves what it means to simplify our wants or needs in a Gandhian manner. It would seem that we can simplify our lives in at least two primary senses. First of all, we can make a concerted effort to reduce the sheer number of encrusted desires and habit-patterns that vitiate our altruistic impulses and fond dreams for others. We self-consciously check the tendency of the aggressive and expansive self to acquire more at the expense of others. But secondly, we take care to do this discriminatingly. We must, like the smelter and the goldsmith, extract and refine the pure metal from the crude ore. We want not just less possessive desires but more benevolent ones. Furthermore, as we cleanse the energy of desire, we purify our imagination. When we gain control over imagination, we establish mind control and render ourselves capable of using all personal, financial and other resources skilfully. We are more earthed, so to speak. With minds unclouded by vain imaginings, we feel more in charge of ourselves and are more responsive to the needs of fellow human beings. Our feeling for what others may attain is gradually enriched, whilst our fantasies about what we hope to acquire wane. We eventually insert our resources into the expanding circle of human interdependence.

Two other factors contribute crucially to our becoming authentic trustees – the art of silence and the ability to put trust in others. Silence or "speech control" is a precondition for all moral and intellectual growth. A trustee must guard his speech if he is to uphold and extend the good. This is not secretiveness but healthy common sense. A trustee's intentions should be as pellucid as crystal and visible to all. But wisdom is needed in all relationships. Hence, a trustee gradually learns not to speak prematurely or out of turn. He fosters a refreshing candour and reserve in speech which enables him to initiate constructive activity in season. He views wise silence and worthy expression as golden keys to maximizing the appropriate use of resources. No one would entrust us with anything precious or worthwhile if we were known to be garrulous, profligate, promiscuous or indiscreet. Nor could we be credible to ourselves and others if our speech is compulsive.

If the ears are the gates of learning and the eyes the windows of the soul, the tongue is the key to the alchemical transmutation of resources and the freemasonry of benevolence. Thus, a benign and intelligent silence is the precursor of effective, beneficial action. It aids mind control and augments true wealth. For example, parents often discern certain admirable qualities in their own children and those of others. These qualities are frequently at a germinal stage. We notice them intuitively but only partially observe them at an empirical level. By a sage-like silence we can help these virtuous traits to grow and luxuriate, thus becoming serene and sacred trustees of the good. Without drawing premature attention to what we perceive, we are ready to acknowledge or welcome the child's unfolding abilities when it seems helpful or important to do so. This makes every man and woman a custodian of the good in others. This is a high responsibility assumable by the poorest and most destitute as well as by the wealthy. Whenever any one of us treasures the finest qualities and exemplary contributions of another, we add to the store of human good. This commonwealth grows unseen but yields great benefits to all. Its value is especially apparent when we help someone going through difficult times. To remind someone gently of the best in himself is to remind him of what is most salutary and what is relevant to the moment of death.

Finally, we strengthen our desire to act as trustees for the good when we imaginatively extend our trust and the sacred responsibility for our riches in relation to others. This is integral to Mahatma Gandhi's idea of trusteeship. But what is the obstacle? According to him, the root of the problem lies in a fearful refusal to relinquish attachments. We often fail to confer equal trust on others or fail to share responsibilities with others because we will not distance ourselves from our suspicions and mental images of them. This is noticeably true with respect to parents faced with granting their own and other children a wider circumference of choice. It seems that a detached love is the only cure because there is no growth unless we expand the circle of opportunity continually and appropriately. This is not always easy, and good results are certainly not automatic. To confer upon the untried or inexperienced that which we have so judiciously cultivated is no simple task. To retire, like the court musicians of Akbar, from the limelight at the right time is a sign of self-mastery, while avoiding the sorry humiliation of hanging on to offices and honours. Such renunciation calls for a great deal of thought and a definite degree of risk-taking, but at least the risks are on the side of the potential good in others.

If every man or woman has some innate recognition of the true and the good, enriched by active participation in a theatre of political interaction, then a collectivity of citizens is a mature moral community. It necessarily rests upon and reinforces social sympathy born of self-awareness and a shared consciousness of "the species nature", the common humanity and essential similarity, of individuals in diverse roles, situations and circumstances. With this wider perspective, it is possible to derive a viable conception of the common good or public welfare from the individual's pursuit of the good in the privileged company of other men and women. This humane pursuit requires a reasoned reflection upon oneself in relation to others and an imaginative empathy with an expanding circle of human fellowship. The germs of noetic change – hidden within the depths of human beings – can become the basis of communities, communes, conceptions of community, at several levels and in concentric circles, in a novel and more intentional sense than any known in recorded history. They serve as the seeds of a rich variety of modes of participation in the politics of perfectibility. An ideal community is as utopian as the ideal man or the ideal relationship. But every human being is constantly involved in some kind of correction from his external environment, so that he engages in criticism of others (often his own way of criticizing and defining himself). Everyone can see through formal laws and coercive sanctions and recognize constructive alternatives among true friendships for an easier, more natural, trustful context in which one can free oneself and grow.

If this is what is involved in becoming better and abler trustees, then what concrete implications could trusteeship have in relation to day-today matters? In other words, if we wish to embody the quintessential principle of trusteeship more fully, how might it affect our attitude and response towards (i) property, (ii) money, (iii) time, and (iv) skills?

Several points should be kept in mind when considering trusteeship and property. In the first place, most of us do not own property, but we all occupy, use and share it. As trustees we should make every effort to look upon all private and communal property with gratitude. We should be grateful for what we have and treat it with respect – whether it be our bodies, our books or the flowers in public parks and private gardens. This mental posture helps us to divest ourselves of the false modern expectation that there is always more, that everything is replaceable, and that there is always someone else available to tend, fix or clean our material possessions – whether a gardener or a doctor. When we treat all matter with respect, we develop an immense appreciation for those who willingly help in the physical upkeep of our homes and grounds. Those who perform this specialized familial and communal service are thereby less likely to fall prey to an often unarticulated resentment when they see our authentic gratitude and the meticulous care we take with all our possessions and resources.

What could it mean for us to be scrupulous trustees of our money? What attitude and conduct are compatible with the living ideal of trusteeship? Money is a means of meeting certain basic needs, and not an end in itself. It must be handled with the same degree of care that we exercise in relation to electricity. We should plan for its proper use so that it fits into the overall purpose and rhythm of our individual and collective lives. It works best when it is in its proper place, and it can be put to noble, mundane and ignoble uses. Balance is required and so are balance sheets. If we specify suitable uses for our funds – from donations to necessities – they can aid private and collective endeavours. Often our bad habits make it seem as though we lack money, and we seek to earn or grab more. This merely creates an unnatural strain. If, however, we study our spending patterns, tracing them back to their roots, we will frequently find the existence of an unacknowledged trait or hidden desire that needs to be transmuted. As we simplify our wants, establish good patterns and set clear priorities, we generate opportunities to build capital for a higher use. Wealth is not itself the source of vice. Its moral meaning depends entirely upon why we seek it, how we acquire it, and how we use or pollute it.

Custodianship of time can confront needlessly possessive and demanding attitudes in relation to time. This appears to be especially true in relation to 'open time' or non-compulsory time. It is undoubtedly true of obligatory time as well. When we are at work or performing necessary responsibilities at home, how conscientiously do we use our time? Is it well thought out? Is it properly coordinated? Are we cheerfully open to unexpected needs? Do we somehow manage to dissipate time through several 'chat sessions' a day? More significantly, how high is our precise level of constant attentiveness? How often does someone have to repeat the same points to us? Time is, to some degree, a function of conscious attention to duty. The more attentive we are, the more we learn and the more helpful we are to others with our time. This is because, paradoxically, the more concerned we are to do our best with and for others, the more we forget ourselves. Our troubles and trials are largely forgotten when we shift our focus of awareness to a higher and more considerate level of human involvement.

How possessive are we about our leisure – limited though it may be? Do we insist that this 'free' time is 'my' time because well earned? We may be quite entitled to what we term our 'private time'. Private time is an elementary human need (although not to the *yogin*, for whom time is a continuous inward state called 'living in the eternal'). But, whilst we are entitled to leisure time, we must, as ethical trustees, be willing to utilize it well. Furthermore, our chaste or corrupt visualization and use of free time often tells us something about the colour and direction of our spiritual will. If, for example, we use our leisure time constructively, then, in fact, time is a friend and not an enemy – either to us or to others. We work with the critical points within time – called cyclic recurrences – to regenerate ourselves within the spacious transcendental realm of the timeless. If we are wholly unable to use voluntary time well, then we sadly diminish ourselves and rapidly subtract from our opportunities to add to the sum of good. *Adharma* inevitably invites destructive Karma, "for whatsoever a man soweth, that shall he also reap".

When we turn to individual skills, we can appreciate the full significance of trusteeship – its subtle power of reconciliation and its ineffable moral beauty. In what sense, we might ask, are our individual skills to be held in sacred trust for others? In what sense can we badly abuse our skills and even use them to exploit others? The litmus test as to whether or not we are true trustees of our skills lies in our expectations of return for using them. Our motivation and our expectations are generally interwoven. In the modern West, and increasingly in the modernizing East, skills and specialized knowledge are felt to be convertible into personal success and personal status. We might suppose that we are too mature to fall for the 'lure of filthy lucre', the cancer of greed, the canker of soulless competition. However, we are often all too susceptible to self-deception in this regard. We are subject to the satanic temptation that our hard-earned skills should purchase some intangible reward – from spiritual salvation to public praise. If we receive no external acknowledgements, then we are almost certain to be insidiously tempted to retreat into the tortured world of self-pity and self-approbation. This is because the tenuous exercise of borrowed knowledge and routinized skills is inescapably bound up with a fragile and fugitive self-image. Our frail sense of self-regard is disastrously opposed to the Aquarian spirit of effortless renunciation and intelligent sacrifice.

In practice, our daily approximation to distant ideals will depend upon the extent to which a substantial number of individuals balance their timid concern with individual claims to freedom against a calm willingness to consider the moral claims of the larger community of mankind. Can even the most ingenious organization of industry be dynamized by the innate desire to serve, not merely the desire to be served, the readiness to hold in trust and not the urge to appropriate? Psychologically, the spontaneous commitment to serve a community selflessly may be a self-conscious development, but the primary impulse to serve others is as much rooted in the universal desire for self-expression as the familiar instinct of self-preservation. The noble impulse to serve others, first displayed in the family, could progressively develop into the Bodhisattvic vow to serve the community of souls. This rests upon the compelling assumption that as citizens mature into creative individuals, the very process of individuation requires the growing recognition of the just claims of other individuals and of concentric communities, as well as a deepening concern with self-transcendence and the pilgrimage of humanity.

There is indeed no external cure for egotism or pride in what we have accomplished – especially when we strive and hope to see that it has truly benefited others. It is only through pain and patience that we learn to enjoy giving freely without expectation. However, if we readily recognize that trusteeship is a form of sacrificial action (*yajna*) natural to man, then it can truly help us to release the exhilarating sense of soul-satisfaction and soul-emancipation taught by the *Ishopanishad* and exemplified by Mahatma Gandhi. Our daily sacrifices merge into the mighty stream of *Adhiyajna* or cosmic sacrifice. Such ungrudging contributions cannot be measured and meted out in the meagre coinage of thank yous and material rewards. Voluntary sacrifice releases its own incomparable spiritual elixir. The sacramental yearning to use everything wisely for the greater welfare of our Teachers and for all Humanity could progressively dissolve the noxious sense of 'mine' and 'thine'. The raging fires of rampant greed, insatiable craving, and demonic possessiveness could gradually subside because there would be less and less fuel to sustain them. There would then arise, Phoenix-like, the incandescent spirit of love and longing for *Lokasangraha*, universal welfare, the ceaseless celebration of excellence and promise. Meanwhile, courageous pioneers could light up all over the globe the sacred fires of creativity, altruism and universal fellowship in the common cause of *Lokasangraha*, human solidarity and welfare, enlightenment and emancipation.

Hermes, August 1985

BUDDHI YOGA AND SVADHARMA

Whosoever knoweth me to be the mighty Ruler of the universe and without birth or beginning, he among men, undeluded, shall be liberated from all his sins. Subtle perception, spiritual knowledge, right judgement, patience, truth, self-mastery; pleasure and pain, prosperity and adversity; birth and death, danger and security, fear and equanimity, satisfaction, restraint of body and mind, alms-giving, inoffensiveness, zeal and glory and ignominy, all these the various dispositions of creatures come from me. So in former days the seven great Sages and the four Manus who are of my nature were born of my mind, and from them sprang this world. He who knoweth perfectly this permanence and mystic faculty of mine becometh without doubt possessed of unshaken faith. I am the origin of all; all things proceed from me; believing me to be thus, the wise gifted with spiritual wisdom worship me; their very hearts and minds are in me; enlightening one another and constantly speaking of me, they are full of enjoyment and satisfaction. To them thus always devoted to me, who worship me with love, I give that mental devotion [Buddhi Yoga] by which they come to me. For them do I out of my compassion, standing within their hearts, destroy the darkness which springs from ignorance by the brilliant lamp of spiritual discernment.

Bhagavad Gita, X

Lord Krishna represents the universality and versatility of boundless joy (*ananda*) and the unconditional love at the core of cosmic and human evolution. Wherever thought has struggled to be free, wherever the human heart has opened itself to the invisible Spiritual Sun, and wherever even a drop of wisdom has been awakened through suffering and pain, courage and persistence, there you will find the immortal Spirit, the sovereign power of the omnipresent *Purusha*. All the *Rishis* and *Mahatmas* reside within the universal form (*brahmanda*) of Vishnu-Narayana-Krishna. In saluting them, one experiences a sense of the timeless, a transcendence that reaches beyond all limits, frontiers and boundaries of manifestation. One may greet the Supreme in the midnight sun, in the dawn of Venus, at midday or in the gathering dusk – the time of memory or the time of reverie. And one must always reach out towards that Divine Darkness which is prior to all worlds and beyond all forms. Myriads upon myriads of worlds of billions of beings arise from that Divine Darkness and reside in the unmanifest light of the invisible form of Vishnu-Narayana.

That light neither rises nor sets, neither waxes nor wanes. It is the same light which, in the words of the Gospel according to John, irradiates every soul that comes into this world. It is the light to be found in the sound of the AUM, uttered, however imperfectly, by every baby at birth. It is the light that descends upon every human being at the moment of death, when he or she stands ready to cast off the external garments of this world and return to the inmost vesture, the *karana sharira*, and come closer to the *Atman*. It is also the light-vibration of the ever-present *Brahma Vach* that pulsates throughout the cosmos, maintained in motion by mighty men of meditation, *Dhyanis*, Rishis, *Mahatmas*, Buddhas and *Bodhisattvas*. All human beings can return, again and again, to sit at the feet of Lord Krishna and so learn how to brighten their lives and awaken compassion in their hearts.

Every pilgrim soul who seeks to increase skill in action for the sake of increasing his or her capacity to add even a little to the sum of human good can benefit from the Teachings of Lord Krishna in the *Bhagavad Gita*. Taken as a whole, the *Gita* is a treatise on *yoga*, the kingly science, of the individual soul's union with the universal Self. That union is, ontologically, ever-existent. But because of the *maya* of manifestation and the descent of consciousness through vestures which seem to create a world of many selves and many forms, the human mind becomes alienated from the true inmost Self in which *Ishvara* resides. It becomes confined within time and space, within past, present and future, and it must struggle to overcome these illusions. Thus the whole of the *Gita* is a summons and challenge to engage in that righteous warfare which every human soul must undertake. In the eighteenth chapter of the *Gita*, Lord Krishna declares that if one will not voluntarily choose to engage in this righteous war, karmic necessity will compel one to do so. The wise are those who cooperate with cosmic necessity, with their own divine destiny, with their own sacrosanct duty or *svadharma*. The wisest are those who choose as firmly and as early as possible, making an irreversible and unconditional commitment, in the gracious manner and generous spirit of Lord Krishna. Without doubt or hesitation, they choose His path, His teaching and His prescribed mode of skill in action.

In the second chapter of the *Gita*, Krishna begins by affirming to Arjuna the eternal existence of one indivisible, inconsumable, inexhaustible Source of all life, light and energy. Having dispelled the danger that Arjuna would abandon through fear the righteous battle and his *svadharma*, Krishna presents before Arjuna the talismanic teaching of *Buddhi Yoga*:

> Yet the performance of works is by far inferior to mental devotion [*Buddhi Yoga*], O despiser of wealth. Seek an asylum, then, in this mental devotion, which is knowledge; for the miserable and unhappy are those whose impulse to action is found in its reward. But he who by means of *yoga* is mentally devoted dismisses alike successful and unsuccessful results, being beyond them; *yoga* is skill in the performance of actions: therefore do thou aspire to this devotion. For those who are thus united to knowledge and devoted, who have renounced all reward for their actions, meet no rebirth in this life, and go to that eternal blissful abode which is free from all disease and untouched by troubles.
>
> Ibid., II

Buddhi Yoga requires a fixity and steadfastness in intuitive intelligent determination which is superior to *Karma Yoga*, the yoga of works, as a means of gaining enlightenment. It involves an eye capable of recognizing essentials, which, once awakened, will give a decisiveness without wavering or wandering. Through this resolute intellect, one's actions may become shadowless – *nischaya*. Even though one may be obscured, as a member of the human family participating in the world's pain, ignorance and turbulence, nonetheless one inwardly preserves the dignity of the power of choice. It is, therefore, possible to touch within oneself that level of absolute resolve which ensures that something essential will never be abandoned, or diluted or doubted, never weakened by careless speech nor lost in the chaos of compulsive acts, but always protected from discursive and dissecting Manasic reasoning. Every human being enjoys such moments of assurance. Otherwise it would not be possible to survive. Even fools and knaves have a few moments of *sushupti* at night inspiring them to awaken in the morning to greet another day. Were it not for this abiding sense of assurance about one's minimum dignity within the core of one's being, one could not go on.

This sense of one's distinct place in the total scheme of things is what Spinoza called the *conatus*, the urge or will to sustain rational and spiritual self-preservation. This is not merely an intellectual notion, but a biological fact. When a person begins to approach death, the *anahata* vibration in the spiritual heart ceases to sound in the *linga sharira*. The Sage or Seer can recognize this cessation of sound and a subtle alteration in the rate of breathing several months before the time of physical death. Throughout this period, the human being is engaged in a protracted review of the whole of his or her life, a review which is too often chaotic and confused, a jumble of recent memories and childhood events. Only at the time of separation from the physical body is the soul enabled to view in an orderly and rapid manner the entire film of an entire life. In the final preparation for this there is an ebbing of the connection between the sound vibration in the spiritual heart and the *karana sharira* and the vibration in the *linga sharira*, and therefore also in the *sthula sharira*. Once this ebbing begins, the person has begun to withdraw or die.

The sense of resolve and human dignity is so weak in human beings today that vast numbers, in the phrase of T.S. Eliot, are only "living and partly living". They have become so disgusted with the world, so confused about the events of our times and the precipitous decline of humane values throughout the globe, that they are hardly incarnated. They are mostly asleep or sleep-walking, drowsy or passive, or they mechanically go about their duties. They maintain none of that minimal wakefulness that is found in many a humble villager who, through desperation and poverty, maintains intact the light in the eyes, the light of *Manas* and human self-awareness. Paradoxically, one can sometimes sense the ray and radiance of pure consciousness in the most desperate and despised of human beings, whilst others have, alas, been educated beyond their capacity to make use of their knowledge. Between the head and the heart there is a terrible chasm, or even a battle. Many tend to be lost and therefore they live and partly live. It is as if the will to live, the *conatus*, has weakened; nothing remains but an automatism of habit and the power of cohesion in the *skandhas*. This is the pitiable condition referred to by Lord Krishna when he speaks of those who are wedded to the fruits of action. The plight of those who have conditioned themselves only to act for the sake of results is an indictment of modern education in *Kali Yuga*. The Iron Age arms too many people to live only in terms of what is perceptible, measurable and tangible. Having reduced all to the terms of a utilitarian consciousness, they come to view their fellow human beings in a crude Lockean fashion: "Every human being is a threat to you, unless you can join interests with him." If a person is neither a threat nor an accomplice in some selfish interest, he is a stranger. Today vast numbers of human beings live in cities of strangers. They live alone amidst humanity, unloved, with no sense of warmth. Such is the tragic condition of 'modern man'.

Over five thousand years ago Lord Krishna anticipated this condition of *varnashankar*, the confusion of castes. Although it will increase and proceed throughout the entirety of *Kali Yuga*, it will also provide an opportunity for those who engage consciously and voluntarily in a discipline of intuitive determination, *Buddhi Yoga*. Human beings who are yoked to *Buddhi* are lifelong exemplars of *Buddhi Yoga*. Preferably before the age of seven, and in rare cases even before the age of three, they have permanently married themselves to the Light of the Logos within the secret spiritual heart. Having so early betrothed themselves and permanently married themselves to the Lord within, they go through the obligations of life with ease, without much expectation, but with a certain lightness and skillfulness in the performance of duty. They do what is needed for their parents and grandparents. They do not despise those who claim to be their rivals or enemies. They do not become too attached to their own siblings, and see themselves as essentially no different from the other children they encounter from poorer families, from humbler circumstances, or even from rich and unhappy families. All of them they recognize as a part of one sacred family.

Between the ages of seven and fourteen, having already secretly betrothed themselves to this inner core of the *Ishvara* within, they become quite ready to engage in the duties of the *grihastha ashrama*. At the same time, they have cultivated that skill in self-education which will last all through the *grihastha ashrama* and take them into the third *ashrama*. Even if they cannot retreat into the solitude of forests, mountains or caves, but remain in the midst of society, they will be like wanderers or *parivrajakas*, preparing themselves for the fourth *ashrama*. They will always be one step ahead of the stages of life. By the age of twenty-one they will have sharpened their powers of reason and by the age of twenty-eight they will have developed sufficient Buddhic insight to be able to synthesize and select. So they are able to let go of what is irrelevant and inessential. They can follow the teaching of Buddha: "O Bhikshu, lighten the boat if you will cross to the other shore." While others who are less wise are engaged in amassing and accumulating, they learn to lighten their claims upon the world and their demands upon others. By lightening their expectations from institutions, their hopes and fantasies in relation either to the opposite sex or in relation to children or parents, they become capable of looking with eyes of wonder each day for what is unexpected. They begin to perceive the unwritten poetry of human life and the silent drama of human existence. Thus they become witnesses to the divine dialectic ceaselessly at work.

Such souls are fortunate, for they have chosen to become yoked to *Buddhi*. Having established true continuity of consciousness in youth, by the age of thirty-five they have already started withdrawing. At the moment of death, whether it come early or late, they are able to engage in a conscious process of withdrawal, maintaining intact the potency of the AUM. In life they have not merely learnt to meditate upon the AUM, but also to enact it. They have learnt the art of will-prayer and gained the ability to act in any and every situation for the good of others, without expectation of reward. They have learnt to cast their actions, like offerings, into the ocean of universal sacrifice in the spirit of the AUM. Thus they are able to experience the AUM, whether in the silence that precedes the dawn or in the noisy rush and din of cities. Even in the cacophony and cries of human pain they hear the AUM. It cries out to them in all of Nature's voices. So they maintain continually an awareness of the AUM, and well before the moment of death they are able to receive the help that will enable them to follow a life of *svadharma* and *Buddhi Yoga* in their future incarnations.

Having given Arjuna preliminary instruction in *Buddhi Yoga* in chapter two of the *Gita*, Krishna conveys in chapter four the correct mental posture of the disciple. He depicts that divine *bhakti* which is the prerequisite for *jnana* and also the true spirit of *Karma Yoga*, because they all fuse into a sacred current of consciousness.

> Seek this wisdom by doing service, by strong search, by questions, and by humility; the wise who see the truth will communicate it unto thee, and knowing which thou shalt never again fall into error, O son of Bharata. By this knowledge thou shalt see all things and creatures whatsoever in thyself and then in me.
>
> *Ibid.*, II

In this depiction of the perfect posture of the *chela*, Krishna stresses the humility of the wise and the silence of the strong, virtues of the Sage whose portrait was given in the second chapter of the *Gita*. Having conveyed this ideal posture, Krishna proceeds in the seventh chapter to present *Buddhi* as an element in cosmic manifestation. Here he goes beyond the teachings of the Sankhya School, which holds that *Buddhi* is a kind of radiant matter or substance present throughout all Nature. Krishna affirms *Buddhi* as wisdom itself and inseparable from himself, something that no human being can develop except by the grace of the Lord.

> In all creatures I am the life, and the power of concentration in those whose minds are on the spirit. Know me, O son of Pritha, as the eternal seed of all creatures. I am the wisdom [*Buddhi*] of the wise and the strength [*tejas*] of the strong.
>
> *Ibid.*, VII

To understand this a human being must be able to insert himself or herself into the whole of humanity, recognizing that there is a cosmic force working in human evolution. This is *Mahabuddhi*, connected with *Mahat* and *Akasha*, the alkahest of the hierophants and magicians. It is the universal solvent and the elixir of life. It is the basis of self-conscious immortality and self-conscious transmutation of the *linga sharira* and the *sthula sharira*. It is the Light of the *Logos*. All expressions of intelligence – whether latent, partial or highly specialized, whether precise, diffused or merely potential, whether in a dog or an Adept –

are drops in one universal shoreless ocean of cosmic *Buddhi*. Therefore, no human being can develop *Buddhi Yoga* on the basis of individualistic conceptions of progress. One cannot simply say to oneself that because one has seen through one's illusions, one is now going to become an apprentice in *Buddhi Yoga*. To say that is to misapprehend the nature of the quest. All forms of yoga require, at some level, what M.K. Gandhi called *anashakti*, egolessness; this is supremely true in *Buddhi Yoga*.

In the practice of spiritual archery one must forget oneself. One can do this meaningfully only if, at the same time, one remains spiritually awake. One must become intensely conscious of one's kinship with all of creation, capable of enjoying its beauty and intelligence without any sense of 'mine' or 'thine'. Wherever there is a display of wisdom, one must salute it. Wherever one finds an exhibition of that true common sense which is helpful in the speech of any human being, one must acknowledge and greet it. This does not mean merely saying "*Namaste*" outwardly, but inwardly bowing down, prostrating oneself before others. At night, before falling asleep, one must count all the benefactors and teachers that one met during the day. No matter how they are disguised, you must be so taken up in rejoicing that you have learnt from other human beings that you have no time to complain of injustice or to become discontented, let alone contentious and cantankerous. In the *Uttara Gita*, long after the Mahabharata War had ended, Krishna told Arjuna that every time one speaks unnecessarily or falsely, one's astral shadow lengthens. If one speaks unwisely, harshly or without thought and deliberation, one expands and fattens the *linga sharira*. So one creates a smoky obscuration of the power of *tejas*, the light within the spiritual heart. The true yogin does the opposite, becoming very conscious and deliberate in the exercise of mental and therefore uttered speech. He learns the art of what D.K. Mavalankar calls self-attenuation. Through this stripping away of inessentials, one becomes capable of maximizing one's every use of life-energy.

Paradoxically, one cannot acquire this self-mastery without recognizing that one cannot do it on one's own. Therefore, Krishna teaches that the power of universal *Buddhi* is an omnipresent essence. Krishna is the radiance in all that is radiant and the intelligence in all the intelligences in the universe. Thus it is only by Krishna's gift that one can arouse that power of devotion which brings the disciple to him. This ultimate paradox, which can be understood in relation to music and love, is vital to spiritual life. It is not only that one must strive and try; a moment comes when one is so absorbed in the object of the quest that one feels the magnetic attraction of that which one seeks. Therefore, the more one enjoys being drawn towards the Lord, the more one can recognize and receive His gift of *Buddhi Yoga*. To prepare oneself to use the gift of the Lord, one must, as the second chapter of the *Gita* teaches, become a spiritual archer, skilled in the art of action. One must become perfected in the precise performance of one's self-chosen duty or *svadharma*. Initially, when Krishna uses the term *svadharma* in the second chapter of the *Gita*, he uses it in relation to the duties of birth, of calling and of caste. He chides Arjuna for forsaking the *svadharma* of a *Kshatriya*. He suggests that if one does not fulfil one's own obligations, chosen and accepted over lifetimes, and if one does not come to terms with the limits, possibilities and opportunities of one's birth, one is moving in the wrong direction and will accrue much evil. Even this initial definition of *svadharma* in terms of one's starting-point in life is much more than a reference to mere occupation and caste.

In the early years of life, most human beings have so little meaningful choice with regard to circumstances that it is difficult to talk credibly of freedom at an early age. Nonetheless, there is for every human being a clear opportunity to accept or not accept that which one cannot alter. In that context, one may be said to choose one's *svadharma*. The concept of choosing that which one cannot change is not fatalism. Rather, it is a critical assessment in consciousness of those elements in one's life which are innate. In the very act of understanding and in the attempt to give meaning to these initial parameters, one must develop and apply some understanding of the karmic field. Moreover, by understanding the karmic tendencies in one's own constitution and confronting one's likes and dislikes, one may come to sense something about one's lower nature and gain some understanding of one's possible behaviour in other lives. Thus, one will recognize that in one's family, for all its obvious limitations, there may be many opportunities for enjoyment and for learning. All true soul-education is an unfoldment through worship and affection, and it is open to every human being to make all life a celebration of learning.

If one really wishes, through the power of worship coupled with affection, to become skilled in the performance of duties, one must recognize that there are those who have gone beyond the initial stages of *Buddhi Yoga*. They have become constant in the power of *Jnana Yoga*, men and women of ceaseless meditation and contemplation. They are the Buddhas and *Bodhisattvas* of ceaseless contemplation, constantly ideating and thereby sustaining the possibility of human aspiration. They are able to do this through their conscious choice of mental solitude and their freedom from attraction and repulsion. Above all, they exemplify perfection of mental devotion. They have become supremely steadfast, like the immovable Himalayas. They are rock-like in their strength of *tapas*, *bhakti* and *dhyana*. Krishna repeatedly gives encouragement to all beginners making their first tentative steps on the path by urging them to discern in themselves something in common with the highest beings who have ever existed. He offers to Arjuna a living portrait, in potent words, of the true Sage. Whilst it is difficult for modern man to understand, there are in fact many more sages, *munis* and *yogins* than guessed by human beings incarnated on earth. Whilst there are billions upon billions of human beings, there are also galaxies of adepts and *Bodhisattvas*. Whilst they are invisible to the physical senses, they nonetheless exist and they all have their roles in the task of cosmic and human evolution.

To become capable of recognizing them and saluting them means that it is possible to gain some light with regard to one's own *svadharma*. Hence, Krishna affirms that it is even better to die in one's own *svadharma* than to be concerned with the duty of another. Even if little is going to change significantly in one's life, the acquisition of wisdom always remains possible and worthwhile. It is a useful mental exercise just to imagine that one is going to die in exactly one's present situation. Then, without giving any room to fantasy and expectation, one must understand how, through this acceptance of immediate *svadharma*, one may strengthen the power of mental devotion or *Buddhi Yoga*. Growth in the power of sacrifice or *Jnana Yajna* is always possible in every circumstance. But that growth requires a turning away from the region of separative consciousness towards the realm of the united hosts of perfected performers of *yoga* who reside within the universal form of Krishna.

To begin to apprehend this is to begin to prepare for the opening of the Wisdom-Eye, a process that is beatified by the realization of the universal vision given to Arjuna by Krishna in the eleventh chapter of the *Gita*. At the end of that vision Krishna makes a statement which is the foundation of all self-conscious transcendence: "I established this whole universe with a single portion of myself, and remain separate." Here Krishna is the paradigm of the Pythagorean spectator, the *Kutashtha*, he who is aloof and apart from all manifestation. He is the fount of those great *Dhyanis* who descend in the dawn of manifestation, knowing its limits and uninvolved while performing their tasks in manifestation. Maintaining their continuity of consciousness and self-transcendence in the Logos, they remain free from the hypnotic spell of *Mahamaya*. What is exemplified by *Dhyanis* in the dawn of manifestation is repeatedly re-enacted in the course of human evolution when human beings, by the power of *vairagya* – true dispassion established by the power of a vow of fixed determination – are able to generate a continuous current of Buddhic insight. Establishing and maintaining this current, testing it in action and correcting themselves by it, individuals may become constant witnesses to the truth. After a while, their minds become so firmly yoked to Buddhic discrimination that it becomes as natural as breathing. In many Buddhist schools and sanctuaries, particularly in the *Hinayana* tradition, neophytes are taught to observe their breathing. When coupled with the *Mahayana* refinement of motive, this can serve as the enduring basis of bare mindfulness and pure attention.

Vinoba Bhave sums up the whole teaching of *svadharma* in the *Gita* in terms of the concept of *chittashuddhi* – purity of consciousness. All human beings, even in *Kali Yuga*, and even surrounded by pollutions, are capable of mental purification. All are capable of maintaining unbroken and intact a stream of pure consciousness, but this requires spiritual food. One must learn to devise one's own rituals and sacrifices, to treat one's body as a temple in which one will greet and bathe in the Light of the Logos. One must learn to consecrate one's own vesture, becoming wholehearted, uncalculating and without expectation in one's relationship with Krishna. When through self-consecration *bhakti* and *Buddhi* come together, *jnana* is released. From *jnana* one may eventually rise to *dhyana*, ceaseless contemplation. Then it is possible to return to *svadharma* and understand it in the salvific sense expressed by Krishna in the eighteenth chapter of the *Gita*. There Krishna puts *svadharma* in terms of a universal formula, independent of birth, of early circumstances, of vocation and calling. It is the art of discovering one's true nature, and therefore becoming creative in one's capacity for self-expression.

Each human being is an original, and each act is unique. Out of enjoyment of the cosmic *lila* and out of veneration for the universal form and omnipresent light of Krishna, a human being can become unrestricted and spontaneous in enacting and delivering *svadharma*. There is a great joy in this and such *ananda* is so all-absorbing that there is no time to interfere with other people or to criticize them. There is no distraction in relation to the demands of *dharma*. Instead, there is full concentration on becoming a servant and instrument of the universal Logos in the cosmos, the God in man, Krishna in the heart.

> With thy heart place all thy works on me, prefer me to all else, exercise mental devotion [*Buddhi Yoga*] continually, and think constantly of me. By so doing thou shalt by my divine favour surmount every difficulty which surroundeth thee; but if from pride thou wilt not listen to my words, thou shalt undoubtedly be lost. And if, indulging self-confidence, thou sayest 'I will not fight', such a determination will prove itself vain, for the principles of thy nature will impel thee to engage. Being bound by all past karma to thy natural duties, thou, O son of Kunti, wilt involuntarily do from necessity that which in thy folly thou wouldst not do. There dwelleth in the heart of every creature, O Arjuna, the Master – Ishvara – who by his magic power causeth all things and creatures to revolve mounted upon the universal wheel of time. Take sanctuary with him alone, O son of Bharata, with all thy soul; by his grace thou shalt obtain supreme happiness, the eternal place.

To become a true votary of *Buddhi Yoga* through the performance of *svadharma* is to become ready to serve the divine will of the *Atman*, the workings of the Logos and the Avatar behind all the turbulent sifting and chaos of the historical process. The *Buddhi Yogin* recognizes the intimations of the divine dialectic in maturing human beings, mellowing minds and hearts, broadening and expanding their quintessential humanity. Cooperating with the Light of the Logos within, they are able to rediscover the germ of purity of consciousness and thereby enter the family of the wise, the fraternity who know all of this and exemplify it ceaselessly. The true hallmark of these Rishis and Mahatmas is the power of devotion and adoration. They are constant in adoration of Krishna, His *lila*, His wisdom, the joy of His dance, the beauty of His unconditionality. They understand from within themselves the way in which Krishna may be seen in Arjuna, in Arjuna's aspiration to reach up to Krishna, and also in Krishna's enjoyment of the seeming separation of himself from himself in Arjuna. This is the mysterious art of the universal diffusion of the one Light, the problem of the One and the many, and the participation of the many in the One. Through *Buddhi Yoga*, *bhakti* and *svadharma* there can be a self-conscious return to the One, but only on behalf of the many. This is the sacred Teaching of Lord Krishna in the *Bhagavad Gita*, given to sustain humanity throughout *Kali Yuga*. All may benefit from the Teaching, returning to it again and again, using it in individual ways, enjoying and appreciating its beauty. Those who are perceptive and appreciate this great gift will make resolute vows to be steadfast in maintaining unbroken a sacred relationship with the Teaching and its great Giver.

Hermes, January 1985

CIVILIZATION, POLITICS AND RELIGION

Mohandas Karamchand Gandhi was too modest to be comfortable with the title of "Mahatma", and too candid to be readily understood by his contemporaries. Throughout his life he saw himself and his ideas distorted or oversimplified by others. Patiently, he kept on affirming and amplifying his ideals so that those who cared might comprehend. Politically, he sought to touch people's hearts so as to awaken their faith both in themselves and in his abiding vision of social transformation. At the same time, he was able to sidestep those contentious pundits who prefer verbal combat to patient assimilation or courageous experimentation. Through his remarkable capacity for self-criticism, his freedom from the complex reactions of others, and his firm insistence on essentials, he nurtured an enormous strength and moral toughness. Revered as a saint and reviled as a demagogue, Gandhi made so powerful an impact that we are still not ready to assess it. If he has already suffered the fate he was anxious to avoid – being lionized at a safe distance, only to be overlooked in daily practice – he nonetheless left mankind a challenging, and even haunting, image of the nobility of self-conquest. This memory will grace the corridors of history for centuries to come. It will long serve to disturb the complacency, and to question the unspoken assumptions, of modern life.

Within the tangled worlds of both politics and religion Gandhi moved freely; challenging sacrosanct dogmas about the limits of the possible, he explored daringly simple alternatives. Owing to his early experience of the meretricious glamour of modern civilization, he could at once declare that its influence was insidious, and deny that it was inescapable. Rather than retreat into stoical aloofness, he lived insistently in the world to show that even an imperfect individual could strive to purify politics and exemplify true religion – thereby restoring the lost meaning of humanity. By holding out at all times for the highest potential in every person, he raised the tone and refined the quality of human interaction.

An unsuspecting reader might be rather surprised at the range of Gandhi's writings. Although he recognized the power of the written word (his collected works fill ninety large volumes), he wrote no extensive treatises, devised no definitive theories, and refused to cultivate a written style in the usual sense of that word. A remarkably pellucid thinker, he was always a man of action, a *karma yogin* devoted to the moral transfiguration of mankind. For himself he asserted, "Action is my domain, and what I understand, according to my lights, to be my duty, and what comes my way, I do. All my action is actuated by the spirit of service." [1]

As a thinker, Gandhi was more resilient than rigorous. Having laid down the foundations of his thought during the pioneering days of his campaigns in South Africa, he elaborated upon its diverse applications as problems arose in his eventful life. With his superb sense of occasion and his assured faith that God provides what is needed by the aspiring soul, he used the enquiries of correspondents, speaking engagements, and the demands of day-to-day business to set the pace and scope of his pronouncements. Convinced that he should never take the next step until he was ready, Gandhi preferred to lead when persuaded, without claiming any messianic mantle. He would not be prompted or pushed; instead he waited for his inner voice to show the way, and often halted large-scale movements because that voice was silent. On one such occasion, when many were clamouring for his counsel, Gandhi simply explained his reticence by saying: "I am trying to see light out of darkness." [2] He was unerring in perceiving opportunities without becoming an opportunist, serving as an effective leader without recourse to expediency.

Gandhi was more inclined to underrate than to overstress the significance of his written words, largely because of his deep distaste for fathering a sectarian cult. Just as he disdained the title of

---

[1] M.K. Gandhi, "Two Requests", *Harijan*, Mar. 3, 1946; reprinted in *The Moral and Political Writings of Mahatma Gandhi*, by Raghavan Iyer, ed., Clarendon (Oxford, 1986-1987), vol. 1, p. 39 (hereafter cited as *MPWMG*).

[2] M.K. Gandhi, "Message to *Bengalee*", *Amrita Bazar Patrika*, Nov. 7, 1924; *MPWMG*, vol. 1, p. 20.)

"Mahatma", he also disowned the notion of anything like "Gandhism". Leaving *The Story of My Experiments With Truth* to stand as his sole account of himself, he unwittingly invited readers to imagine him as an unusually honest, but self-absorbed, individual. In his pathbreaking social experiments, Gandhi saw himself as an ethical scientist conducting an incomplete laboratory study of an imperfect specimen. He was, he stressed, an ordinary man who evolved by setting himself extraordinary, seemingly impossible, standards. As he wrote in more than one place, *The Story of My Experiments with Truth* was never intended to serve as an autobiography. It originated, rather, as a series of short notes on his life, written in gaol during the twenties, and subsequently issued in book form. By themselves, these fragments portray a deeply sensitive personality, but they do not, of course, touch upon the last twenty-five years of his life. A thoughtful reader can gain a more rounded perspective of Gandhi by consulting his wide-ranging correspondence, his significant speeches and his weekly essays.

Gandhi's moral and political insights grew out of a coherent set of concepts, the nuances of which he explored over six decades. Even the claim that he was a man of action rather than of introspection could be misleading. Gandhi worked from within outwardly. Through praying each day, repeatedly consulting his "inner voice", probing his own motives, he would reach general conclusions. Then, after carefully considering the views of others, he would decide upon a course of action. This elusive and indefinable process, which he called "heart churning", itself arose out of his unwavering conviction that constructive thought and timely action are inseparable. If skill in action can clarify and correct thought, soul-searching deliberation can purify action. Gandhi stressed fidelity to the greater good even when it remained hidden from view, together with the perseverance that springs from trust. Maintaining such faith was for Gandhi true *bhakti* He also demonstrated that this practice need involve neither indecisiveness nor ineptitude in worldly matters. A keen alertness to detail can, he showed, be accompanied by a cultivated disinterest in immediate results. Upon a basis of unalterable conviction, one can confidently refine thoughts and redirect action. For Gandhi, this bedrock was spiritual truth gained through intense search and deep meditation; a developed art of fundamental commitment to *satya* and *ahimsa*, a moral dedication to self-chosen vows and sacrificial action.

Gandhi did not think that all human beings are alike, but he did fervently believe that all humanity originates in the same transcendental godhead. Recognizing that he could not define that sacred source, he found in *satya* or truth its best expression. God is Truth, and Truth is God. Since every human being can know and exemplify some truth – and indeed cannot live otherwise – every human being participates in the Divine. From this conviction, one is compelled to affirm universal brotherhood while attempting to enact it through authentic tolerance, mutual respect and ceaseless civility. If Truth is God, man, who cannot exist without some inward truth, must at some level be sincere. Each individual enjoys both the ability and the sacred obligation to grow in Truth whilst acknowledging disagreements.

Gandhi could say without exaggeration that his all-absorbing goal in life was to seek and to serve God as Truth. Longing to obtain *moksha*, spiritual freedom, he maintained that it could not be won through great learning or preaching, but only through renunciation and self-control *(tapascharya)*. Self-control was to be won through action, and the course of action to which Gandhi gave his life was the service of the downtrodden. Service of humanity alone could generate the disinterested self-control essential to spiritual emancipation. Through the selfless embodiment of *ahimsa* and *satyagraha*, Gandhi believed theophilanthropists could ameliorate human misery whilst freeing themselves from worldly hopes and fears. Freedom, he felt, lies in *anasakti*, selfless service. He was certain that he could never be a votary of principles which depended for their existence upon mundane politics or external support. While even social work is impossible without politics, political work must ever be judged in terms of social and moral progress, which are in turn inseparable from spiritual regeneration.

Gandhi viewed civilization as that which assists moral excellence, moving individuals and society to truth and nonviolence. True civilization aids self-realization and nurtures universal brotherhood. Gandhi decried modern civilization because he felt that it is less an instrument for soul-growth than a supposed end in itself. Its vaunted intellectual and technological achievements deflect it from any authentic concern with moral welfare. Its "isms" and social structures, sciences and machines, are not evil in themselves – though in a true civilization many of them would not exist – but they actively participate in the contagion of corruption that pervades it. Modern civilization is diseased in the Socratic sense because it blinds the soul and eclipses the truth. It is, as Tolstoy also thought, bondage masquerading as freedom.

Gandhi contended that the earth has enough resources to provide for human need, but not human greed. He held, therefore, that every man, woman and child would eat adequately, clothe and shelter themselves comfortably, if there were a greater sharing of wealth in all parts of the world. Spurning equally the insatiable acquisitiveness of capitalism and the mechanistic materialism of communism, Gandhi condemned the very basis of modern civilization. In his notion of authentic civility, a sense of spiritual and social obligation is fused with a spontaneous sense of natural reciprocity. He further upheld the belief, steadily undermined since the eighteenth century, that social institutions and political actions are by no means exempt from ethics. For social institutions are, he felt, the visible expression of moral values that mould the minds of individuals. It is therefore impossible to alter institutions without first affecting those values. Since modern civilization is one complex tissue of intertwined evils, no plan of partial and gradual reform from within the system can produce a lasting remedy. Gandhi sought to destroy systems, not persons; but he argued that the "soulless system" had to be destroyed without its reformers themselves becoming soulless.

Holding that one should repudiate wrongs without reviling wrongdoers, Gandhi could not bring himself to condemn the British for their mistakes and even their misdeeds in India. They too, he felt, were the hapless victims of a commercial civilization. The theme of Hind *Swaraj* was not just the moral inadequacy and extravagant pretensions of modern civilization, but its treacherously deceptive self-destructiveness. "This civilization is irreligion", he concluded, "and it has taken such a hold on the people of Europe that those who are in it appear to be half mad." ³ Yet, he added, "it is not the British that are responsible for the misfortunes of India but we who have succumbed to modern civilization." ⁴ For Gandhi, the villain is hypocritical materialism, the judge is he who frees himself from the collective hallucination, and the executioner is the Moral Law (Karma) which inexorably readjusts equilibrium throughout the cosmos. ⁵

Gandhi did not preserve his feeling for common humanity by remaining conveniently apart from it. He knew poverty and squalor at first hand; he knew too the desperate violence found in those who have lived on the edge of starvation. Yet he could still extol the Indian peasant with ringing authority:

> The moment you talk to them and they begin to speak, you will find that wisdom drops from their lips. Behind the crude exterior you will find a deep reservoir of spirituality.... In the case of the Indian villager an age-old culture is hidden under an encrustment of crudeness. Take away the encrustation, remove his chronic poverty and his illiteracy and you have the finest specimen of what a cultured, cultivated, free citizen should be. ⁶

Gandhi's longing to transform contemporary civilization was mirrored in his political thought and action. No more than civilization is politics an end in itself. Gandhi invoked Indian tradition in rejecting the modern dichotomy between religion and politics, but he went much further than most classical Indian thinkers in dispensing entirely with notions of *raison d'etat* and in hoping to counter the propensity of politics to become corrupt. Even if all wished to shed their pretensions and nurture the "enlightened anarchy" of an ideal world community, politics would be necessary since human beings differ in their perspectives, needs and desires. Accepting, then, that politics cannot

---

³ M.K. Gandhi, *Hind Swaraj*, ch. VI; *MPWMG*, vol. 1, p. 214.
⁴ M.K. Gandhi, Preface to second Gujarati edition of *Hind Swaraj*, May 1914; *MPWMG*, vol. 1, p. 277.
⁵ For a fuller treatment, see by Raghavan Iyer, *The Moral and Political Thought of Mahatma Gandhi (MPTMG)*, Oxford University Press (New York, 1973, 1978); second edition, Concord Grove Press (Santa Barbara, 1983), chs. 2 and 3.
⁶ M.K. Gandhi,"Discussion with Maurice Frydman", *Harijan*, Jan. 28, 1939; *MPWMG*, vol. 3, p. 530.

simply be abolished, Gandhi sought to purify politics by showing that its sovereign principle is neither coercive nor manipulative power, but moral and social progress.

Gandhi rejected collectivist theories of both State and society. He argued that only the individual could exercise conscience, and, therefore, morally legitimate power. Refusing to hold political office himself or to endorse those compatriots who did, he saw power as a by-product of social activity at the family and community level. Through *satyagraha* he sought to introduce religious values into politics by extending the rule of domestic life into the political arena. Ascribing the underlying continuity of mankind to the sacrificial exercise of soul-force within families, he was convinced that the same energies could be brought to bear self-consciously in the larger sphere of life. For the *satyagrahi*, the individual committed to Truth, the only power that can be legitimately exercised is the capacity to suffer for the errors of others and on behalf of the welfare of all whether it be the family, the nation or the world.

The individual is therefore always to be treated as an end in himself, while social institutions are always to be treated as corrigible means to some greater end. The *satyagrahi* should be active in politics if he can stand firmly for social justice and initiate constructive change. Where he cannot, he must practise non-cooperation. One can at least refuse to participate in evils that one cannot directly alter, even if the *satyagrahi* soon finds that he can alter more than he previously supposed. Far from denying the existence of conflicts of interest, Gandhi evolved *ahimsa* so as to resolve such conflicts by limiting, if not wholly removing, their *himsa* (violence). Gandhi further advocated voluntary poverty as an essential prerequisite for any social or political worker who wished to remain untainted by the wasteful greed of power politics. He even maintained that possessions are anti-social: it is not enough to continue possessing goods in practice under the sincere illusion that one has given them up in spirit. Possessions, he believed, should be held in trust at the disposal of those who need them. Furthermore, those who trusted the community to provide for essential needs could come to experience true freedom.

Firmly believing in the fundamental unity of life, he rejected any distinction between public and private, between secular and sacred, and ultimately, between politics and religion. Religion, for Gandhi, signifies a spiritual commitment which is total but intensely personal, and which pervades every aspect of life. Gandhi was always concerned more with religious values than with beliefs; more with the fundamental ethics that he saw as common to all religions than with formal allegiance to received dogmas which hinder, rather than aid, religious experience. He staunchly refused to associate religion with sectarianism of any kind. "Isms", he thought, appeal only to the immature; through religion he sought nothing less than the Truth itself. In his vision, each soul resembles a drop of water from the ocean of divinity, fallen into a muddy pool. To experience consanguinity with God it must cleanse itself of the mud. Whatever its tenets, assumptions or practices, every true religion holds out this hope of self-regeneration. All true religions are therefore equal in Gandhi's estimation. He regularly advised enquirers to discover the true meanings of the faiths they were born into under karma. The seeker pledged to Truth must, however, abstain from proselytizing others. He should rather encourage, or inspire, others to elevate the inner and outer practice of their own faiths. Different religions and sects emerge only because no tradition and no individual can be the exclusive receptacle for boundless Truth.

Gandhi found no difficulty in accepting his own religion, while also acknowledging that he was at heart a Christian, a Jain, a Muslim and a Buddhist. He thought that accepting the *Bible* did not require rejecting the *Koran*, just because one scripture speaks more directly to an individual than another. The *Bhagavad Gita* was Gandhi's "spiritual dictionary", [7] but his continued recourse to it did not negate any other sacred texts. He thought that the *Bhagavad Gita* was the most accessible text in the Indian tradition. As it affirmed that God represents perfect Truth, and that imperfect man, whatever his path, can follow its precepts and come closer to God, the *Gita* has universal application. Gandhi felt that enduring help could come only from within, from

---

[7] M.K. Gandhi, Preface to *Gitapadarthakosha, Harijanbandhu*, Oct. 25, 1936, *MPWMG*, vol. 1, p. 97.

what one learns through *tapascharya*.

For Gandhi, religions and religious concepts grow through human experience just as individuals mature morally, socially and spiritually. No religion can claim to be complete in time. No formulation is final. He could thus say, without condescension, that Hinduism included Jainism and Buddhism, while freely criticizing Hindu sectarian disagreements and dogmatism; he praised Islamic brotherhood, while decrying the intransigence of some Muslim zealots; he upheld Christianity as a "blazing path of *bhakti yoga*" and the Sermon on the Mount as a model, while dismissing most theology because it invidiously tends to explain away what should be taken to heart and applied. Gandhi's radical reinterpretation of Hindu values in the light of the message of the Buddha was a constructive, though belated, response to the ethical impact of the early Buddhist Reformation on decadent India.

Given such beliefs, religion is ultimately priestless, because the capacity for prayer lies latent within human nature. Prayer and all devotion *(bhakti)* are, for Gandhi, a kind of petition. The noblest and purest petition is that one should become outwardly what one is inwardly – that one's thoughts, words and deeds should ever more fully express the soul's core of truth and non-violence. Prayer is to God as thought is to Truth, but since God and Truth are beyond all limiting conceptions, they cannot accommodate egotistic petitions. Prayer is truly an intense supplication towards one's inmost ineffable nature, the source of one's being and strength, the touchstone of one's active life. Just as politics and religion should endeavour to reduce the gap between theory and practice, so too prayer must narrow the gulf between one's real being and one's manifest appearance.

Gandhi's heartfelt reverence for all religions and for their spiritual founders and exemplars, together with his restraint in attributing to any of them uttermost divine perfection, arose from his concept of Deity. God is alien to no human being, not even the atheist who risks sundering himself from his own source. "To deny God", Gandhi believed, "is like committing suicide." [8] Since the divine is reflected

---

[8] M.K. Gandhi, Letter to Hanumanprasad Poddar, *Mahadevbhaini Dairy*, vol. 1, p. 82; *MPWMG*, vol. 1, p. 587.

within every individual as his inalienable core of Truth, God will appear in as many forms and formulations as there are possibilities of human thought. There are, at least, as many definitions of God as there are individuals, and God transcends them all. Beyond the boundaries of reason and imagination, God is ineffable, indescribable, without form or characteristic. Gandhi thought that the concepts and images used to express the divine, including his own formulations, were at best derived from glimpses of immense but partial truths. As aids, these images may assist human growth; but as dogmas, they tend to breed sectarianism and violence. As aids, they may foster the universal religion of duty and detachment (*dharma* and *vairagya*); but as dogmas, they tend to reinforce a harsh insistence upon rights and privileges. For Gandhi, all conceptions of God are merely means to be used in the service of Truth.

By upholding vows, any person, Gandhi held, can align his conduct to the motionless centre of the wheel of life. But the individual must first adopt stern measures to control the mind in its everyday vagaries, monitoring or even selecting his every thought. Only in this way can one become single-minded and so incarnate one's beliefs in one's sphere of *dharma*. Gandhi felt that conscience is kept alive not by a preoccupation with intention, but by concern for rectitude of action. He deliberately shifted emphasis from the spiritual emancipation of the individual to the collective benefit of all.

Gandhi's fundamental convictions constitute a world-view of far-reaching dimensions. They cannot be proved, for "truth is its own proof, and non-violence is its supreme fruit." [9] But Gandhi never doubted that if these ideals were practised with sincerity and humility, aimed not at the applause of the world, but at the support of the soul, they would gradually prove to be self-validating, helping the individual, painfully but assuredly, to mature into a joyous state of spiritual freedom and self-mastery. It is awe-inspiring, but hardly surprising, that upon receiving his assassin's bullets, Gandhi made a final gesture of forgiveness and whispered, "Hey Ram! Hey Ram!"

Gandhi did not wish to be considered an inspired prophet. His

---

[9] M.K. Gandhi, "Meaning of the *Gita*", *Navajivan*, Oct. 11, 1925; *MPWMG*, vol. 1, p. 80.

metaphysical presuppositions only deepened his disarming faith in a human solidarity that admits of no degree. He persisted in seeing himself as a somewhat unworthy exemplar of his exacting ideals. And yet, by his lifelong fidelity to his vows, Gandhi demonstrated the liberating and transforming power of any attempt to fuse metaphysics and conduct, theory and practice, through an enormous effort of the will. A few months before the assassination, Sarojini Naidu, the poetess who had played a leading role in the Salt March, tried to capture something of the enigma of Gandhi in the context of the twentieth century:

With Christ he shares the great gospel that love is the fulfilling of the law. With the great Muhammad he shares the gospel of brotherhood of man, equality of man and oneness of man. With Lord Buddha he shares the great evangel that the duty of life is not self-seeking but to seek the truth, no matter at what sacrifice. With the great poets of the world, he shares the ecstasy of the vision that the future of man is great, that the future of man can never be destroyed, that all sin will destroy itself but that love and humanity must endure, grow and reach the stars. Therefore, today, a broken world ruined by wars and hatred, a broken world seeking for a new civilization honours the name of Mahatma Gandhi.

In himself, he is nothing. There are men of learning, greater than his, and there are men of wealth and power, and men of fame, but who is there that combines in one frail body the supreme qualities of virtue enshrined in him: courage indomitable, faith invincible, and compassion that embraces the entire world? This transcendental love of humanity that recognizes no limitations of race, no barriers of country but gives to all, like a shining sun, the same abundance of love, understanding and service. Every day – today and yesterday and tomorrow – every day is the same story of the miracle of Gandhi in our own age.

Who said that the age of miracles is past? How should the age of miracles be past while there is such a superb example of embodied miracle in our midst? . . . He was born like other men, he will die like other men, but unlike them he will live through the beautiful gospel he has enunciated, that hatred cannot be conquered by hatred, the sword cannot be conquered by the sword, that power cannot be exploited over the weak and the fallen, that the gospel of non-violence which is the most dynamic and the most creative gospel of power in the world, is the only true foundation of a new civilization, yet to be built. [10]

Hermes, February 1988

---

[10] D.G. Tendulkar, *Mahatma*, vol. 8, p. 144; *MPWMG*, vol. 1, p. 12.

SAT AND SATTVA

> *In one sense, Oeaohoo is the "Rootless Root of All"; hence, one with Parabrahmam; in another sense it is a name for the manifested ONE LIFE, the Eternal living Unity. The "Root" means...pure knowledge (Sattva), eternal (Nitya) unconditioned reality or SAT (Satya), whether we call it Parabrahmam or Mulaprakriti, for those are the two aspects of the ONE. The "Light" is the same Omnipresent Spiritual Ray, which has entered and now fecundated the Divine Egg, and calls cosmic matter to begin its long series of differentiations. The curds are the first differentiation, and probably refer also to that cosmic matter which is supposed to be the origin of the "Milky Way"– the matter we know. This "matter", which, according to the revelation received from the primeval Dhyani-Buddhas, is, during the periodical sleep of the Universe, of the ultimate tenuity conceivable to the eye of the perfect Bodhisattva – this matter, radical and cool, becomes, at the first reawakening of cosmic motion, scattered through Space; appearing, when seen from the Earth, in clusters and lumps, like curds in thin milk. These are the seeds of the future worlds, the "Star-stuff".*
>
> The Secret Doctrine, i 68-69

The eternal life *(Sat)* and pure knowledge *(Sattva)* of the perfected *Bodhisattva* transcend the boundaries of cosmic manifestation. They have their pristine root in a realm that precedes and encompasses the universe, a realm that is undisturbed by its eventual passing away. During the night of *Maha Pralaya* – "the periodical sleep of the Universe" – the spiritual eye of the *Bodhisattva* bears eternal witness to the slumbering veils of rarefied cosmic matter. This state of exalted spiritual wakefulness *(Turiya)* lies at the farthest end of the path of pure knowledge, the Bodhisattvic path of self-sacrifice, self-correction and self-regeneration in the service of universal enlightenment. It is the serene fulfilment of both mind and heart, the self-conscious intelligence of the Manasa and the spiritual intuition of the *Dhyani-Bodhisattva*. It is a path of self-sanctification travelled through honouring the sanctity of all beings. The supreme realization of the one ray of Spirit in the Bodhisattvic heart rests upon the recognition of the presence of that ray in the heart of every atom and every creature throughout the entirety of manifestation. Yet it depends too upon the realization that the spiritual ray, in essence, is uninvolved in any manifestation or any differentiation.

This supernal understanding of the *Bodhisattva* is at once a cognitive concept of the mind and a mystical conception of the heart. It is compassionate understanding, transcending the seeming otherness of "other" beings. However intense one's concern, one cannot ever understand another human being through egotism alone. To understand one's parents, for example, one must set aside lower *Manas*. True understanding of human beings is different from personal love or hatred. It consists, rather, of an active sense of moral bonds between human beings and a willingness to engage in sacrifice to deepen one's understanding and observance of those bonds. Such understanding is akin to that of a parent for a child. While the child is swept along by the vicissitudes of change that accompany infancy and youth, the parent offers an understanding born of pain and sacrifice. Ordinarily, however, this is mostly involuntary and not enriched by wisdom. The understanding of the *Bodhisattva* is rooted in wisdom which comes from a long and arduous path of deliberate sacrifice of memories and expectations, of self-image and the sense of will, of the very conception of success and failure. To enter this path means to sacrifice much more than people normally think they should or even could sacrifice. Yet every vestige of the separative self must be renounced to sanctify the field of one's awareness and prepare it for the awakening of pure understanding.

Every day human beings enjoy innumerable opportunities to touch the Buddhic stream of intuitive understanding that underlies their lives as incarnated souls on earth. At twilight it is possible to take stock of the day and to welcome into the sanctuary of one's inner understanding wise thoughts and compassionate feelings that come unbidden. Through cleansing one's motivation and transcending the egotistic sense of likes and dislikes, one may avail oneself of life's innumerable opportunities to sanctify and deepen the power of understanding. Authentic understanding of anything at all, whether it be of the events of the day or of other human beings, reaches towards that which is hidden within the surface and succession of events, behind the dense veil of likes and dislikes, beyond predilections and habits. To understand that which is truly at the heart of a situation is to pass beyond and behind all names and forms, to become the object of one's scrutiny. Sometimes people use the colloquial expression "understanding what makes somebody tick". One cannot know what makes a human being tick unless one becomes receptive to the inaudible vibration in the imperishable heart of a human being. That *anahata* heart is inseparable from the eternal vibration – AUM. Ultimately, to understand another human being one has to become that human being. Though perfectly possible, this involves a tremendous act of the imagination.

One cannot persist in looking at the world in terms of sights and sounds and external forms. One's sensations, perceptions and conceptions must all be transcended, not only in their successive multiplicity, but also at their genetic core. Distant and difficult as this may seem to ordinary understanding, this exalted state of transcendence and knowledge is inherently possible. That pure knowledge or *Sattva* enables the soul to gain full and true understanding of anything and everything.

> The original for Understanding is *Sattva*, which Sankara(acharya) renders *antahkarana*. "Refined", he says, "by sacrifices and other sanctifying operations."... *Sattva* is said by Sankara to mean *buddhi* – a common use of the word.... Whatever meaning various schools may give the term, *Sattva* is the name given among Occult students of the *Aryasanga* School to the dual Monad or *Atma-buddhi*, and *Atma-buddhi* on this plane corresponds to *Parabrahm* and *Mulaprakriti* on the higher plane.
>
> Ibid.

Buddhi is no other than direct perception, divine discrimination and spiritual intuition. Very often people ignorantly associate intuition with inexplicable hunches or vague guesses. Self-indulgence and self-rationalization of such psychic tendencies are quite harmful to the true awakening of *Buddhi*, and should never be confused with it. It is far better to be humble than to pretend to have exact knowledge when one does not. It is even better, in fact, to avoid talk about *Buddhi* and Buddhic awareness than to be involved in the shadowy world of pseudo-speculative knowledge. True Buddhic understanding is real knowledge, which comes in the Silence. At times, it comes with a laser-like flash of instantaneous directness and recognition so exact that one might call it microscopic omniscience. This is, however, nothing alien to human nature. It is none other than the highest subtlest material field within the hebdomadic human vestures. *Buddhi* is to *Atman* like spiritual subliminal and noumenal matter lit up, made radiant in relation to the perpetual motion and light-energy of the *Atman*. *Buddhi*, activated and aroused, is pure *Sattva*, refined pure knowledge, free from all taint of separateness, all taint of selfhood. It is totally unblemished by any trace of partiality, any bias of partisanship, any vestige of attachment and possession. As pure knowledge, it is a principle entirely independent of the standpoint, or even the existence, of the lower self. It is the living wisdom of eternal life itself.

The teaching of the *Aryasangha* school of the great *Yogacharya* tradition regards *Buddhi* not only as the highest principle of understanding in human nature, but also as inseparable from the principle of Universal Wisdom in the cosmos. *Sattva*, taken as the Atma-Buddhic duad, is itself only an analogue within the human field to that in the cosmic field which represents the unity of primordial cosmic substance and cosmic ideation. *Atma* and *Buddhi* are two in one, just as *Parabrahm* and *Mulaprakriti* are inseparably one. *Parabrahm* is the Absolute, and *Mulaprakriti* is similar to a veil upon the Absolute. In the highest fusion of ideation and substance, at the cosmic level, which is theoretically accessible to every human being, one finds the ultimate root of the Bodhisattvic standpoint which is identical to the basis in *Atma-Buddhi* of the highest pure knowledge. To understand the sense in which this knowledge transcends even the manifested cosmos in its entirety, though subtly diffused throughout it, one must understand the relationship between cosmic ideation and its many differentiated vestures.

> Cosmic Ideation focussed in a principle or *upadhi* (basis) results as the consciousness of the individual Ego. Its manifestation varies with the degree of *upadhi*, *e.g.*, through that known as *Manas* it wells up as Mind-Consciousness; through the more timely

differentiated fabric (sixth state of matter) of the *Buddhi* resting on the experience of *Manas* as its basis – as a stream of spiritual INTUITION.

Ibid., i 329

In its ultimate sense cosmic ideation has no necessary connection with forms or events, with succession or simultaneity, nor indeed with any of the terms belonging to a differentiated world of subjects and objects in space and time. Thus, *Gupta Vidya* speaks of pre-cosmic ideation, the conceptual correlate of pre-cosmic root substance. In relation to both ideation and substance, there is that which is pre-existent. This pre-existence is ontological and not temporal. It is not merely at some prior point in time, but comes before the existence of the cosmos in the order of being itself. Cosmic ideation, in order to focus, requires a lens or instrument – an *upadhi*. At the subtlest conceivable level this basis is cosmic substance, an extended purely spiritual quality called *suddhasattva*, the subliminal matter that makes up the subtle vestures of *Mahatmas*. It is only by focussing pre-cosmic ideation upon an *upadhi* that there is individuation, the active capability of consciousness to take an individual standpoint in relation to a world. To begin to imagine what this Bodhisattvic standpoint might be like, one could attempt to visualize what it would be like to see omnidirectionally. This could be helped by meditative exercises, in which one visualizes oneself as a point of perceptivity radiating in every direction throughout space, reaching towards the surface of an ever-receding and infinite sphere. Such pure vision cannot be trammelled by limits that apply to sense-objects, whether on the gross physical plane or the subtle astral plane.

It is an understanding capable of tracing back causes to their root, and of anticipating from that root cause the entire series. It is like knowing the seed and limit of a series, and all the intervening stages and rates of transformation in its expression. This is merely an imperfect mathematical analogy to a transcendental process of consciousness which far outstrips the sluggish structures of rationality. *Buddhi* is one with the finely differentiated spiritual substance of the sixth plane of matter. Differentiated from it and at a greater degree of differentiation of the same fabric of substance is the principle of *Manas* on the fifth plane of matter. Supported by the refined experience of *Manas*, "by sacrifices and other sanctifying operations", according to Shankara, *Buddhi* emerges as a stream of pure spiritual intuition having a quality of unbroken continuity of perception. The Buddhic individual carries within him through day and night, through dreaming and sleeping and waking, a knowledge of the *Atman*. He is awake in dreams and can anticipate before sleeping his first thought upon waking. These are, in effect, nothing but minor applications of the developed capacity to overcome the discontinuities that arise through separate states of consciousness. These common interruptions arise out of inherent imperfections of the vestures, the fabric and matrices through which cosmic ideation is refracted. If one views human nature prismatically, *Buddhi* may be compared to golden yellow light, which is the closest ray to the one pure white colourless Light. Transcending the more extreme contrasts in the spectrum, it synthesizes them and sees their apparent differentiation as merely an illusion within a single, undivided and unbroken stream of pure spiritual intuition.

The capacity for such unbroken vision is seen in the eyes of a child. The ray of lower *Manas* enters the lower vestures during the seventh month in the womb, and the ray of *Manas* enters the child around the seventh year. But out of the eyes of a baby, where *Manas* has not been aroused, radiates the light of Atma-Buddhic awareness. It is this intensity and integrity of focus that makes an infant's eyes eloquent. That same directness is apparent when a baby grasps an object, feels it and seeks to know what it is. This same capacity is latent, though lost, in every human being. It persists through sleep and through all the ageing processes, and if it is not pursued on the basis of separative personal consciousness, it can be recovered. All such notions of individual spiritual progress are bound up with differentiations and inversions of consciousness on the lower planes of matter. Through meditation, one must reach beyond all these to the cosmic core of human identity, saluting this principle of Buddhic awareness at work throughout the entirety of Nature. One must through discipline attempt to enter the mind of the Adept, the *Bodhisattva* and the Buddha.

One must extend one's conception of the principle of *Buddhi* in every direction, encompassing all objects, forms and beings on the subtlest planes of matter, because ultimately matter itself is the entire range of all possible objects of perception. Pure Buddhic understanding, as an analogue of *Mulaprakriti*, is the noumenal ground of substance underlying the entire collective range of differentiated objects and perceptions. This notion of Buddhic substance is so abstract and philosophical that it could scarcely be appreciated during the nineteenth century. In the twentieth century contemporary notions of matter and space are beginning to converge with arcane knowledge, although they lack philosophic clarity and moral relevance. For the student of *Gupta Vidya* who is able to link metaphysics and meta-psychology, the concept of spiritual ideation inhering in *Mulaprakriti* begins to reveal the extraordinary possibilities in human consciousness.

The fundamental obstacle blocking the realization in consciousness of the Bodhisattvic possibilities of human nature is identification with personal name and form *(namarupa)*. It is the problem of the ego. The Jains say that to acquire all virtues yet not conquer the ego is to achieve nothing. Perhaps one is kind to cats, contributes to charities, pays all dues and performs every mundane and religious duty. Perhaps one even assumes the role of a neophyte on the Path, seeking to honour one's vows and be a true companion to others. Yet if at the moment of death one has not overcome the ego, one has gained nothing. This is why the Path is not easy, and this is why to grasp the problem is not to simplify it. Through hydra-headed salvationism, through desperate pursuit of *moksha*, through frenetic attempts to escape, people have all too often tried to opt out of the difficult stages of authentic inner growth. Inevitably, these misconceptions arise from a fundamental misunderstanding of self-existence, self-consciousness and hence of individuation.

The mere knowledge that one's most fundamental spiritual problem is egotism in no way dispels that egotism. In fact, a focus upon one's own ego problem is itself a manifestation of that problem. Instead, one should attempt to see the problem of the ego in impersonal terms, in relation to the entire cosmos. "I-am-I" consciousness exists in individual human beings only as a reflection of universal egoity.

> *Ahamkara*, as universal Self-Consciousness, has a triple aspect, as also *Manas*. For this conception of "I", or one's *Ego*, is either *sattwa*, "pure quietude", or appears as *rajas*, "active", or remains *tamas*, "stagnant", in darkness. It belongs to Heaven and Earth, and assumes the properties of either.
>
> Ibid., i 335

From a philosophical perspective one might say that the entire universe has an ego problem. That is why it exists. Yet at its core there is no differentiation and no fragmentation. That is why the ground of the universe is held to be beyond the spectral rays of light, beyond even the one white Light that synthesizes the colours. The true ground of self-existence is the Divine Darkness. If this is true of the universe as a whole and of universal self-consciousness as a principle in invisible Nature, one can imagine in that universe beings who stand outside the stream of differentiated existence. They are fully aware of the limits of existence in reference to the whole universe, in reference to solar systems and in reference to worlds like the earth. They can, like Prospero in *The Tempest*, contemplate the "great globe itself". The universal self-consciousness which they realize in themselves as their perfected *Manas* is nothing but a ray of *Mahat*. Conversely, *Mahat*, the cosmic mind, is the consciousness of perfected beings who together, by their ideation, give expression to the Divine Thought in the Divine Mind. Self-consciousness of self-existence at the Mahatmic level is the highest *Ahamkara*, pure *Sattva* or quietude.

During the long night of non-manifestation, such perfected *Bodhisattvas* may be conceived of as thinking of pure possibilities. Even during the long period of manifestation they can see beyond everything that exists. Their vision transcends not merely that which is actual, but also that which is potential, and through a negation of everything that relates to even the possibility of manifestation, they experience pure quietude. It is as if the ego problem of the universe is put to rest, falling into deep dreamless sleep. Such perfected beings should not be confused with the host of creators, who, early in the dawn of manifestation, became captive to the cosmos. Extraordinarily important as these creative beings are, they still become trapped in the process of the emerging cosmos through the quality of their wonderment at its appearance out of the night of non-manifestation. By greeting the cosmos with a sense of otherness, they fell away from pure quietude into a more active state. At the same time, the wisest beings shared in the thrill of the dawn of manifestation, but stood apart from it, and resisted enthralment.

To begin to understand what it might mean to stand apart from an entire period of cosmic manifestation, one might apply the principle of negation to one's entire life. Instead of being caught in the details of the present incarnation, one might think of how one should live one's next life. Before the age of seven one would want to do all that can negate the unnecessary illusions of later life. One would want to become so strong within oneself that even the most demonic environments of corrupt societies could not distort or interrupt one's tranquillity. For most human beings, even to consider such a possibility is extraordinary. It would involve being ready before the age of seven for the opportunities that exist at the age of fourteen. By fourteen one would be ready for the opportunities at the age of twenty-one, by twenty-one for the opportunities at the age of twenty-eight, and by twenty-eight for those that come at the age of thirty-five.

To live life in such a Promethean manner, neither appearing pretentious to others nor becoming anxious about being considered foolish, one must anticipate myriad illusions. One must purge oneself of a brittle personality dependent upon likes and dislikes. One must free oneself from psychic vicissitudes, imagining oneself an untouchable one day and a saint the next. In principle, the capacity to cut through all the psychic froth stems from the possibility of awareness of the night of non-manifestation. Practically, as an individual aspirant, one must rescue the notion of one's being from deep sleep or *sushupti*. The capacity to withstand the bombardment of events and situations during the day is directly proportional to one's ability to bring back from deep sleep an awareness of formless self-existence.

This continuity of consciousness has its cosmic basis in pure quietude or *Sattva*. It can also involve activity and an acceptance of ceaseless cosmic motion. This is actionless action. It is like a dance. If one experiences actionless action, then one can sleep undisturbed by the noisy traffic of the world. For one has gained a more exalted view of motion than known to the ordinary world. One has learnt to see behind that which is stagnant, or *tamasic,* finding there some sort of mirroring of the Divine Darkness. One is able to reach up to heaven, while keeping one's feet on earth. Mahatmic self-consciousness spans heaven and earth and is capable of assuming the properties of either. The perfected *Bodhisattva* is able to reach to the empyrean, the rarefied altitudes of *Akasha,* where pure substance exists in its ultimate tenuity, and to enter into the maximum field of differentiated matter. He can move at will from one state to another, freely passing in and out of vestures, not captive to them nor concerned to escape them.

When the egoic principle is purified of all positive and negative desire, it is possible to experience universal selfhood. Sometimes enlightened beings say that they do not sleep, but rather that when the body wants to sleep, it does so and has nothing to do with them. They are always awake. This is a mirroring of the total uninvolvement in the modifications through the mind in the body and in the lower planes of existence of the perfect *Bodhisattva.* From this extraordinary state the *Bodhisattva* is able to witness the birth of worlds. Rooted in pure knowledge and unconditioned reality – *Sattva* and *Sat* – such a one is *Parabrahmam* and *Mulaprakriti* – *Atma-Buddhi* – and knows that

> "the one Universal Light, which to Man is *Darkness,* is ever existent".... From it proceeds periodically the ENERGY, which is reflected in the "Deep" or Chaos, the store-house of future worlds, and, once awakened, stirs up and fructifies the latent Forces, which are the ever present eternal potentialities in it. Then awake anew the Brahmâs and Buddhas – the co-eternal Forces – and a new Universe springs into being.
>
> *Ibid.,* i 337

Such a *Bodhisattva* understands that there is a difference between darkness and light. From one perspective it seems possible to look at everything either as Absolute Light or as Absolute Darkness, but this is due to the contrast of light and darkness that human beings ordinarily experience relative to planes of extreme differentiation. These contrasts are relatively unreal. In a sufficiently homogeneous universal medium, there is a crucial difference between radiance and darkness. The wisest beings refuse to be impressed even by the most radiant and beautiful atom in pregenetic space. They have a metaphysical basis for appreciating beauty, whether in the flower of womanhood, in a glorious sunset or in the serene Himalayas, while at the same time not being captivated by any of these in concrete manifestation. Like Gandhi, they will not travel to the Himalayas, but rather extol the Himalayas of the heart which can be found in dusty crowded villages. They do not indulge themselves by surrendering to radiance because, through their metaphysics, they have come to contemplate Darkness, pure negation, and have recognized that the deeper one goes into the Darkness, the more one experiences pure Spirit.

> DARKNESS is the one true actuality, the basis and the root of light, without which the latter could never manifest itself, nor even exist. Light is matter, and DARKNESS pure Spirit. Darkness, in its radical, metaphysical basis, is subjective and absolute light; while the latter in all its seeming effulgence and glory, is merely a mass of shadows, as it can never be eternal, and is simply an illusion, or Maya.
>
> *Ibid.*, i 70

However beautiful, light is still matter. It is not spirit. Darkness is pure Spirit, and that is why one can experience most spiritual wakefulness, the greatest heights of meditation, in the night especially around the dawn of Venus. In the darkness it is possible to come closer to reality than in the bright light. Those who are metaphysically wise do not like the glare of the sun. They always seek the shade; they have no need of radiance on the physical plane. They know that at the moment of death, when one has the opportunity to leave the prison-house of the lower vestures, one will need to transcend the temptations of noumenal subtle light which have to do with the *rupa devas*. At an even higher stage, one must be able to transcend the subtler temptations associated with the hosts of the *arupa devas* and enter into the absolute Divine Darkness of total negation.

No progress can be made in this direction at the moment of death unless one prepares for it now during life. That is why Plato and Shankara insisted on the importance of seeing the whole of life as a ceaseless preparation for death. Life should be lived as a continual transcendence of the illusion of being connected with a name and form, with the five sense-organs and with the subtler astral senses. One must move beyond the entire kaleidoscopic world of beautiful and radiant dreams bound up with the concept of a personal ego. One must see instead that there is nothing more real, nothing more radical or primordial, nothing more invisible and eternal, than Darkness as pure Spirit. The soul must realize that Light in its highest philosophic sense has nothing to do with what is normally called light on the physical plane. But it must also necessarily go beyond light in this exalted sense.

Ultimately, even when one salutes *Daiviprakriti* – *Brahma Vach*, Wisdom itself in the unmanifest, which is like radiant light – one should see it from behind, from within without. If one stands before the radiant veil of Wisdom, one may adore it. But when one abides behind it, one may see it from the standpoint of Divine Darkness *(SAT)*. Then one may appreciate it all the more. And one may also see that aspect of it which is illusory, relative to a vast manvantaric period of manifestation. Rooted in that Darkness, one can understand and aid the travail of all beings engaged in the universal quest for enlightenment and so help them along the Path.

Hermes, May 1984

TRUTH

It is common to make a sharp separation between knowledge and being, truth and reality, between what we affirm to be true or false and what exists or is non-existent. This distinction, which we have inherited from the Greeks, is valuable in itself and is fundamental to modern thought. On the other hand, in classical Indian tradition as in pre-Socratic thought echoed in Plato, truth and reality are often used as interchangeable terms and we are taught that there is a higher level of awareness and apprehension beyond the sensory field in which our knowing and what is known are united and even transcended in a sense of immediate vision and absorption in what is seen. This identification of truth and reality was reaffirmed by Gandhi in his insistence that truth is that which *is* and error that which *is not*. Most of what we normally call knowledge has clearly nothing to do with truth as Gandhi understood it, and we are right to distinguish it from being. The modern man is neither willing nor able to grasp reality; he has been trained to develop and use his reason and his feeling in a manner that can give partial formulations of the truth or passing sensations of particular sense-objects. Once we accept the notion that man can be separated and detached from nature, human knowledge and sensation cannot attain to an intuitive insight into the *Tattwas*, the essences of things. If, however, we start with the ancient axiom that man is the microcosm of the macrocosm, then we can see that the extent of truth that is available to any man is connected with the plane of reality on which he functions. Hence the importance of H.P. Blavatsky's advocacy of the Platonic standpoint which was abandoned by Aristotle, who was no Initiate, and who has had such a dominant influence upon subsequent thinking in the West.

In theosophical thought we start with a clear conception of the notion of absolute abstract Truth or Reality, SAT, from which is derived *satya* or truth. The First Fundamental Proposition of *The Secret Doctrine* urges us to set out with the postulate that there is one absolute Reality which antecedes all manifested, conditioned being, which is attributeless, which is "Be-ness" rather than Being and is beyond the range and reach of all thought and speculation. *Paranishpanna,* the *summum bonum,* is that final state of subjectivity which has no relation to anything but the one absolute Truth *(Paramarthasatya)* on its plane. Sooner or later, all that now seemingly exists will be in reality in the state of *Paranishpanna,* the state which leads one to appreciate correctly the full meaning of Non-Being or of absolute Being. But there is a great difference between *conscious* and *unconscious* "being." "The condition of *Paranishpanna,* without *Paramartha,* the Self-analyzing consciousness (Svasamvedana), is no bliss, but simply extinction."

The Greeks were then right to distinguish between reality as it presents itself to finite human minds and reality as it is or would be to the Divine Mind. "Divine Thought" does not necessitate the idea of a single Divine thinker. The Universe is in its totality the SAT, with the past and the future crystallized in an eternal Present, the Divine Thought reflected in a secondary or manifest cause. However, as man is indissolubly linked with the universe, and his *Manas* is connected with MAHAT, it is possible for man to bridge the gap between truth and reality, between knowledge and being, by *conscious* effort. As man becomes more and more self-conscious, and less and less passive, in his awareness of the universe, he must abandon the distinction between truth and knowledge and redefine his notion of truth so as to make it identical with reality. The real distinction is between head-learning and soul-wisdom. What the *pundit* or the ignoramus regards as truth is error to the sage and the Adept. The Adept has realized the non-separateness of all that lives and his own unity with the "Rootless Root" of all, which is pure knowledge *(Sattwa,* which Shankara took to mean Buddhi), eternal, unconditioned reality or SAT.

The world in which we live is itself the shadow of a shadowy reflection, twice removed, of the "World of Truth" or SAT, through which the direct energy that radiates from the ONE REALITY reaches us. That which is manifested cannot be SAT, but is something phenomenal, not everlasting or even sempiternal. This "World of Truth" is described as "a bright star dropped from the heart of Eternity; the beacon of hope on whose Seven Rays hang the Seven Worlds of Being." The visible sun is itself only the material shadow of the Central Sun of Truth, which illuminates the invisible, intellectual world of Spirit. The ideal conception of the universe is a Golden Egg, with a positive pole that acts in the manifested world of matter, while the negative pole is lost in the unknowable absoluteness of SAT or Be-ness. The first cosmic aspect of the esoteric SAT is the Universal Mind, MAHAT, "the manifested Omniscience," the root of SELF-Consciousness. The spirit of archaic philosophy cannot be comprehended unless we thoroughly assimilate the concepts of SAT and *Asat*.

> *Asat* is not merely the negation of *Sat*, nor is it the "not yet existing"; for *Sat* is in itself neither the "existent," nor "being." *SAT* is the immutable, the ever present, changeless and eternal root, from and through which all proceeds. But it is far more than the potential force in the seed, which propels onward the process of development, or what is now called evolution. It is the ever becoming, though the never manifesting. *Sat* is born from *Asat*, and *ASAT* is begotten by *Sat*: the perpetual motion in a circle, truly; yet a circle that can be squared only at the supreme Initiation, at the threshold of Paranirvana.
>
> *The Secret Doctrine*, ii 449-50

The Theosophical Trinity is composed of the Sun (the Father), Mercury or Hermes or Budha (the Son), and Venus or Lucifer, the morning Star (the Holy Ghost, *Sophia*, the Spirit of Wisdom, Love and Truth). To these three correspond Atma, Buddhi and *Manas* in man.

It is useful to distinguish between absolute and relative truth, between truth and error, between reality and illusion, between *Paramarthasatya* and *Samvritisatya*. *Paramartha* is self-consciousness and the word is made up of *parama* (above everything) and *artha* (comprehension); and *Satya* means absolute true being, or *esse*. The opposite of this absolute reality, or actuality, is *Samvritisatya*, the relative truth only, *Samvriti* meaning "false conception" and being the origin of illusion, *Maya*; it is illusion-creating appearance. The two obstacles to the attainment of *Paramarthasatya* are *Parikalpita*, the error of believing something to exist or to be real which does not exist and is unreal, and *Paratantra*, that which exists only through a dependent or causal connection. As a result of *Parikalpita*, we get *tamasic* knowledge or "truth," which is based upon an obsession with the sole reality of a single object or thought, which is, in essence, unreal and non-existent.

As a result of *Paratantra*, we get *rajasic* knowledge or "truth," based upon a concern with the differences between seemingly separate, but interdependent and ephemeral, things.

When we have developed the faculties necessary to go beyond *Parikalpita* and *Paratantra*, we begin to get *sattvic* knowledge or truth, based upon the recognition of the unity of all things, their common identity on a single plane of universal, ultimate reality. This is itself only an approximation, imperfect and inadequate, to absolute Truth. Whereas relative truth is ephemeral and can be the subject of controversy and is eventually extinguished, absolute Truth is enduring, beyond dispute and can never be destroyed. Whereas relative truth will triumph over error, absolute Truth ever shines, regardless of whether there are martyrs and witnesses ready to vindicate it and die for it. Hence "the failure to sweep away entirely from the face of the earth every vestige of that ancient Wisdom, and to shackle and gag every witness who testified to it." And yet, in the world of manifestation, every error proliferates other errors rapidly, while each truth has to be painfully discovered. "Error runs down an inclined plane, while Truth has to laboriously climb its way uphill," says an old proverb.

The Theosophist is, in a sense, a Berkeleian phenomenalist and holds to the axiom, *esse est percipi* (to exist is to be perceived), in regard to all relative truths. Everything that exists has only a relative reality since the appearance which the hidden noumenon assumes for any observer depends upon his power of cognition. *Maya* or illusion is an element which, therefore, enters into all finite things. The cognizer is also a reflection and the things cognized are therefore as real to him as he himself is. Nothing is permanent except the one hidden absolute existence which contains in itself the noumena of all realities. Everything is illusion outside of eternal Truth, which has neither form, colour, nor limitation. He who has placed himself beyond the veil of *maya*, the Adept and Initiate, can have no *Devachan*. Whatever plane our consciousness may be acting in, both we and the things belonging to that plane are, for the time being, our only realities. Relative truths are relative to our plane of perception at any given time in any particular situation.

> As we rise in the scale of development we perceive that during the stages through which we have passed we mistook shadows for realities, and the upward progress of the Ego is a series of progressive awakenings, each advance bringing with it the idea that now, at last, we have reached "reality"; but only when we shall have reached the absolute Consciousness, and blended our own with it, shall we be free from the delusions produced by Maya.
>
> *The Secret Doctrine*, i 40

Ideologies or systems which claim to be the absolute Truth are clearly *tamasic*, static and doomed to atrophy and decay and final extinction. Dogmas and claims to uniqueness are *rajasic*, partial and ephemeral, ever changing and destined to disappear. In ideologies and dogmas are to be contained the seeds of violence because they violate the absolute truth of unity and endow relative truths with the evil aura of the dire heresy of separateness, the greatest of all sins and their common source. When one party or another, when one sect or the other, thinks itself to be the sole possessor of absolute Truth, it becomes only natural that it should think its neighbour absolutely in the clutches of error or of the "devil," requiring to be redeemed by force or threats or intimidation, *i.e.*, to be shocked into acquiescence by verbal or physical violence. Alternatively, it may attempt to seduce the unwary by subtle propaganda and theological or political bribes.

> But once get a man to see that none of them has the *whole* truth, but that they are mutually complementary, that the complete truth can be found only in the combined views of all, after that which is false in each of them has been sifted out – then true brotherhood in religion will be established.
>
> *The Key to Theosophy*

Further,

> unless every man is brought to understand, and accept as *an axiomatic truth* that by wronging one man we wrong not only ourselves but the whole of humanity in the long run, no brotherly feelings such as preached by all the great Reformers, pre-eminently by Buddha and Jesus, are possible on earth.

That which is true on the metaphysical plane must also be true on the physical plane. *Satya* entails *ahimsa*, and the degree of *ahimsa* that a man possesses is the measure of the *satya* that he embodies.

THEOSOPHIA is identical with SAT or Absolute Truth, and Theosophy is only a partial emanation from it, the shoreless ocean of universal Truth reflecting the rays of the sun of SAT. In *The Secret Doctrine*, H.P. Blavatsky declared that only the outline of a few fundamental truths from the Secret Doctrine of the archaic ages was now permitted to see the light after long millenniums of the most profound silence and secrecy. "That which must remain unsaid could not be contained in a hundred such volumes, nor could it be imparted to the present generation of Sadducees." The great truths, which are the inheritance of the future races, cannot be given out at present, as the fate of every such unfamiliar truth is that, if it falls into the hands of the unready, they will only deceive themselves and deceive others, as the Masters have warned. As esoteric truth is made exoteric, absolute Truth is not only reduced to the illusive plane of the relative, but casts a shadow on the delusive plane of error. Occult Wisdom, dealing with eternal truths and primal causes, becomes almost omnipotent when applied in the right direction; its antithesis is that which deals with illusions and false appearances only, as in our exoteric modern sciences, with their immense power of destruction.

The ancients managed to throw a thick veil over the nucleus of truth concealed by archetypal symbols, but they also tried to preserve the latter as a record for future generations, sufficiently transparent to allow their wisest men to discern that truth behind the fabulous form of the glyph or allegory. The whole essence of truth cannot be transmitted from mouth to ear, nor can any pen describe it, unless man finds the answer in the innermost depths of his divine intuitions. No religious founder invented or revealed a new truth as they were all transmitters.

> Selecting one or more of those grand verities – actualities visible only to the eye of the real Sage and Seer – out of the many orally revealed to man in the beginning, preserved and perpetuated in the *adyta* of the temples through initiation, during the MYSTERIES and by personal transmission – they revealed these truths to the

masses. Thus every nation received in its turn some of the said truths, under the veil of its own local and special symbolism.

The Secret Doctrine, i xxxvi

Those who do not relish the distinction between esoteric and exoteric truth, the elect and the multitudes, do not really appreciate the tremendous practical potency of pure truths, and the danger of their misuse. In the *Milindapanha* we are told about the magical power of an act of truth, the power of a pure soul who has embodied a truth and enacted it in his daily life and who can work magic by the simple act of calling that fact to witness. In Theosophical literature, we are clearly told that a man must set and model his daily life upon the truth that the end of life is action and not thought; only such a man becomes worthy of the name of a Theosophist. "The profession of a truth is not yet the enactment of it." But truth, however distasteful to the generally blind multitudes, has always had her champions and martyrs. Endless is the search for truth, but we secure it only if we are willing to incarnate it in our own lives. "Let us love it and aspire to it for its own sake, and not for the glory or benefit a minute portion of its revelation may confer on us."

Theosophy thus teaches the transforming power of truth and affirms the teaching of the Gospel, "Ye shall know the Truth and the Truth shall make you free." The early Gnostics claimed that their Science, the *GNOSIS*, rested on a square, the angles of which represented *Sige* (Silence), *Bythos* (depth), *Nous* (Spiritual Soul or Mind), and *Aletheia* (Truth). The cultists are fighting against divine Truth, when repudiating and slandering the Dragon of esoteric Wisdom. But

> no great truth was ever accepted a *priori,* and generally a century or two passed before it began to glimmer in the human consciousness as a possible verity, except in such eases as the positive discovery of the thing claimed as a fact. The truths of today are the falsehoods and errors of yesterday, and *vice versa.*

The Secret Doctrine, ii 442

It is only in the Seventh Race that all error will be made away with, and the advent of Truth will be heralded by the holy "Sons of Light." Meanwhile the Golden Age of the past will not be realized in the future till humanity, as a whole, feels the need of it. In *The Key to Theosophy* we are told:

> A maxim in the Persian "Javidan Khirad" says: "Truth is of two kinds – one manifest and self-evident; the other demanding incessantly new demonstrations and proofs." It is only when this latter kind of truth becomes as universally obvious as it is now dim, and therefore liable to be distorted by sophistry and casuistry; it is only when the two kinds will have become once more one, that all people will be brought to see alike.

Truth, in the former sense, is identical with reality and cuts across the distinction between knowledge and being. Truth, in the latter sense, presupposes this distinction, but also requires us to transcend it, for we cannot effectively demonstrate truth until we embody and become the truth, until we carry out the injunction: "Become what thou art."

> O Teacher, what shall I do to reach to Wisdom?
>
> O Wise one, what, to gain perfection?
>
> Search for the Paths. But, O Lanoo, be of clean heart before thou startest on thy journey. Before thou takest thy first step, learn to discern the real from the false, the ever-fleeting from the everlasting. Learn above all to separate Head-learning from Soul-wisdom, the "Eye" from the "Heart" doctrine.
>
> Yea, ignorance is like unto a closed and airless vessel; the soul a bird shut up within. It warbles not, nor can it stir a feather; but the songster mute and torpid sits, and of exhaustion dies.
>
> But even ignorance is better than Head-learning with no Soul-wisdom to illuminate and guide it.
>
> The seeds of Wisdom cannot sprout and grow in airless space. To live and reap experience, the mind needs breadth and depth and points to draw it towards the Diamond Soul. Seek not those points in Maya's realm; but soar beyond illusions, search the eternal and the changeless SAT, mistrusting fancy's false suggestions.

For mind is like a mirror; it gathers dust while it reflects. It needs the gentle breezes of Soul-wisdom to brush away the dust of our illusions. Seek, O Beginner, to blend thy Mind and Soul.

The Voice of the Silence

Hermes, September 1975

LOVE

No word has perhaps been so much abused in our age as "love," thus fulfilling the celebrated prophecy about *Kali Yuga* in the *Vishnu Purana*. In view of the unfortunate but undeniable fact that "love" is more loosely used today than "truth," Gandhi preferred to adopt truth rather than love as the highest value although he repeatedly stressed that the two are inseparable and even identical in the ultimate analysis. Relative truth may masquerade as absolute truth, but the mere existence of contrary claims and the continual violence of controversy cast doubt on the universal validity of all partisan standpoints. On the other hand, when selfish, personal love, often based on passing passion, wears the mask of selfless, impersonal, dispassionate and immortal love, it is far more difficult for deluded victims to discern the true from the false, the everlasting from the ephemeral. Earthly love is indeed an alluring and deceptive shadow, and sometimes a perversion, of ethereal love. Just as untruth invariably requires some form of violence for its instrument, so too blind and selfish love, which contains the seeds of violence and even hatred, is based upon untruth and uses it to further its immediate ends. Our main difficulty here is that, as Socrates points out in *The Symposium*, we isolate a particular kind of love and appropriate for it the name of love, which really belongs to a wider whole. . . . The generic concept embraces every desire for good and for happiness; that is precisely what almighty and all-ensnaring love is. But this desire expresses itself in many ways, and those with whom it takes the form of love of money or of physical prowess or of wisdom are not said to be in love, or called lovers, whereas those whose passion runs in one particular channel usurp the name of lover, which belongs to them all, and are said to be lovers and in love.

In *The Secret Doctrine* H.P. Blavatsky explains that *Fohat* or *Eros* in the phenomenal world is that "occult, electric, vital power, which, under the Will of the Creative Logos, unites and brings together all forms, giving them the first impulse which becomes in time law. But in the unmanifested Universe, *Fohat* is no more this, than *Eros* is the later brilliant winged Cupid, or LOVE."

The universal aspect of Love was embodied in the Puranic conception of Brahma's "Will" or desire to create, and it was affirmed in Phoenician cosmogony as the doctrine that desire is the principle of creation. In the *Rig Veda Kama* is the personification of that feeling which leads and propels to creation. "Desire first arose in It, which was the *primal germ of mind;* and which sages, searching with their intellect, have discovered to be the bond which connects Entity with Non-Entity." As *Eros* was connected in early Greek mythology with the world's creation, and only afterwards became the sexual Cupid, so was *Kama* in his original Vedic character the primeval creative urge, *Atma-Bhu* (self-existent), *Aja* (unborn), sometimes regarded allegorically as the son of *Dharma,* the moral Law, and of *Shraddha,* faith, but elsewhere depicted as *Agni,* the fire-god. Harivansa makes him a son of Lakshmi or Venus. *Aja* is the Logos in the *Rig Veda.* Venus Aphrodite or Lakshmi, the Celestial Virgin of the Alchemists and the Christian Virgin Mary, is the personified Sea, the primordial Ocean of Space, *Akasha,* on which *Narayana,* the self-born Spirit, moves. Venus is the generator of all the gods, the mother of *Kama*deva, the god of Love, Mercy and Charity.

True love is a creative force that emanates from the One Logos and its expression is under the universal law of cosmic and human interdependence. The love of which Christ spoke cannot be grasped without reference to the law of love, which is set forth in *The Key to Theosophy:* "As mankind is essentially of one and the same essence, and that essence is one – infinite, uncreate and eternal, whether we call it God or Nature – nothing, therefore, can affect one nation or one man without affecting all other nations and all other men."

True love can never be a divisive force but always has a universally beneficent and unifying effect. It leads in the end to that love of wisdom, the worship of the Logos, which has been extolled by the Platonists and the great mystics of all ages. This true love was expounded in Porphyry's long letter to his wife, Marcella, when the time came for them to part and for him to resume his wanderings as a pilgrim. He wrote that every disturbance and unprofitable desire is removed by the love of true philosophy.

> In so far as a man turns to the mortal part of himself, in so far he makes his mind incommensurate with immortality. And in so far as he refrains from sharing the feelings of the body, in such a measure does he approach the divine. . . . Neither trouble thyself much whether thou be male or female in body, nor look on thyself as a woman, for I did not approach thee as such. . . . For what is born from a virgin soul and a pure mind is most blessed, since imperishable springs from imperishable. . . . They who do not use their own bodies, but make excessive use of others, commit a twofold wrong, and are ungrateful to nature that has given them these parts . . . it is impossible that he who does wrong to man should honour God. But look on the love of mankind as the foundation of thy piety.

True love is constant and immortal because it springs from the immortal and steadfast nature of the human soul.

Finite love, on the other hand, is born of the perishable part of man and becomes a chain of enslavement rather than an abiding bond of communion and cooperative endeavour. If we are glamoured by the meretricious fascination of this chain of possessive, personal love, we cling to it until we invite unnecessary suffering and inevitable frustration. Dante shows Paolo and Francesca locked in an eternal embrace which is anguish rather than ecstasy, the condign punishment for selfish lovers. Such love is what H.P. Blavatsky calls *égoisme à deux*, an exclusive and destructive love, whether shown between husband and wife, mother and child, between brothers or between friends. Such love may bring temporary pleasure for the personality, but it is displeasing to the Ishwara within as it could sunder the soul from its divine parentage and true mission, as it hinders more than it helps the love of Beauty of which Plotinus spoke, the intellectual love of God of which Spinoza wrote, the constant love of wisdom extolled by ancient sages from Krishna to Shankara, Buddha to Santideva, Pythagoras to Porphyry.

Does this mean that there is no place for the human affections and for the affinities between kindred souls and that we must eliminate every element of personal love? Certainly not, for this can only lead to pure egotism or to spiritual selfishness and the quest for personal salvation. He who loves only himself lives in hell, the hell of loneliness, ambition and despair. On the other hand, he who loves only one other person lives entirely on earth, and all such earthly love must come to an end; at best, it could only correspond to the idealization and illusion which characterize *Devachan*. He who loves his fellow men lives on earth in a heavenly condition, but as long as his philanthropy and altruism are purely personal, his only reward is a long *Devachan*, a prolonged and beautiful dream, an illusory condition that brings the soul no nearer to its true quest, the love of the SELF of all amidst the conditions of earthly life. Finite, personal love is not bad in itself but it is frustrating and useless to the human soul unless it can gradually purify and make more impersonal and unselfish the force of *Kama* in its material manifestations through the incarnated personality. Only thus can love be transformed from a violent and divisive tendency in human relationships into a non-violent, unifying power that produces strength and peace. The evils wrought by lust and selfish love have been nowhere more forcefully depicted than in Tolstoy's indictment of modern marriages in *The Kreutzer Sonata* or in Gandhi's *Self-Restraint versus Self Indulgence*. The Theosophical ideal of marriage has been clearly stated by W.Q. Judge in "Living the Higher Life" and also hinted at in *The Dream of Ravan*.

In *The Secret Doctrine* H.P.B. gives the key to the transmutation of finite love when she repeats the ancient teaching that *Manas* is dual – lunar in the lower, solar in its upper portion. It is attracted in its higher aspect towards *Buddhi*, the seat of true love and real compassion, but in its lower aspect it descends into and listens to the voice of its animal soul, full of selfish and sensual desires.

> The human *Ego* is neither *Atman* nor *Buddhi*, but the higher *Manas*: the intellectual fruition and the efflorescence of the intellectual self-conscious *Egotism* – in the higher spiritual sense. The ancient works refer to it as *Karana Sarira* on the plane of *Sutratma*, which is the golden thread on which, like beads, the various personalities of this higher *Ego* are strung.
>
> *The Secret Doctrine*, II, 79

The imperishable thread of radiance which is *Manas* serves man as a medium between the highest and the lowest, the spiritual man and the physical brain. When the lunar aspect of *Manas* is positive, *Kama* in man, like the *Barhishad Pitris*, is possessed of creative fire but devoid of the MAHAT-mic element. When the solar pole of *Manas* is positive, *Kama* becomes Agni or divine fire and is capable, like the *Agnishwatta Pitris*, of conserving its energy as well as of sacrificing itself to the good and salvation of Spiritual Humanity. The distinction here is between finite love and the more enduring love which is a link between passion and compassion and which finally culminates in the highest spiritual love.

When *Kama* in man overcomes and enslaves *Manas*, love becomes violent and cunning, or a mere form of sentimental wish-fulfilment. In the former case, it tears the individual to pieces. It becomes a volcanic and tempestuous force, an explosion of all the passions pent up in man; it knows neither law nor restraint and its pressure drives the deepest undercurrents of the animal nature in man to the surface. Love is then a leaping, a devouring fire, but a fire that can be turned to ice, doomed to a tragic end, death-dealing and futile. On the other hand, the love that is romanticized, the love sung by the troubadours, the love of Tristan and Iseult, the love poured forth in the letters of the Portuguese nun, Marianna Alcaforado, is the pathetic attempt of *Kama* to masquerade as *Buddhi*, a psychic effusion, a product of delusion and self-pity, a fragile if seductive flower under which the serpent of selfishness is coiled. Tamasic love, as *The Dream of Ravan* points out, is devoid of the light of knowledge and ideality, for it is content with illusions and idealization and could turn into cold indifference and hatred or into self-destructive morbidity. When *Kama* influences without overpowering *Manas*, we have rajasic love which can sting the beloved into an emulating pursuit of cherished ends, which is animated by a keen intelligence, and which shows a lofty scorn of every divergence or shortcoming.

Sattvic love has been well depicted in *The Book of Confidences:*

> When thou shalt find true Love, shalt find one homogeneous to thy nature; to whom all Life is consecrate, who will have ardency to take with thee the Bright Track of the Soul. And in that

embodiment of thine own love, shalt find all others for thy love, thy joy, thy patience, and compassion.

Such love can only arise when *Kama* is under the influence, even if intermittently, of a *Manas* that tends upwards to *Buddhi*. This love is silent rather than clamorous in its expression, marked by inward depth rather than by outward display. The silences of love lie in wait for us, night and day, at our threshold, and those who have loved deeply in this way come to learn many secrets that are unknown to others, the secrets of sharing and sacrifice and duty well done.

Love is the moving power of life itself, and nothing can exist without the love which drives everything towards everything else that is. He alone who loves lives. Love is the drive towards the unity of the separated, and separation presupposes an original unity. The restlessness in love is only a dim reflection of the divine discontent of the soul, but it could act as a barrier to the union of the soul with nature if it is channelled merely through personal and material forms of expression. The active and creative element in love is the urge of the human soul to participate in the work of cosmic and human evolution, a form of *kriyashakti* which enables man to emulate the gods, the Dhyan-Chohanic host of creative intelligences. Human love could become a bridge between the animal and the divine aspects of love provided the desire to ascend through lower to higher forms of love is continually nourished and sustained.

The *Narada Bhakti Sutras* and *The Voice of the Silence* point to the highest kind of love which transcends the three qualities, the constant love of the Absolute, Eternal Truth, the attributeless Compassion which is the law of laws, embracing the entire universe, ceaselessly filling the world with its benedictory and magical power. We can progress gradually from *Dana*, "the key of charity and love immortal," to *Paramarthasatya* and *Karuna*, the Universal and Absolute Compassion that is rooted in Eternal and Absolute Truth. The *Gita* warns us against the rajasic and downward tendency of *Kama*, the constant enemy of man, but it also points to the process by which we could perfect our power of devotion and become worthy of the Divine Grace that flows from the Lords of Love who reflect the Power and the Compassion of the Creative Logos in the cosmos. The *Narada Bhakti*

Sutras list the following eleven different forms of *Bhakti* or Divine Love: Love of the glorification of the Lord's blessed qualities, Love of His enchanting beauty, Love of worship, Love of constant remembrance, Love of service, Love of Him as a friend, Love of Him as a son, Love for Him as that of a wife for her husband, Love of self-surrender to Him, Love of complete absorption in Him, Love of the pain of separation from Him. If we wish to go beyond "love" and "hate," we must use all our loves as a preparation for *amor dei* or true *Bhakti,* the total and endless Love of the Logos in the cosmos, God in man.

Hermes, October 1975

THE SEVEN DEADLY SINS
I. The Historical Context

He that is without sin among you, let him first cast a stone.   John 8:7

Throughout Christian history, sin has functioned as the Archimedean lever of orthodox Christian morality. From the patristic period to the close of the Middle Ages, sin and its progeny exercised the imaginations of laymen and theologians alike, so much so that European society and culture are unintelligible to those unacquainted with sin. From the refinements of scholastic philosophy to the exuberance of popular fancy, sin functioned as a common measure of man for all alike and in every arena. Suffice it to say, this is not the case in the twentieth century. Indeed, any enquiry today into the seven deadly sins must have a certain quaintness which would itself be entirely unintelligible to an officer of the Inquisition. Even where there were doubts about the right response to sin and even its detailed nature, there was no more doubt of its reality in general than there is today regarding notions like progress. To enquire into sin today can, however, be instructive. Sin is, so to speak, a geologic formation in human history, largely obscured by recent deposits of events, but still there, not far beneath the social surface and obtruding visibly in certain places. To understand it in the past is to understand something of the supports of the present, as well as certain possibilities for the future. Not to understand it is like being haunted by the ghosts of dead ideas.

The Christian notion of sin is, naturally, a successor to previous cultural conceptions. In particular, as one can see through the derivations of terms in the Indo-European tongues, sin and the sins reflect a crystallization of moral ideas around certain aspects of human nature and action. Activities and conditions that were morally neutral became charged with the electric force of sin and salvation, while other elements of human life once regarded as central to spirituality and ethics fell into conceptual and practical eclipse. Since the Renaissance and the Reformation, sin has been displaced by other conceptions and modalities, disclosing the pre-Christian era in a light that was not accessible during the period of Christian dominance, and also putting the era of sin in a not entirely favourable perspective. Hence, one can begin to examine the concept of sin not simply as a possession of Christianity and not simply as the precursor of certain contemporary moral and spiritual ideas, but as a specific approach to the articulation of elements in human life which antedate Christianity and also will be a part of the future. Viewed in this manner, one may ask what sorts of conceptions and ideas about human nature were assembled into the notion of sin. How were they modified in the process? What is there in the history of the idea of sin that illumines the timeless elements of human nature? And is there some way in which the collective experience of sin, the cultural living out of the idea over centuries, can be assimilated to serve the needs of the present?

These and other related questions could be given a sharper focus by attaching a more specific meaning to the idea of contemporary moral and spiritual need. In particular, owing to the massive and pervasive violence of the twentieth century in every sphere, from the political to the social and psychological, it would be helpful to explore the historic development of the idea of sin and then to apply this enquiry to an understanding of violence. Despite the moral anomie of the present century, the idea of violence comes as close as any to arousing a universal moral concern comparable to that evoked by sin in earlier centuries. At least, like sin, violence is scarcely valued for its own sake. This cannot be said, however, for each of the specific modes of action and attitude identified in the past as deadly sins. Pride, for example, is often treated as an integral component of self-respect, a definite contemporary good. Gluttony, though not good for health and perhaps unattractive to spectators, certainly has its unabashed coterie. Such facts underline the necessity of recovering the historical meanings and content of sin and the seven deadly sins before attempting to relate them to contemporary moral realities such as pervasive violence. If one merely engages in perfunctory reflections on pride, avarice and the rest, this will neglect totally the force and substance of their lost status. Thus, one would overlook the longer-term threads of moral meaning once expressed in the notion of sin and now surrounding the notion of violence.

To begin with the linguistic evidence, "sin" comes from the Latin *sons*, "guilty", (stem *sont*-, "existing", "real"), originally meaning "real". It is akin to the Old Norse *sannr*, "true", "guilty", from which come *santh* and eventually "sooth" or "the truth". In Latin thought, according to Curtius, "Language regards the *guilty* man as the man *who it was.*" The Old High German *sin*, "to be", has the zero-grade form *snt-ia*, "that which is", from the Latin root *esse*, "to be", the Latin *est*, "he is", the Greek *esti*, "he is", the Sanskrit *asti*, "he is", and perhaps also the Sanskrit *satya*, "true" and "real". (The twenty-first letter of the Hebrew alphabet is *sin*, a variant of *shen*, "tooth", from the shape of the letter, but is not related to the Indo-European "sin". Also, Sin, or *zu-en*, the Sumerian moon god, often rendered as *en-zu*, "lord of wisdom", is unrelated to the term "sin". Furthermore, the relation to the Latin *sinister*, "left", "evil" and "inauspicious", is an etymological speculation of unknown merit.)

In Greek thought there is a significant distinction between the early Homeric conception of sinister acts which vitiate the relation between the agent and his or her environment, and the later conception of sinful acts considered in themselves morally wrong and hence offensive to the gods. Whereas the first meaning seems akin to the idea of ritual impurity, the second idea definitely involves the notion of specific moral misconduct. Thus, Theognis said that *hubris* — overweening disregard of the rights of others — arises out of *koros* — a satiety such as when too much wealth attends a base man. Sophocles added that *hubris* results in a moral and prudential blindness, *ate*, where the evil appears good. Aeschylus explored the relation between such deeds and the rectifying principle of *nemesis* acting over successive generations, whilst the Orphics and Pythagoreans depicted its activity through successive reincarnations of the soul. In Roman thought there is also an older non-moral notion (*scelus* — ill luck attendant upon violation of taboos — and *vitium* — a shortcoming in the performance of a ritual), which later gave way to a moral notion attached to misdeeds. Virgil portrayed heaven, hell and purgatory as the exclusive theatres for the experience of the consequences of moral misdeeds. Perhaps, like Plato, he thought misdeeds were equilibrated in both this world and the afterlife, but he was often misunderstood by Christian thinkers who took a one-life view.

In the *New Testament* the Greek term translated as "sin" is *hamartia*. It comes from the root *hamart* and the verb *hamartano*, originally meaning "to miss", "to miss the mark", and by extension "to fail", "to go wrong", "to be deprived of", "to lose", "to err", "to do wrong" or "to sin". As a substantive *hamartia* means generally "failure", "fault", "sin" or "errors with most Greek authors, but also includes "bodily defect" and "malady" as well as "guilt", "prone to error", "erring in mind" and "distraught". In the four canonical Gospels, the term *hamartia* occurs three times in *Matthew*, all in contexts speaking of the forgiveness of sins. It occurs fourteen times in *John*, where it is likened to a form of blindness or incapacity and is connected to the ideas of forgiveness and non-condemnation. It occurs not at all in *Mark* or *Luke*. In the Acts and various letters there are about eighty occurrences. This distribution suggests that *hamartia* was perhaps a Gnostic term of reference, so far as the *Gospels* are concerned, and a point of interest or concern more to the disciples than it was to Jesus. Certainly he never speaks of *hamartia* in a harsh or violent manner.

In subsequent history the Latin term *peccatum*, from the verb *peccare*, meaning "to stumble", "to commit a fault" and thus "to sin", became the principal designation for sin in Christian theology. It is found, for example, in the formula of confession, *"Peccavi "~* meaning "I have sinned." The Latin verb derives from *peccus*, "stumbling", "having an injured foot", itself from the comparative form *pejor*, "worse", of the verbal root *ped*, meaning "to fall". This is the same root as the noun *ped*, "foot", and traces to the Greek stem *pod*, "foot", and the Sanskrit *pada*, "foot", and *padyate*, "he goes" or "he falls". The same family also produces the English "pejorative", "impair" and "pessimism".

The enumeration of the seven deadly sins as specific categories of active moral transgression took place sporadically through the general development of Christian theology. While a popular notion in the patristic period, it did not gain a precise and permanent delineation, probably because of the open texture of theological disputation. In principle, the deadly sins are the causes of other and lesser forms of sin. They are fatal to spiritual progress. The distinction between mortal and venial sins is not a distinction of content such as separates the seven deadly sins from each other. Rather, as in the writings of St. Augustine, it is a juridical distinction of degree of gravity in any sinful act. Mortal sins are either sins serious in any instance or lesser sins so aggravated in their circumstance or degree of wilfulness as to become grave. Mortal sins involve spiritual death and the loss of divine grace. Venial sins are slight offenses against divine law in less important matters, or offenses in grave matters but done without reflection or without the full consent of the will. Actual sin is traceable to the will of the sinner, whereas original sin *(peccatum originale)* is an hereditary defect transmitted from generation to generation as a consequence of the choices made by the first members of the human race.

The classification of sins was ordinarily, during the Middle Ages, part of a system of classification of virtues and vices. Whilst such efforts owed something to classical Greek ideas, they were also varied and distinctly Christian. In the twelfth century monastics like Bernard of Clairvaux and mystics like St. Hildegard of Bingen presented rich visionary descriptions of personified virtues and vices. Hildegard, in her *Liber Vitae Meritorum*, described "cowardly sloth":

Ignavia had a human head, but its left ear was like the ear of a hare, and so large as to cover the head. Its body and bones were worm-like, apparently without bones; and it spoke trembling.

She was also witness to the hellish consequences of various sins:

> I saw a hollow mountain full of fire and vipers, with a little opening; and near it a horrible cold place crawling with scorpions. The souls of those guilty of envy and malice suffer here, passing for relief from the one place to the other.

Thus, through an array of boiling pitch, sulphur, swamps, icy rivers, tormenting dragons, fiery pavements, sharp-toothed worms, hails of fire and ice and scourges of sharpened flails, Hildegard traced out a catalogue of the varieties of sin and their consequences.

With equal imagination, Alanus Magnus de Insulis, in his complex religious allegory *Anticlaudianus*, showed man protected by a host of more than a dozen virtues, clothed in the seven arts, and engaged in a complex struggle against a corresponding host of besetting sins and vices. Nature calls upon the celestial council of her sisters to aid in forming a perfect work. Led by Concord, they come forth to help — Peace, Plenty, Favour, Youth, Laughter (banisher of mental mists),

Shame, Modesty, Reason (the measure of the good), Honesty, Dignity, Prudence, Piety, Faith, Virtue and Nobility. Despite all this assistance, Nature can produce only the mortal, albeit perfect, body of man. The soul demands a divine artificer. Reason praises their plan to place a new Lucifer upon the earth to be the champion of all the virtues against vice, and he urges the celestial council to send an emissary to Heaven to request divine assistance. *Prudence-Phronesis* agrees to go, and Wisdom forms for her a chariot out of the seven arts: Grammar, Logic, Rhetoric, Arithmetic, Music, Geometry and Astronomy. Reason attaches the five senses to the chariot and then mounts it as its charioteer. He is able to bring *Prudence-Phronesis* to the gate of Heaven, but can go no further. There, Theology, the Queen of the Pole, takes Prudence into her care and conveys her, supported by Faith, into the Presence. She cannot bear the vision directly, but must look into a reflecting glass, wherein she adores and worships the eternal and divine All. Then she explains Nature's plight and asks for aid. Mind is summoned and ordered to fashion the new form and type of the human mind. Mind constructs the precious form in the reflecting glass, including in it all the graces of the patriarchs. Then the new form is ensouled and Prudence-Phronesis is entrusted with it. She returns in the chariot with Reason to the celestial council of Nature, where Concord unites the human mind with the mortal, though perfect, vesture formed by Nature.

Unfortunately, when news of this new creature reaches Alecto in Tartarus, she is enraged. She summons the masters of every sin — Injury, Fraud, Perjury, Theft, Rapine, Fury, Anger, Hate, Discord, Strife, Disease, Melancholy, Lust, Wantonness, Need, Fear and Old Age. She exhorts them to destroy this new creature who threatens their dominions. First, Folly — accompanied by her helpers, Sloth, Gaming, Idle Jesting, Ease and Sleep — attacks the man, but the virtues with which he is endowed repel the assault. So it goes until the final onslaught by Impiety, Fraud and Avarice, but the man, protected by all the virtues of Nature, by Reason and all its arts, and above all by his divine mind, prevails. Love and Virtue banish Vice and Discord, and the earth adorned by man springs forth in flowering abundance. With this, Alanus closes, observing that all good flows from the invisible and unmanifest source of All.

The doctrinal structuring of this profusion of mystical and literary variety into a standardized set of seven deadly sins had begun earlier with St. Ambrose and St. Augustine, who spoke of pride, avarice, anger, gluttony and unchastity, as well as envy, vainglory, gloominess *(tristitia)* and indifference *(acedia,* from the Greek *akedos,* "heedlessness"). It was Aquinas who, in his *Summa Theologica,* depicted a systematic series of seven specific virtues, coupled with corresponding gifts, and opposed by seven specific vices or sins. In this scheme there are three theological virtues — *fides, spes* and *caritas* — and four cardinal virtues — *prudentia, iustitia, fortitudo* and *temperantia. Fides,* "faith", is accompanied by the gifts of *intellectus* and *scientia* and opposed by the vices of *infidelitas, haeresis, apostasia, blasphernia* and *caecitas mentis* ("spiritual blindness"). *Spes,* "hope", has *timor* as its corresponding gift and *despratio* and *praesumptio* as its opposing vices. *Caritas,* "charity", is accompanied by the gifts of *dilectio, gaudium, pax, misericordia, beneficentia, eleemosyna* and *correctio fraterna.* It is opposed by the vices of *odium, acedia, invidia, discordia, contentio, skhisma, bellum, rixa, seditio* and *scandalum.*

Then comes the first of the purely moral cardinal virtues, *prudentia,* "prudence", which is accompanied by the gift of *consilium* and opposed by the vices of *imp rudentia* and *neglegentia. Justitia,* justice", the second cardinal virtue, has as its general gift *pietas* and is opposed to *iniustitia.* It comprehends ten lesser virtues as its parts. First comes *religio,* enacted through *devotio, oratio, adoratio, sacrificium, oblatio, decumae, votum* and *iuramentum,* and opposed by *superstitio, idolatria, tentatio Dei, periurium, sacrilegium* and *simonia.* Second is *pietas,* "piety", along with its opposite, *impietas.* Third is *observantia,* enacted through *dulia,* "service", and *oboedientia* and opposed by *inoboedientia.* Fourth comes *gratia* and its opposite, *ingratitudo.*

Fifth is *vindicatio* or "punishment". Sixth is *veritas,* "truth", opposed by *hypocrisis, iactantia,* "boasting", and *ironia.* Seventh is *amicitia,* coupled with the vices of *adulatio* and *litigium.* The ninth is *liberalitas,* and its vices are *avaritia* and *prodigalitas.* The tenth and last of these virtues subordinate to *iustitia* is *epieikeia* or *aequitas.* Then comes the third of the cardinal virtues, *fort itudo,* enacted through *martyrium* and opposed by the vices of *intimiditas* and *audacia. Fortitudo* has four subordinate parts — *magnanimitas, magmficentia, patientia* and *perseverantia* — each with the evident opposing vice. Finally, the fourth cardinal virtue, *temperantia*, "temperance", has as its opposite, *intemperantia*, along with the lesser constituents *verecundia, honestas, abstinentia, sobrietas, castitas, dementia, modestia* and *humilitas*, each of these having in turn its own appropriate vice. Despite the complexity of this system, or perhaps because of it, it did not lead to a popular designation of the virtues and vices, although it endorsed the idea that the mystical number seven should be employed in enumerating the sins.

When the King James translation of the Greek *New Testament* was done, the following terms emerged as the English names of the seven deadly sins: pride, covetousness, lust, anger, gluttony, envy and sloth.

1. *Pride:* From the Anglo-Saxon *prut*, "proud"; the Old French *prod*, "valiant", "notable", "loyal", as in *prud 'homme;* the Late Latin *prode*, "advantageous"; and the Latin *prodesse*, "to be beneficial"; the compound *pro + esse*, literally "to be before". *Pro*, "before", is from the Greek *pro*, "before", "ahead", and akin to the Sanskrit *pra-*, "before", "forward". In *Mark* 7:22, *huperephania*, "haughtiness", is spoken of as one of the things that come out of a man, thus polluting him. There are two other references to pride in the *Epistles*.

2. *Covetousness:* From the Old French *coveitier*, "to desire"; the Latin *cupiditas*, "desirousness", and *cupere*, "to desire"; the Greek *kapnos*, "smoke" (from which comes the Latin *vapor*, "steam"); and the Sanskrit *kupyati*, "he swells with rage", "he is angry", having to do with smoking, boiling, emotional agitation and violent motion. In *Mark* 7:22, *pleonezia*, "taking more than one's share", is included in the list of things that come out of a man, thereby polluting him. In *Luke* 12:15, the same term is used when Jesus points out that abundance in life does not arise from possessions. This and similar terms for covetousness occur about fifteen times in the non-Gospel portions of the *New Testament*. (The term "avarice", which is now often preferred to "covetousness", is not part of the vocabulary of the King James version. It is a Latin term, *avaritia*, "covetousness", from the verb *avere*, "to long for", "to covet", and *avidus*, "avid", related to the Greek *enees*, "gentle", and the Sanskrit *avati*, "he favours". Similarly, "greed", from the Gothic *gredus*, "to hunger", and the Old English *giernan*, "to yearn", and the

Old Norse *giarn,* "eager" or "willing", is not a common term in the King James and does not occur at all in the four Gospels. Its Latin roots are *horiri* and *hortari,* "to urge", "to encourage" and "to cheer", from the Greek *khairein,* "to rejoice", or "to enjoy", and the Sanskrit *haryati,* "he likes" or "he yearns for".)

3. *Lust:* From the Anglo-Saxon *lust,* "pleasure"; the Old Norse *losti,* "sexual desire"; the Medieval Latin *lasciviosus,* "wanton", "lustful"; the Latin *lascivus,* "wanton", originally "playful" as applied to children and animals; the Greek *laste,* "a wanton woman", *lasthe,* "a mockery", and *lilaiesthai,* "to yearn"; and the Sanskrit *lasati,* "he plays", and *lalasas,* "desirous". There is no reference to lust in the four Gospels. However, the terms *orezis,* "appetite", *epithumetas,* "desire of the heart", and *hedone,* "pleasure", occur about two dozen times in the *Epistles,* almost always in a negative context.

4. *Anger:* From the Old Norse *angr,* "sorrow", "distress", and *angra,* "to grieve"; akin to Old English *enge,* "narrow", and the Germanic *angst* and *angust,* "anxiety"; the Latin *angor,* "strangling", "tight", "anguished", and *angere,* "to distress", "to strangle"; the Greek *agkhein,* "to squeeze", "to embrace", "to strangle"; and the Sanskrit *amhas,* "anxiety". There is one reference, in *Mark 3:5,* to *orges,* irritation", (on the part of Jesus) in the four Gospels. There are two other references to anger in the *Epistles.*

5. *Gluttony:* From the Middle English *glotonie,* "gluttony"; the Middle French *glotoier,* "to eat greedily"; the Old French *gloton,* "a glutton"; the Latin *glutto,* "a glutton", derived from *gluttire,* "to swallow", from *gula,* "the throat" or "gullet" (see "gullible"); and the Greek *delear,* "a bait", and *deleazo,* "to entice" or "catch by bait". In *Matthew* 11:19 and *Luke* 7:34, Jesus, contrasting the crowd's reactions to himself and John the Baptist, says that they regard him as a *phagos,* "a glutton" or "man given to eating" (unlike John, who neither ate nor drank). There is no other mention of gluttony in the *New Testament.*

6. *Envy:* From the Old French *envie,* "envy"; the Latin *invidere,* "to look at askance" or "to see with malice", from *in,* a prefix connoting an intensification of the term modified, and *videre,* "to look" or "to see", hence "to look intensively"; with the Latin root *videre* arising from the Greek *eidos,* "form", and *idea,* "appearance" or "idea", and eventually the

Sanskrit *veda* and *vidya,* expressing "knowledge" and "vision". Both *Matthew* 27:18 and *Mark 15:10* refer to the *phthonon,* "envy" or "ill-will", towards Jesus of the crowd that chose to have Barabbas freed instead of Jesus. There are a dozen references to envy in the non-Gospel portions.

7. *Sloth:* From the Middle English *slowthe,* "sloth"; the Old English *slaw,* the Old Saxon *sleu* and the Old High German *sleo,* "slow", "dull" or "blunt"; and perhaps allied to the Latin *laevus* and the Greek *laios,* "the left", and the Sanskrit *srevayati,* "he causes to fail". In *Matthew 25:26,* Jesus uses the term *okneros,* "shrinking" or "hesitating", to refer, in the parable of the talents, to the man who hid his portion under the ground out of fear. There are two other references to sloth in the *Epistles.* (Among Catholic writers, the Late Latin Aquinan term *acedia,* "sloth", is sometimes preferred to the Saxon term. *Acedia* stems directly from the Greek *akedos,* "careless", from *a,* "not", and *kedos,* "care", "grief" and "anxiety", derived from the Avestan *sadra,* "sorrow".)

Generally, there is no enumeration or theory of the seven deadly sins in the *New Testament.* Pride, covetousness, gluttony and sloth are the only ones mentioned directly by Jesus. Even these are passing single references. Of these four deadly sins, pride and sloth are each mentioned only a few times in the non-Gospel portions of the *New Testament.* Gluttony is totally neglected in the *Epistles.* Only covetousness seems to be a major concern, receiving mention in approximately twelve places. Anger and envy as such are not spoken of by Jesus at all, although they are mentioned in the Gospels. In the *Epistles,* however, envy is mentioned twelve times. Lust, which is not even mentioned in the Gospels, is referred to more than twenty-four times in the various *Epistles.* Overall, Jesus pays little direct attention either to sin or to the species of sin, whilst the disciples, particularly in the *Epistles,* draw a great deal more attention to sin and, in particular, lust, covetousness and envy. Such, at least, is the testimony of the Greek text of the *New Testament* as rendered in the King James Version.

It is at this point, where the seven deadly sins receive their authoritative delineation in the English language, that their significance began to wane. The forces of the Renaissance and the Reformation initiated the fundamental moral mutation in European culture that led to modernity. The England of Queen Elizabeth gave way to the England of King James, and it was not so long from there to the Long Parliament. There and elsewhere people started to take a less sacrosanct view of sin and the seven deadly sins. Most important, the effort to reground morality independent of theological conceptions had taken root. It is not necessary here to go into the post-history of the notion of sin, which includes both the reaction against it as well as the effort to salvage some meaning out of it, and a great deal else. Rather, this is the point at which the structure of the concept should be examined, internally, in relation to what went before, and in relation to the present conception of violence.

Hermes, November 1985

THE SEVEN DEADLY SINS
II. Sin and Violence

One of the most striking facts about sin and its division into seven cardinal forms is the general historical disarray and lack of agreement on this point. Perhaps the list of the seven deadly sins has been reasonably stable in the English language for the past three hundred years precisely because the topic has no longer been a focus of active cultural interest. Certainly, in the preceding sixteen hundred years the list varied immensely. Put in another way, despite the efforts of systematizers, there was no broadly accepted basis for an exhaustive classification of the sins, or of the virtues, for that matter. No doubt there is something arbitrary about any scheme of classification. For example, to say that all directions may be defined in terms of north, south, east and west is not to argue that they must be so defined. Yet from a certain perspective that is readily reached by most human beings, in relation to their idea of location on the earth, this seems an orderly and exhaustive scheme. Unlike the four cardinal directions, the seven deadly sins enjoyed no such widespread self-evidence. Even the division into seven seems to have been but a self-conscious effort to reflect the intellectual ways of classical antiquity, but without a compelling grasp of its logic.

When Plato has Socrates refer, without argument, to the four cardinal virtues as Justice, Wisdom, Courage and Temperance, he does so with a definite basis for the division in mind. Each mode of *arete* or "excellence" exists as a quality or property of a human faculty, or relationship of faculties, which enables it to perform its natural function well. Thus, Wisdom is the virtue of the mind. Courage is the virtue of the spirited nature. Temperance is not the virtue of the appetitive nature, but rather its agreeable governance by the higher faculties. Justice is the principle that each faculty in man should perform the function which it is, by nature, suited to perform – nothing in excess or defect of this mean. Justice is thus the principle of virtue itself. This relationship between the system of psychology and the system of ethics is crucial to the Platonic view of man. It is more than an analogy. It is a primary basis for connecting human welfare and meanings with the broader activities of Nature, since the elements of the human *psyche* are inseparably derived from Nature, including its root ordering principle or *logos* and its fundamental moving causes or *theci*. Hence, human virtues and vices represent aspects of the art of living well or ill, which is founded upon a knowledge of the *psyche* in the *kosmos*. The same principles can be traced out in Orphic and Pythagorean thought, as well as in Buddhist philosophy. To put it in borrowed Christian terms, simply to draw out the contrast with Christian orthodoxy, because man is God moving as Nature, when man realizes God as himself he is the master of Nature.

This is a view not easily accommodated to the Augustinian formula of the two cities and the burden of irredeemable sin. At the same time, there is in the Augustinian view a clear division of the human constitution into body and soul, and this serves the purposes of moral classification by giving a clear locus to sin. Since, *contra* Pelagius, no set of virtues can offset the alienation from God, the *peccatum originale*, represented by incarnation into the bodily nature, there is really no theoretical point to a classification of the moral faculties of the incarnated soul. Thus, there is equally no sound basis for a systematic classification of sins and vices. There is simply the chthonic mass of sin irredeemably divorced from the ordering influence of the Deity, and from which the soul must be plucked by the instrumentalities of grace and the sacraments. Hence, even if there is in the seven deadly sins an imitation of classical schemes of the virtues and vices, there is not the psychology to make this borrowing consistent over centuries. This, however, was not felt as a disadvantage. In fact, the absence of the niceties of Graeco-Roman philosophies could be understood as a more forthright and less effete coming to grips with the hydra-headed problem of sin.

It is now clear that sin is quite different and much more intractable than any of the moral disorders contemplated in the classical world. The very shifts in the meanings of terms used to describe these disorders, as well as the fact of moral disorder itself, show it. The juridical and accusatory flavour of sin as guilt; the conversion of the mild and even pitiable *hamartia,* missing the mark, into a heavy moral pejorative; and the adoption of the relatively innocuous *peccus*, stumbling, to express the irredeemable moral fall of man, all suggest a hardening of moral categories and attitudes. Despite the absence of any such attitude on the part of Jesus in the New Testament, who only mentions sin as something to be forgiven or left behind, later writers lent sin monumental proportions, making it a prime focus of thought, speech, action, even meditative prayer, and above all, moral education. In fact, there seems to be a kind of violence brought into the notion of sin that was not part of the classical conception of moral failings or part of the *Gospels*. A comparison with Buddhism is helpful, wherein the monk is encouraged to meditate with courage and compassion upon the sufferings of birth, death, sickness and error. It would alter the entire aura of the Buddhist way of life to substitute "original sin" for "error". It would be almost as though one were to give up the hope of enlightenment and submerge the consciousness in a dark mass. The same point could be made by examining the Platonic notion of ignorance or the Hindu conception of *avidya*. It would be foolish to argue that these are categories shallow in their implications for moral life, but they do not convey the almost stifling sense of heaviness of sin. Perhaps it was the relative lightness or unburdened nature of a number of Eastern moral cultures that left morally serious Europeans, missionaries and laymen alike, with the impression that non-Europeans lacked a proper sense of morality. But then again, the average twelfth-century resident of Paris would probably have a similar complaint about the contemporary residents of London or Los Angeles.

If we turn to the particular deadly sins, several curious points emerge. For example, pride, which heads some orthodox lists and is omitted from others, is now more admired as a virtue than a vice. This is because nobody thinks, anymore, of the terrible fall of Adam and Eve from grace when they speak of "pride of accomplishment", "proud parents" or the like. Nor are they thinking of the Greek *hubris*. Generally, like most of the seven deadly sins, pride is today simply one among a host of psychological or behavioural states which are relatively acceptable or unacceptable, depending upon circumstances. It is simply difficult to put oneself in Lucifer's putative position and get a sense of what awful thing the medieval mind saw in him. Worse yet, from an orthodox standpoint, the Renaissance restored a portion of the classical admiration for Lucifer-Prometheus, so that the supposed arch-villain of pride is converted into a folk hero of sorts against the violent depredations and tortures of the Inquisition. To say that a heretic was "proud as Lucifer" became a compliment among individuals committed to the spread of light and learning in the Renaissance. Since the word "pride" itself had originally meant "valiant", "loyal" and "notable", one wonders whether the entire history of pride as a deadly sin is actually a history of the removal from power of various prominent nobles who opposed the social and political advance of the Church. The saying "Pride cometh before a fall" may have been used more as a political *verbum sapienti* than as a principle in moral philosophy. The issue of pride is still complex, as the Shelleys show – Mary pointing to the darker side in *Frankenstein* and Percy to the brighter in *Prometheus Unbound*. Victor Frankenstein, like Faust, seems more a case of *hubris* than of Adamic disobedience. There is no one for Victor to disobey. Yet he does display an arrogant disregard for other men and even Nature, releasing violent forces beyond his control. His pride has become an accepted token of the new *hubris* and the threat of violent doom it wantonly imposes on masses of human beings.

Covetousness too has undergone a sea change in the modern era. As a term, it has largely died out, to be replaced by "avarice" and more commonly by "greed". Where the original term pointed to a psychological state of being smoked out by the boiling of one's desires, modern attention, as in so many things, has moved to the correlative exterior object. Greed is defined in relation to material possessions, not interior ferment. Desire is generally accepted as necessary, and seen as requiring not elimination but equitable management in relation to resources and expectations. There is support in the New Testament for this concern with equity in relation to covetousness, though usually the term connotes an unregulated appetite. The contemporary Gandhian maxim that the world has enough for man's need, but not his greed, points to the significance of old-fashioned covetousness. It was also Gandhi who said that poverty, the consequence of some people taking more than their share of the commonwealth, was the worst form of violence. It may be some time, however, before mental and spiritual poverty and dispossession are recognized along with their corresponding modes of violence, owing to our contemporary concentration on externals, itself a symptom of inner poverty. The violent attempts of the have-too-muches to dominate and enslave the have-not-enoughs is central to covetousness in any age. Psychologically, it is a failure of self-government of the appetites by humanity, a loss of Platonic temperance or *sophrosyne*, resulting in a self-destructive civil war.

Of all the seven deadly sins, lust seems to be the one most widely rejected today as a failing, and therefore most commonly embraced in practice. The theory of repression is set forth as a proof of the unhealthiness and impossibility of overcoming lust. Hence lust is generally held to be a mistaken and outmoded category, representative of an era of ignorance about human nature. The fact that lust was not originally restricted to the sphere of sexuality, but applied to the entire field of pleasure and pain, is now ignored. It began to be ignored, though for different reasons, from the time of Augustine. Thus, the classical meaning of lust is considerably narrowed in orthodox thought, even as compared with its meaning in the New Testament. Actually, Mill and Bentham could be seen as restorers of the full conception of lust, except that they came to praise pleasure, not to overcome it. Even Mill, however, speaks of higher pleasures, suggesting that physical pleasures represent a kind of inferior good. But in the democracy of the contemporary *psyche*, it is difficult to make the case against any pleasure that seeks its day, and even pains vie for equal consideration. The notion that attraction and aversion have some end beyond themselves is difficult to grasp, and the discussion of them is often pitched at the most vulgar level, in the name of honesty and accuracy. This sort of relentless reductionism of the motives of the *psyche* is itself a kind of violence, a lusting in one's lusts, so to speak. The relationship between overcharged sexuality and explosive violence is all too familiar in our time.

One might expect a straightforward relationship between anger and violence. The origin of the term points to the constriction and tightening of the *psyche*. Anger is the buildup of internal pressure before a volcanic eruption. The terms *angst* and "anxiety" are readily connected to these phenomena. What are less familiar or accepted are the subtler aspects of this contraction or constriction of the nature called anger. Franz Anton Mesmer diagnosed a variety of illnesses directly in terms of such a contraction, while an earlier era bore witness to the unhealthy effects of a choleric disposition. Despite these ideas, which support a fairly continuous judgement in history that anger ought to be dispensed with, there is nevertheless a school of thought which holds that anger is acceptable, if only it is released regularly. Like steam in a boiler, it can do a lot of work, but when it is not put to work, it can accumulate to dangerous levels. In this view, the violence associated with outbursts of anger is not to be held against anger itself, but is seen as the unregulated letting off of otherwise valuable steam. This notion then gives rise to a theory of creativity based upon anxiety, tension and conflict, in effect a refined anger. This outlook is further complicated by the dual meaning of the term *animus*, which is vital energy on the one hand but the basis of animosity on the other. To have a strong *animus* is to have great energy, but also to run a great risk of anger and conflict. Hence the contemporary confusion of aggressiveness, assertiveness and fighting with individuation. Perhaps neither anger as a sin nor anger as a modern psychological fact really gets at the core of the phenomenon. The nature and qualities of the energies themselves which flow through the individual and which are reflected in anger must, however, be considered. Since energy, whether physical or psychological, remains a morally neutral category, it is helpful to turn to the *Sankhya* conception of the three *gunas* – *sattva*, "light", *rajas*, "restlessness", and *tamas*, "darkness". These three pervade all Nature, including man, and give a definite inherent moral quality to all thought, feeling and action. There may be certain types of psychic energy that are inherently violent in their expression, or inevitably explosive when mixed, no matter how one proposes to handle the relief valves, whether individual or collective.

If anger has to do with violent outbursts, perhaps gluttony may be thought of as a contrasting state of unregulated, even violent, intake. As with many of the other deadly sins, both orthodoxy and modernity seem to have narrowed the associated ancient connotations of the term. Gullibility, the etymological cousin of gluttony, conveys a wider scope and suggests a general lack of discrimination. The image of a fish snapping at the bait and thereby becoming caught has at least as broad a moral application as that of a pig feeding at a trough. There is an obvious relationship between gluttony and inability to follow ascetic discipline – whether in relation to the mind, the heart or the body. The single reference to gluttony in the *New Testament* is the ironic reference of Jesus to himself, when he drew a contrast to the sternly ascetic John the Baptist. In a similar vein, Gandhi made control of the palate a prerequisite to *brahmacharya*, chastity at every level or the devotion of one's entire being to the realization of *Brahman*. Anyone who has ever attempted to learn, whether about a specific situation or a general idea, has seen the need to narrow the focus of attention, concentrate on essentials, and not snap at everything that comes by. To be a glutton is to fill oneself with inessentials and overwhelm one's power of assimilation, thus doing a good deal of violence to one's constitution.

Envy, on the other hand, is the will to do harm, evil or violence to others. This sin has been almost entirely misunderstood by modernity. It is evident from the original meaning of the term that it is equivalent to the evil eye, an unfortunate but prevalent fact of life, according to many ancient and traditional cultures. Plato, like Patanjali, suggested that there are emanations of the eye involved in vision, along with the reception of external influences. Paracelsus, Mesmer and a host of others elaborated the same point. Indeed, the whole history of healing seems to give direct or grudging acceptance to the power of unspecifiable influences flowing from the physician to the patient. Envy is the other side of the coin. Christian theology early adopted the view that healing was a supernatural and miraculous process, involving divine intervention. It also rejected the notion of the malevolence of envy, attributing its force to possession by the devil. As the entire notion of sin has declined, and hence interest in the devil, the notion of envy has shifted from the idea of active ill-will to the idea of a desire to usurp the possessions of others. Thus, envy is now understood as a desire to have things that belong to others – whether material goods or more abstract ones – and is often conflated with covetousness or greed. This displacement of envy from the other person to their possessions and properties masks the nature of the violence implicit in the older conception. In fact, envy would appear to be the deadly sin most directly connected with violence in the sense of a conscious volition or will to do harm, injury and murder to another. In Gandhian terms, envy comes closer than even anger to pure *himsa*.

The contemporary impression that envy has to do with objects, not persons, and that it is a form of desire for some good, masks its vicious and unjustifiable antecedents. From a classical perspective it would be a serious error to dismiss envy as an innocent but understandable disappointment of bourgeois expectations regarding denied access to economic goods.

Turning finally to sloth, it is in its ancient antecedents certainly the most elusive of the seven deadly sins. Sloth itself seems to be almost an aboriginal Teutonic conception. As such, it was rejected by Latin writers who, like Aquinas, preferred the term *acedia,* a neologism from the Greek invented for the purpose. But the term *akedos* clearly represents, at least in Greek, an absence of anxiety, and is thus akin to the absence of anger. Thus there seems to be a dilemma: one must choose between anger and sloth. Later criticism of the idea of religious tolerance as being a form of sloth suggests that there should be righteous anger directed towards wickedness. The Hamlet problem persists in a variety of forms. It has to do with the ability to release the will, and this is perhaps the essence of sloth. On the other side, the Teutonic notion of that which is slow, dull and blunted also conveys an image of the depotentiated will. If it is correct that the old Teutonic "sloth" is akin to the Greek *laios,* or left, this would connect sloth with classical conceptions of impurity and pollution of the will. This was a powerful idea in the ancient world, but since it has to do with the capacity to invoke divine potencies, it is not a theme upon which Christian orthodoxy encouraged speculation. Hildegard's vision of sloth as lacking a spine is very suggestive to anyone familiar with Patanjali's *Yoga Sutra.* Perhaps the old Celts and Teutons retained an awareness of certain rites and ceremonies which could not be performed if the proper will was lacking in the officiant. From the standpoint of orthodox Christian theory, however, the sacraments could be performed by any officiant properly vested by a consecrated bishop. The success of the ceremony did not depend on the will of the officiant, but was ordained from without. Naturally, the priest was expected to live a pure life and could be defrocked, but so long as he remained a priest in name, all sacraments conducted by him were held to have succeeded. There is here a considerable question of the source and polarity of the forces that are supposed to act through the officiant.

In the ancient view, they flow from the inner divinity of the man. In the orthodox view, they are called from without. Unfortunately, this debate has become almost meaningless to modern thought, though there are remnants of the idea in the contrasts of dependency and self-reliance, slavery and freedom, cowardice and strength.

Put more philosophically, the issue of sloth would have to do with reliance upon the external, the material and the manifest, amounting to a resignation of initiative, will and power of choice. This is much more than laziness. In fact, it is a kind of killing oneself, and in classical terms, it is making oneself the focus of misfortune which can, when given an opening, wreak terrible devastation upon human society and well-being. In this sense, sloth is the deadly sin most allied to the Homeric conception of a violation of that which is *hieros* or holy. The interleaved Greek concepts of *akrasia*, "a bad mixture", *akrateia*, "incontinence", *akrates*, "impotence" and *akratos*, "unmixed" or "pure", may be allied with this idea of sloth as an inversion *(anatrope)* and atrophy *(atrophos)* of the will. This is an even more morally vital consideration than the Aristotelian *akrasia* or "weakness of will". Jesus declared that the Kingdom of Heaven must be taken by storm, and Dostoyevsky's Grand Inquisitor disdainfully remarked that heaven is certainly not for a flock of servile geese.

If many classical conceptions of human moral nature are preserved in the notion of sin and the set of seven deadly sins, others no less important are ignored or reversed. The passage of time has witnessed an erosion of the concept of sin itself. The modern estimate of moral defects and misdeeds is nowhere near as harsh and judgemental as the medieval assessment, nor is it so pessimistic. At the same time, it is much less theoretic and thoughtful, having little or no access to ontology, and hence no secure psychology. Perhaps some of the nostalgia moralists feel for the certainties of sin arise from a recognition that the moral problems of the twentieth century cannot be solved in a way that is psychologically or metaphysically cheap.

Gandhi, the exemplar in this century who has, more than any other, confronted the gravity of human moral failings in a profound and powerful fashion, found it necessary to elaborate out of Hindu, Buddhist, Muslim and Christian sources, not to mention a great array of secular reformers and theorists, a whole new metaphysic of Truth, enacted and embodied through the master virtue of non-violence. One might expect that the corresponding master vice or sin in such a view would be violence, but it is not. The besetting sin of humanity and civilization is not violence but untruth. Violence is the universal expression of untruth, and all the more specific moral failings of mankind are ultimately traceable to it. Here Gandhi is in agreement with Jesus, who affirmed that knowledge of truth will make men spiritually free. Plato and Shankara taught the same view, attributing moral error to ignorance or *avidya*. The obvious judgemental and retributive concern with sin and its varieties during a large portion of the history of Christian orthodoxy is quite distant from these more compassionate conceptions. In fact, seen from a modern perspective, the net result of European involvement in the concept of sin was a tremendous release of violence in the name of religion. While the future may well require a degree of moral self-consciousness considerably higher than present slothful attitudes, it would be unfortunate, and fortunately unlikely, to resuscitate the seven deadly sins in all their medieval splendour. It is also unlikely that there will be a return to classical modes of culture. Instead, and this is perhaps the lesson to be learnt through twenty centuries of experience of sin, perhaps there will finally be an appreciation of the proposition "Judge not, that you be not judged. For with the judgement you pronounce, you will be judged, and the measure you give will be the measure you get." How could it be any other way in a universe of Law?

Hermes, December 1985

THE SEVEN DEADLY SINS
III. Non-Violence and Regeneration

The seven deadly sins can be viewed independently of their historical and theological interpretations. They may be seen as an open-textured set of human actions, attitudes and dispositions related to each other through their common participation in an underlying spiritual condition of the soul. In particular, in a Gandhian perspective they may be seen as complex instances and ramifications of violence deriving from untruth. One may leave open the question whether all forms of violence are comprehended within the moral connotations of the seven deadly sins. Certainly, a broad and important range of ethically problematic action does arise through what we understand as pride, avarice, lust, anger, gluttony, envy and sloth. Each of these terms has a rich penumbra of meanings, and each at the core represents the obscuration of an essential aspect of human strength (or virtue, in the classical sense of the word). In a Spinozist analysis they are passions, passive reactions of the human being informed by inadequate ideas – a lack of fullness of spiritual vision of the wholeness of Nature, the wholeness of Man and the wholeness of God. In a Kantian sense they are all fallings off from the ideal of a purely good will. They are forms of moral self-contradiction, inherently non-universalizable, and therefore constituting corruptions of the soul's faculty of reason. In a Pauline sense they are failures of love, of charity and of sympathy. They display the lifelessness, coldness and cruelty that are inescapable so long as the soul lies bound in the coils of mortality and is unable to ascend through an intimate adoration of the divine – that in which we live, move and have our collective being.

All three of these themes – blinded vision, corruption of will and erosion of sympathy – are crucial to an understanding of contemporary moral, psychological, spiritual and social violence, whether one considers the small circle of friends and family, the wider circle of the city and nation, or the great circle of the globe. These three tendencies are like powerful vectors flowing from the centre of one's nature and forming a kind of inverted constellation of force. Where there ought to be vision, strength and love, there is instead blindness, weakness and hatred – a sort of dwarfed and perverted caricature of human nature, a tragic realization of a Hobbesian view of man.

This condition is no doubt pervasive in modern civilization, which Gandhi compared to the South American *upas* tree, a maleficent tree that emanates noxious vapours, choking out life for miles around. But the crucial question is whether this is the natural and inevitable condition of humanity, or whether it is, as Spinoza, Kant, St. Paul and Shankaracharya would affirm, a superimposition upon underlying powers of wisdom, courage and love. The latter view, like its opposite, is unverifiable and therefore also unfalsifiable. Neither optimism nor pessimism about human nature can be given an unexceptionable warrant on narrowly empirical grounds. Yet as Plato observed in the *Republic,* it makes all the difference in the world whether we tell small children that Nature is inherently consistent with human good and also non-deceptive, or the reverse. We either encourage the child's sense of responsibility and natural capacity to learn, or we cripple them. Where there is a firm optimism about Humanity, Nature and History, there will be a lifelong inclination to learning and self-correction. No man or woman would willingly harbour in the heart an untruth, a falsehood, a lie about the most important things, since this would subvert at the core all one's attempts to realize any good in life. Paradoxically, the worst falsehood one could clutch to one's bosom would be the pessimistic doctrine that evil and ignorance are the inevitable moral condition of man. No matter how ugly the moral visage of humanity may seem in an age obsessed with murder, rapine and deceit, and terrified of mass self-annihilation through foolish or self-righteous misadventure – nevertheless, despair and doubt are the most disabling dangers. Perhaps this is why faith and hope are mentioned before charity, even though charity is greatest of all.

In a similar manner Gandhi displayed a marked reluctance to begin with an affirmation of the power of love and then to derive from it all other modes of human strength and goodness. Instead, he began like Plato with an affirmation of the centrality of the vision of truth in one's life and the necessity of unwavering adherence to the truth as one knows it in one's heart. Without this devotion to truth, one's life is worth nothing. It is like a vessel with no compass. It cannot lead one to any fair haven. Yet the Gandhian idea of truth is much more than any merely cognitive state of mind. It is first and foremost an ontological precondition. In Indian thought, *Sat* is absolute reality, beyond the realm of genesis and corruption. It is the ineffable ground of all truth and existence, the source both of differentiated subjectivity and objectivity. The *satya* in a human being is his or her relative and partial realization of the abstract ideal of Truth, what one might call the tap-root of one's true being. According to many cognate metaphors, the life of true Nature is stifled and choked out by a secondary and sporadic growth. In the *Bhagavad Gita* this is powerfully expressed in terms of the great *Ashwatha* tree of the world, growing downwards from its roots in heaven and branching out to fill all space with its mayavic or illusionary foliage. To reach wisdom, one must hew down this tree with the sharpened blade of discrimination. In Chaucer's *Parson's Tale* the whole assemblage of the seven deadly sins is seen as the trunk of a great tree from which ramify all the hosts of sinful acts. In either case, what is necessary is to cut this false growth at the root so that the true individual may flourish. The vision, strength and compassion needed to do this are themselves aspects of the higher life of humanity, and their awakening is the obverse of the extinction of spiritual ignorance, impotence and malice.

Like Gautama Buddha, Gandhi held that "Hatred ceaseth not by hatred but by love", and like Jesus Christ he held that the direct measure of one's love, and therefore truth, was in one's daily conduct in relation to others. One treats everyone with whom one comes in contact either with violence, or *himsa,* arising out of one's own untruth or *asatya,* or with *ahimsa,* non-violence, arising out of one's realization of truth or *satya.* There is no intermediate course, according to Gandhi, and thus human nature either sinks or soars at every moment. There is an earnestness to human life, a moral significance that is either sensed and seized through self-discipline, or allowed to slip away through the insidious influence of the elements of untruth in oneself.

This is an especially dynamic view of moral life, and whilst perhaps explaining in part the amazing intensity of Gandhi's own life, it also draws attention to the volatility of the various vices and virtues with which moral self-discipline is concerned. Every situation brings with it fresh opportunities for learning and new tests and trials in one's grasp of truth. What one may have understood yesterday is valuable but insufficient to meet the challenge of today. Gandhi, therefore, readily recognized that "sufficient unto the day is the evil thereof", and he often recited the invocation in Cardinal Newman's hymn, "Lead, kindly Light, one step enough for me."

This willingness to take an incremental view of moral growth while holding to the exacting universality of truth and non-violence as twin moral absolutes is the Gandhian key to progressive self-transformation rooted in self-transcendence. In this way, one avoids the Scylla of self-righteousness and the Charybdis of despair. No attainment can exhaust the potentiality of truth and non-violence. Hence, every realized good must point beyond itself. No failing can divest truth and non-violence of their vital relevance to the future. Hence, every misdeed must also point beyond itself. By holding to the possibility of progressive growth, and thereby recognizing the possibility of moral regression, one can avoid the static smugness of those who are too confident of their salvation, as well as the stagnant inertia of those who are too assured of their damnation. Either extreme extinguishes initiative. Unlike any conception of a fixed or homeostatic mean between two extremes, Gandhi sought a dialectical balance between theory and practice, ideal and act, which could release the energies of the soul and of truth itself. No doubt this vision of life is both exacting and elusive. But it holds the promise of the amelioration of human misery, transmitting hope and human dignity to the civilization of the future.

If the ontological core of *ahimsa* or non-violence is *satya* or truth, then the various forms of violence must be seen as varieties of untruth manifesting with differing degrees of intensity. Just as one can adopt the ideals of truth and non-violence at a minimal or mundane level and also at a maximal or mystical level, one will find that the moral afflictions of human nature have their grosser and subtler forms. One might exemplify truth and non-violence in certain limited contexts and in one's relations, while at the same time one may have far to go inwardly. This is perhaps what Gandhi meant by saying, when asked whether he had no vices, that he had no *visible* ones. Whilst anyone could overcome one or another of the seven deadly sins outwardly, this would be but a preparation for a more intensive internal struggle. This is only common sense, and it is also the essential teaching of every great tradition of spiritual training, such as that of Gautama Buddha and John of the Cross. Both warn against the subtle recrudescence of the sins awaiting the spiritual seeker. One is never safe until the diseases of the soul are removed at the root. It would clearly represent a tremendous improvement in human affairs to remove physical violence, especially rape, murder and warfare. But this advance means little if it is purchased at the price of a psychological reign of terror and the spiritual murder of souls. It is not so much that the contemporary theory of repression is wrong about human nature, which it is, but rather the reason that it is wrong: it is simply another case of treating the symptoms and not the disease. The roots of ignorance, egotism and attachment must be cut if the poisonous tree of deadly sins is to die and the tree of life is to spring up in its place.

Classically, pride signifies spiritual blindness, overweening self-concern, and arrogant disregard of others in the pursuit of one's own supposed good. Spinoza called pride a species of madness, thereby suggesting that it springs from a fundamentally delusive conception of one's own existence. The image of the tower as the isolated haunt of pride points to its divorce from reality. Pride is the opposite of the sagely posture portrayed in the *Bhagavad Gita,* wherein the wise man is said to be content in the Self through the Self – the universal *Atman.* Instead of this divine sufficiency and transcendent unity, the proud man is restlessness incarnate, holding forth against the world but also hopelessly entangled in snares of his own making. The story of Alexander and the Gordian knot is a parable of pride, and so too is Milton's study of *Samson Agonistes,* doomed to toil "eyeless in Gaza". In both cases, pride seizes upon seeming strength to undo the soul. Even the tragic grandeur of such failures has a magnetic attraction for the proud, a higher self-destructiveness or violence of the soul towards itself. According to John of the Cross, spiritual neophytes take pride in their fervour and diligence, taking on a new layer of false identity directly from their sincerest endeavours. This is known in Buddhist practice as the shadow of oneself outside the Path. To become fascinated by it is fatal to inner growth, since it involves turning away from the source of one's being – the metaphorical and noumenal inner light – towards the image cast by oneself on the field of one's awareness. As Patanjali stressed, the underlying ignorance or *avidya* gives rise to the false idea that the ephemeral non-self is the enduring Self. This false sense of identity is subject to myriad vicissitudes, lifted up and cast down by turns through attraction and aversion. Because of this involuted posture, the capacity of the will is subverted and the power of sympathy for others is blocked. What begins in a form of violence towards one's true Self results in an obsessive self-regard which sees others merely as means to one's own selfish ends. As a form of madness, pride is the root of self-destruction.

All the other deadly sins may be seen as arrayed around the core of pride, some related to its subjective and some to its objective manifestations, obscuring the powers of vision, strength and sympathy. Thus, one may think of avarice, anger and envy as a turning outwards of pride into the objective field. Avarice represents the ignorant attempt to compensate for the felt insufficiency of the false self through external goods. Anger represents the impotent assertion of the unregulated centrifugal force of desire turned outward by the ego into the hall of mirrors of the phenomenal world. Envy represents the loveless striving, contention and opposition of the separative personal will against the seeming otherness of other wills in the world. On the other side, lust, gluttony and sloth may be thought of as manifestations of pride turned inward upon the subjective field of awareness. Lust seeks to fill up the void in the centre of one's being that is due to the ignorance of the joy of awareness of supernal unity with a riot of subjective fantasies of pleasure. Gluttony represents the imbalanced operation of the centripetal force of desire turned inward into an all-consuming vortex. Sloth is the careless indifference of will even to one's own well-being, a perverse inattention to the health and purity of the soul, and a sick lovelessness towards oneself that is rooted in the corruption of the will through despair. In practice, of course, any such systematic conceptualization should function as an aid to reflection and a guide to thought. Nonetheless, it would be useful to trace out the specific relations of the deadly sins to non-violence according to this schema.

Ignorance of the true nature of things, for Plato and Jesus, for Spinoza and Gandhi, is the source of all the futile attempts to fill up life with one or another form of compensatory activity. When these pursuits focus upon external outlets, they involve the acquisition of objective possessions from a deceptive realm wherein to divide is definitely to take away. This striving after external goods is insatiable, since it is a pointless persistence in seeking spiritual fulfilment through material means. Thus, avarice inevitably draws the individual into recurrent conflicts with others. Socrates remarked, after depicting the origin of the luxurious society, that herein lay the cause of expropriation and warfare. Proudhon simply defined property as theft. Gandhi elaborated a similar conception by extolling the virtues of *asteya*, non-stealing, and *aparigraha*, non-possession, as essential to the votary of non-violence. His own individual stance towards personal possessions is well known, but he also put forth a subtle theory of trusteeship for all external goods as an ethically superior alternative to the violence of aggressive capitalism as well as militant communism. When this ontological and psychological sense of deficiency is internalized, there is a futile effort to compensate for it through subjective claims and ideological propaganda. This quest for gross or subtle pleasures is, as contemporary psychology has discovered, extremely malleable and elusive, and is able to adjust itself internally to virtually any external conditions.

Pleasure and pain are not simple terms with stable referents, but amount to a pair of concepts convertible in denotation, depending upon circumstances. In all cases, however, whether one is caught in the attractive or repulsive side of the effort to compensate for a sense of non-being, the direction of attention is away from the centre and towards the elusive focus of desire. For Gandhi, the letting go of all these lustings and longings involved the practice of *brahmacharya*, a term that certainly includes chastity in the ordinary sense, but also means the pursuit of *Brahman*, identical with *Sat*, with one's whole being. True inward chastity is full devotion to the truth, and therefore essential if one is to release the active energy or force of truth through *ahimsa*. According to Patanjali, true *brahmacharya* releases *virya*, inward strength, the strength needed to persevere in one's pursuit of the truth. This strength is vital in the face of the innumerable distractions and snares that trap the ego, annoying and disheartening it. Typically, anger and gluttony are seen as failures of self-control in the face of provocation from without or seduction from within. We sometimes speak of them as connected with sore spots and weak spots in our nature, certain points of vulnerability. They are like apertures through which energies violently rush out or rush in.

For Gandhi, anger and gluttony, *krodha* and *lobha,* are manifestations of a deceptive reliance upon that which is false. They are essentially opposed to true sovereignty and freedom of the will, *swaraj,* and also true self-reliance, *swadeshi.* Where there is reliance upon the truth, it is possible to release the non-violence of the brave and fearless. Where there is true freedom, there is joyous self-mastery. In their absence one will be beset by anger towards those who seem to threaten one's weakness or by a gluttonous craving for whatever seems to veil it from one's view. The oscillation between these two can itself be quite violent and extreme. As John of the Cross noted, anger at others, owing to their perceived virtues, is the reverse of an impatient ambition to see oneself as a saint. When anything happens to challenge the seductive image of one's own goodness that one has swallowed, this is quickly vented in indignation against the merits of others. At a grosser level, everyone is familiar with the infantile and impotent attitude which says, "If I cannot have it, none else can have it." Whether this is said of a plate of cookies or the entire world, the interplay of anger and gluttony is the same, though the degree and scope of violence involved may differ. Essentially, the forces of violent striking and grasping are substituted for the continuous and harmonious noetic energies of the spiritual will.

The strength of the will cannot be separated from the spiritual and moral texture of one's conception of oneself as an ego or individuality in the world. For Gandhi, the question of the ego resolved itself into two complementary ideals. The first involves the reduction of oneself to a zero or cipher. The second involves training oneself as a champion of truth in the world, an exemplar of heroic non-violence, a *satyagrahi.* Gandhi's conception of beatitude is not a state of exile or stoic aloofness, but rather of incessant striving on behalf of universal welfare, *sarvodaya.* At every point, there are unexpected opportunities for service to others and for relieving their spiritual distress. It is through humility, tolerance, and a willingness to work for the welfare of others that the constructive force of *ahimsa,* or love, is released. To abolish the separative ego is like removing an obscuring disc in front of the sun, allowing its beneficent light to stream forth. The absence of obscuration is not anything to be reified in and of itself, in contrast to the reality of the light released. But from the standpoint of the soul seeking to individuate and realize its true relation to the rest of humanity, the removal of this disc blocking the aperture of the inner light is the crucial task. Every thought of envy towards the light of others, and every trace of slothful indifference to the obscuration of the light within oneself, does violence to the life of the soul. It is perverse, as well as loveless, to deny the light of others. It is suicidal to deny one's own light or, what is the same, to insist that it be kept apart from that of others in the name of the separative ego. True individuation involves the universalization of the heart and the mind in what Spinoza called *amor Dei intellectualis,* the intellectual love of God, and what Jesus called the love of God with all one's soul, heart and mind. This is the existential prerequisite to realization of the concrete ability to love one's neighbour as oneself, as well as the Pauline apotheosis of the finest and fullest love.

Clearly, it is not possible categorically to compartmentalize all the vices, sins and misdeeds that arise out of ignorance and to sharply separate them from their effects upon one's strength of will and one's ability to sympathize with the lives of others. This is part of what is meant by saying that all the seven deadly sins arise through proud ignorance manifesting as egotistic violence. The root of the *Ashwatha* tree is not to be understood through any set of analytic terms derived from the phenomenal world. It can be known only by rising in consciousness to the noetic realm of pure ideation, sublime tranquillity and universal benevolence that is hidden deep within the heart of every man and woman alike. Then, descending again into the field of moral action *(Dharmakshetra),* one may use conceptual tools and categories, not for their own sake or for intellectual sport, but rather as practical tools in the tending, refining and purifying of one's habitual nature. One may see oneself as agitated by many modes and manifestations of violence, arrayed in terms of the seven deadly sins. But all of this, like the physician's diagnosis, is only for the sake of applying curative powers to the soul. Bringing forth all violent tendencies into the light of self-awareness is itself a great therapeutic.

In no case, however, should one allow oneself to become hypnotized by the essentially banal and boring assemblage of one's sins and vices. It is like the story Gautama Buddha told of the man wounded by a poisoned arrow. Instead of pulling it out, he succumbed while asking many questions about the arrow maker, the material of the shaft, the type of poison and the feathers with which the arrow was fletched. In thinking of the seven deadly sins in relation to non-violence, the emphasis should be upon the ability to awaken spiritual vision, to recover the lost virtues of the soul, and to release a current of healing sympathy and love towards all other human beings. This was always the focus and intent of Gandhi's life, and the basis of his indomitable goodwill to all. Rather than make one's failings, however portrayed, the immutable centre of one's metaphysical and psychological perspective, one should instead meditate upon the potential of the good, in oneself, in others and in Nature. Then, even if one cannot at once go forth to sin no more, one can at least go forth to sin less and less.

For Gandhi, however, non-violence or *ahimsa* is an infallible and immediately available means to the arduous task of cutting down the ever-expanding tree of sinfulness with the axe of selflessness in word and act, as well as in thought and feeling. *Ahimsa* becomes no less than the gateway towards *moksha* or emancipation from man-made illusion and delusion. Gandhi regarded the aim of human life as *moksha,* liberation from impure thought, and the total elimination of impure thought is possible only as a result of much *tapasya.* The utter extinction of egoism is *moksha* and he who has achieved this will be the very image of Truth or God. "Government over self is the truest *swaraj* (freedom); It is synonymous with *moksha* or salvation." He also said that "*ahimsa* means *moksha* and *moksha* is the realization of Truth". "The test of love is *tapasya* and *tapasya* means self-suffering. Self-realization is impossible without service of, and identification with, the poorest. The quest of Truth involves *tapas* – self-suffering, sometimes even unto death. *Satya* then requires the *tapas* of *ahimsa* and this means self-suffering and self-sacrifice in the midst of society . . . ."

Gandhi's interpretation of *moksha* as the full realization of Truth and his justification of *ahimsa* as an exercise in *tapas,* the self-suffering and service needed for the attainment of *satya,* gave traditional values a new meaning and a fresh relevance to politics and to society. In deriving *satya* and *ahimsa* from what were essentially religious notions he not only gave spiritual values a social significance but also infused into his political vocabulary an other-worldly flavor. His emphasis on suffering as an intrinsic good needed to secure the *summum bonum* is somewhat reminiscent of Kierkegaard's assertion of the concreteness of suffering men against the concept of man as an *animal rationale*. Kierkegaard held that as gold is purified in fire, so is the soul in suffering. Unlike passive and impotent suffering, active and meaningful anguish takes away the impure elements in human nature. It is always man himself that stands in his own way, who is too closely attached to the world, to the environment, to circumstances, to external relationships, so that he is not able to come to himself, come to rest, to have hope, "he is constantly too much turned outward, instead of being turned inward, hence everything he says is true only as an illusion of the senses". If a man has love beyond all measure, he has thereby been laboring for all. All the time he was laboring for his own sake to acquire love, he has been laboring for all others. "It is required of the sufferer that he call a halt to his erring thought, that he reflect what the goal is, that is to say, it is required of him to turn himself about . . . . The difference between man and man is whether they succeed or not in attaining it." [1]

Hermes, January 1986

---

[1] *The Moral and Political Thought of Mahatma Gandhi*, pp. 237-239.

THE SOUL OF TIBET

Many of us were deeply moved by the tragic happenings in Tibet which led to the dramatic escape and exile of the Dalai Lama. Here was a harmless, happy people, with a distinctive culture and a traditional society totally different from that existing anywhere else in the world. To some of us this society seemed to be an archaic survival, an anachronism in the modern world, a "theocratic" system which Europe had rejected long before the Enlightenment and the French Revolution. And yet, in spite of all our attempts to label Tibet, many of us had a feeling of deference towards a religious culture that we could not claim to understand. Despite all the travellers' tales, the many volumes written by scholars and by people interested in Tibet, we still felt that the essential truth had not been told, that perhaps it never could be told by anybody inside that remote and close-knit community to anyone outside it. A few of us went so far as to follow Burke's maxim: "We must venerate where we cannot understand." But even the most insensitive of persons, willing to write off Tibet and dismiss its traditions, had somewhere deep down in his mind a sense of not knowing what he was talking about.

All of us, ranging from the troubled sceptic to the ardent admirer and even to the believer – all of us felt that there had taken place a sudden confrontation, unprecedented in history, between a way of life centred on spiritual concerns – which could be criticized in terms of modern criteria but none the less had a radiant integrity of its own – and the crude forces of aggression and the destructive passions of politics which are all too familiar in the outside world. It seemed as though Tibet was a test case: can a spiritual tradition survive if it does not arm itself against aggressors who are ruthless, who care nothing for the tradition they are prepared to tear apart or for the culture they are willing to destroy in the name of modernization? This is a question which still troubles many of us.

The Dalai Lama is fortified by his faith that in the end Tibetan tradition, embodied in the way of life of which he is the custodian and the conscience, will survive, will even eventually triumph. He is also convinced that, as time goes on, more and more people will come to see that Tibet has a profound political and spiritual significance for us. Elementary human rights have been flagrantly violated by aggressors among a people who were not linked with any foreign power, who were not involved in any sense in the cold war or giving cause for offence to any neighbouring nation.

Here, then, is a test case of the vindication of human rights, and the Dalai Lama pins his hopes on people everywhere who think about this, who read the reports of the International Commission of Jurists, who seriously try to get some idea of the implications, for a people such as the Tibetans, of the desecration of their monasteries and hamlets, and of a stable religious and social order in need of internal reform. His Holiness feels that if men continue to be silent about Tibet they will be betraying their very humanity.

We find that on the political plane the issue has been so sharply and squarely stated that it ultimately touches upon those fundamental decencies which make life meaningful. But, also, the Dalai Lama is convinced that the tragedy of Tibet has a spiritual significance and a meaning even for those who are not primarily interested in Buddhist tradition. Even for them it must appear tragic that there should have been this brutal interference with the beliefs of a gentle and tolerant people. Do the virtues of tolerance and civility for which Europe fought so hard, and which were finally enshrined in the seventeenth century – do these virtues mean nothing to people who may not necessarily share in the beliefs of the Tibetans?

The Dalai Lama speaks with a faith and confidence akin to that of the Encyclopaedists, the great humanists and the religious prophets, and it would be wonderful for any of us to get something of this faith. How this could be translated into immediate political action is a question which is not a matter for casual discussion. Although nowhere more than in England was there an immediate response in the way of sympathy and material support for the Tibetans in their plight, yet already, in a short time, many people even there have begun to take the subjugation of Tibet for granted, and sometimes to talk as though the Tibetan cause were wholly lost. The Dalai Lama has spoken very warmly about England as the leading spiritual and cultural centre of the whole of Europe. He thought that the British Government, more than any other Government in the West, was aware of the historical background of Tibet and the implications of all that had happened. He also felt that the admirable work of the Tibet Society in England was a pointer to the kind of sympathy and support which could be fruitful.

It is indeed distressing that we should come across the feeling that Tibet is a lost cause, an irretrievable tragedy, and that perhaps the time has come to write Tibet's epitaph. Some of us are keen to do what we can for the refugees and to assist the Dalai Lama, while still regarding the cause of Tibet, at least in a political sense, as hopeless. This feeling of hopelessness is unwarranted but perfectly understandable in our time. Whatever we may feel about the legitimacy of the survival of the Tibetan way of life, we are all affected by the tremendous increase in historicism, determinism and fatalism in the modern world, and especially in our own century, even though we instinctively condemn these attitudes when they are couched in their crudest Marxist form. Many of us think that there is something irreversible about the process of modernization, something titanic and totally irresistible about the Industrial Revolution, the march of science and technology. We consequently feel that when any country, but especially a country with an archaic society and a simple economy, with a monastic culture and old-fashioned ideas of government, comes up against a modern aggressor, be he communist or anyone else, the traditional system must necessarily give way to the forces of modernization.

When the British entered Tibet at the time of the famous Younghusband Expedition, and even earlier – going back to the emissary sent out in the eighteenth century – there was a willing recognition that Tibet was no worse for being different. It is Britain, more than any other power that has moved out into far places, which has preserved that due respect for differing cultures and traditions which comes naturally to a people steeped in a traditional culture that has set a high value upon tolerance and the acceptance of diversity. The British failed in the assimilation of people who were racially and culturally different, but they were able to play a protective role in many areas of the world where they were in power. Even in countries where they unwittingly launched the process of modernization they had doubts and reservations; they were never too certain that this was the universal panacea.

But when a country such as Tibet comes into violent contact with fanatical believers in the gospel of material progress and ruthless modernization, can it survive? If we are convinced it cannot, then we can do no more than merely deplore the actual methods used by the Chinese, which indeed are ghastly. And here we have the cruel paradox of modernization introduced by methods which take us right back to the Middle Ages, methods which beggar description. Sickening details of the heinous things that are being done in Tibet in the name of modernization are to be found in the objective reports prepared by the International Commission of Jurists.

Are we going to be content with deploring the pace, the cost, the pains and the ruthlessness of this compulsory modernization? Has not the time come for us to re-assess our high valuation of the very process of modernization? If we do this, we shall become less inclined to accept without question the notion that it is inevitable and unavoidable in every part of the world. We may even come to distrust the dogmatism or fatalism with which people declare Tibet to be a lost cause.

If we wish to appreciate the significance of Tibet, we must not merely have second thoughts about the blessings and inevitability of modernization but also discard at least one version still in vogue of the doctrine of Progress. No doubt the idea of progress is an ancient one, derived from several sources of the Western tradition, different from the cyclical views of history of the East, but it assumed a wholly new form in the last sixty years. All the early apostles of progress – Herder, Kant, Condorcet, Renouvier – regarded it mainly as a moral concept, an ethical ideal towards which modern man was moving. Renouvier clearly condemned the deterministic notion of progress. There is, after all, no religious warrant for the belief that the Kingdom of God will inevitably appear on earth in the foreseeable future. There is no scientific proof for the belief that technological and scientific developments will necessarily ensure better social relations, happier and more harmonious human relationships. There is no economic basis, either, for the belief in indefinite and automatic expansion.

But none of these doubts entered sixty years ago into the minds of those who took the permanency of their political universe for granted.

Then, for the first time, as a result of the Darwinian theory of evolution, a new and specious form of the doctrine of progress came into being: the idea of inevitable, automatic, cumulative and irreversible progress achieved purely through technological inventions, economic betterment and the raising of living standards. This idea, although it was powerfully attacked and rejected by several leading thinkers and writers in Europe, still lingers on in people's minds even if they disavow it. This lingering latter-day notion of progress is a serious obstacle to our appreciation of the significance of Tibet.

If we look at Tibet with this idea in our minds, there is no chance of our really understanding it. Tibetans have lived in a land rich in mineral resources but refused to develop them because they believed that this would be an unnecessary and undesirable interference with the soil. These are people willing to spend a significant proportion of their meagre earnings upon the maintenance of a vast number of monasteries; a people completely happy to accept that the only education available to them (and it was generally available in Tibet) was an essentially religious education. It is true that those who did not wish to become monks went to these ancient monastic universities and got some kind of secular learning, but not what we would today call secular learning. They might acquire a little knowledge of elementary mathematics, indigenous medicine, traditional arts and crafts and practical skills. But how could such people be fitted into any scale of values we might have?

It is not going to be easy for "progressive" people to seize on the true significance of Tibet, and to realize that they are confronted not just by helpless exiles pleading for sympathy but by a moral challenge to many assumptions they normally would not question. As the Dalai Lama has said in his book *My Land and My People*, one cannot understand Tibet if one has no feeling for religion.

What is religion to the Dalai Lama, to Tibetans?

Religion, he says in his book, has got everything to do with the mental discipline, the peace of mind, the calm and poise, the inner equanimity achieved by any human being, which is bound to show in his daily life. The Dalai Lama says explicitly that religion is not a matter of merely going into retreats and monasteries. No doubt when this is done it has its value, but religion is not a matter of outward profession or formal observance. His Holiness does not even use the word "Buddhism" with anything like a sectarian sound. He is simply not interested in making claims of any sort. Religion means for him something quite different from what it means to almost all of us in the modern world. For him, and for the Tibetans, religion means what it meant in Carlyle's definition – the beliefs by which a man really lives from day to day, not the beliefs to which he merely gives verbal or even mental assent.

The Tibetan view of religion is indeed something totally different from our ordinary response to religious as opposed to secular thought. How many of us really believe that even more important than material advancement and the utilitarian criterion of physical pleasure, is the possession of priceless truths concerning the numerous inhibitions and tendencies which afflict the human *psyche* and of which we have hardly any definite and exact knowledge? If we do believe this, we will be prepared to approach in a spirit of humility the thousands of Buddhist texts in Tibet that came from India, Nepal and China. Tibet is a repository of the real wisdom of the East – a much abused phrase. It has been the home of thousands upon thousands of manuscripts, scrolls, and volumes in which we have not only profound spiritual truths but also examples of a highly developed system of logic and dialectics that was primarily put to a metaphysical and a religious use but which in itself provides a unique discipline to the mind. Tibet has no parallel in this sphere. Of course, no one would admit that he does not care for logical processes. But how much thought do we give simply to perfecting the art of enquiry and disputation? How much time do we give to evolving a technique of constructive discussion? Do we really know how it is possible to resolve the apparently contrary standpoints of relative truths in religion and philosophy and our human relationships?

This technique was highly developed in Tibet. It was founded upon the doctrine of what the Dalai Lama calls the Dual Truth: the distinction between a Platonic archetype of absolute truth, which is unknown to mortal man but can always be held up as an ultimate ideal, and the relative truth every human being embodies, acquired purely by reference to his own experience. We have here the basis of an epistemology which in its higher flights enters into mysticism and metaphysics, but which at the same time is firmly grounded in undogmatic empiricism. The resulting attitude of mind enshrines the belief that a man can only speak authentically in the name of the experience he himself has had. That is why to the Dalai Lama and to the Tibetans it would be irrelevant what one calls oneself or how one is labelled, and this is as true on the political as on the religious plane.

It is simply not possible for people who rely largely on their own direct experience to make a general issue out of Communism or to generalize about the Chinese, though they have had to suffer acutely from acts of aggression performed by particular people calling themselves Communists and Chinese. This does not mean that they are "soft" on Communism or blind to the developments in China, but it is a generally shared attitude to life in Tibet – a willing recognition of the inherent worth and true measure of any man, as well as of his stature as a soul, manifested through his acts and gestures, his face, his smile, his total self. There is also an immediate recognition of the evil, separative tendencies in all of us which cause violence, but with this recognition there is a spontaneous compassion for the evil-doer. It is quite literally possible, in the case of Tibetans, for thousands upon thousands of people to say, in their daily lives, "Lord Buddha, forgive him for he knows not what he does." The doctrine of renunciation, of universal salvation and collective welfare, a doctrine embodied in the ideal figure of the *Bodhisattva*, is meaningful to the ordinary man in Tibet. It is not just a mysterious truth to which a chosen few have privileged access. It is significant that the Dalai Lama in his book does not wish to make special claims on behalf of Gautama the Buddha. He casually states that the Buddha is one of a thousand Buddhas. But this makes no difference to the inward gratitude and profound reverence that he has for the Buddha as the transmitter and exemplar of truths that have become part of the way of life of millions of people in the world.

So the very idea of renunciation is absorbed into the consciousness of ordinary people: the idea that a man reveals himself by the extent to which he can shed what he has, and not by how much he acquires. This is an idea which we might put under the label of Christian charity, or Buddhist compassion, or something else – but the fact of the matter is that modern society is founded, as William Morris saw, upon the opposite principle. It is only in the modern world with its shallow moral values that the very spirit of acquisitiveness has given us a new and dominant criterion of judgment, so that we feel if a person acquires more and more of this or that – be it degrees or titles, wealth, or property shares, fame or influence – he is worthy of admiration and imitation. He may at best use his assets in the service of some exclusive cause. It is very difficult for a man to pretend that he is acquiring something for the sake of the whole of humanity; it is not so difficult to pretend that he is acquiring something for the sake of a particular nation, or group – to identify his own personal ambition with a narrow conception of collective self-interest. And we all know how easy it is indeed for us to say that we wish to get ahead for the sake of our children and our families. But once the acquisitive instinct becomes deep-rooted, there takes place a total transvaluation of values – something that is so subtly pervasive that we do not notice the resulting corruption in our natures and in the society to which we belong.

Once this happens, inevitably we begin to set up new idols and false gods. We gradually come to abandon the heroic ideal as well as the very notion of intrinsic value and merit. The heroic ideal which was precious to the Greeks and to the ancient Indians has been applied by the Tibetans to the unseen odyssey of the human soul. We cannot easily imagine what it means to live by the idea that an individual can by his self-discipline dare all, that the world is a place of probation, that he does not have to take what does not belong to him, that he can take freely from nature and put his own talents to a use that may compel admiration and evoke emulation but dispenses with the cruder forms of competition and conflict. This heroic ideal, which even in its worldly form did so much good to Europe and to England even as late as the nineteenth century, has gone – some feel for good.

In Tibet, then, there have been large numbers of people who were shown a technique of creative thinking based upon the doctrine of the Dual Truth, a technique perfected by lamas in the great monasteries of Drepung and Sera. Among the Tibetan people the doctrine of renunciation, as opposed to the notion of personal salvation, is deeply rooted, more than anywhere else even in the East. In India, the original home of the Buddha, the doctrine of *Moksha* or *Mukti* , the quest for personal salvation, became so deeply rooted for centuries that it engendered a selfish individualism, a subtle kind of spiritual isolationism. As a result, most people are not wedded to a living ideal of renunciation, although it is to be found in the Indian scriptures. But this ideal did mean, and has continued to mean, a very great deal to a large mass of people in Tibet. So here is a claim to uniqueness that we may make on behalf of the Tibetans, though they have no interest in making any claims to uniqueness, unlike people less deeply rooted in their cultures and religions.

This is not the occasion to go into all the Tibetan beliefs. The moral values that flowed from their system of beliefs were richly reflected in their daily lives, despite their human failings. Many visitors to Tibet in the course of centuries were much struck by the gentleness, humility, humour and dignity of the people, such as they had not seen anywhere else. These endearing qualities were combined with the rare virtue of intense devoutness to which there is no parallel, as was freely admitted even by the missionaries who went to Tibet. Tibetans are men of quiet faith, but also men of cheerful simplicity; not men of words, not men obsessed with the idea of personal development or any activity that merely enhances the ego. These men were constantly retreating within, training themselves to meditate and to maintain peace of mind in daily life, preparing themselves for the tests that are brought to light by intense suffering. It is not then surprising that the Dalai Lama should now say in effect: "This is the hour of our trial, this is the time when we must show our faith." In his book he extols the creed of *ahimsa* or non-violence and salutes Gandhi as the greatest man of the age.

This does not mean that the Dalai Lama has no use whatever for the small but brave Tibetan army. He recognizes, as indeed any person who believes in the Dual Truth must, that while we must keep clearly before our minds the unadulterated ideal, we must also be prepared to allow others to show their courage and their integrity in differing ways – each human being in a sense being a law unto himself. This is implicit in the very notion of the doctrine that each person has to find out his own way and his own sphere of duty. In his book the Dalai Lama's plea is somewhat like this: "This is our great moment of trial; we have had such moments in our history, but more than ever before we are being tested in our capacity to endure immeasurable suffering with courage and compassion. We must show our willingness to speak the truth until men may hear it in all quarters of the globe, but at the same time preserving, with deliberate intention, freedom from hatred of the people responsible for our suffering." Almost everyone who reads the Dalai Lama's book will be deeply moved by the last paragraph, in which he clearly conveys this spirit of detachment, non-retaliation and of active compassion. At the same time he does not flinch throughout the book to state courageously what is at stake.

Mr. Hugh Richardson has pointed out, in his excellent book *Tibet and Its History*, that although one may deplore the blunder committed by the Indian Government in its handling of the entire Tibetan question in 1950 – in allowing itself to be mesmerized by the word "suzerainty" while not laying down the full implications of the word "autonomy" – it has at least atoned, if atonement were possible, by doing all it can, freely and generously, for the Tibetan refugees. And yet not enough could be done by any Government. Other Governments gave money – Australia and England, initially, and some assistance has also come from other countries. The scale of the problem is so vast, however, that unless we can organize effective international action to provide the material basis for the scattered community of Tibetans outside Tibet, we will not really be doing our bit for Tibet.

All this only refers to the sheer physical survival of an uprooted community. But is this all that will be left of the old Tibet? Is it not possible that ancient Tibet may rise again? In India, or perhaps elsewhere? Or will there be several little Tibets? We are here faced with large questions, and it is because these occur at the most practical level that it has been necessary to look a little at Tibetan values and beliefs. In rendering elementary assistance to these Tibetans we must not forget that it is also our duty to help them to maintain their spiritual independence and the integrity of their way of life.

Of course, the eminent monks who have come from Tibet and who represent the efflorescence of the Tibetan tradition do not need to be cushioned and protected. But what of the children? Mr. Christmas Humphreys, in two lectures which he gave in London, spoke with very great feeling about the problem of the Tibetan children, who are now beginning to receive Tibetan education but are being approached on every side by swarms of missionaries. The very idea is repellent – of children being looked upon simply as religious cannon-fodder, and actually being approached, not because their souls are to be saved (for which of us is going to fall for that kind of self-deception?), but just so that the egotistical claims of some people may be statistically fulfilled to their own satisfaction. If the whole world were to become Catholic or Protestant or Communist, the outcome would only be that we should find the largest number of lapsed Catholics or Protestants or Communists in world history. The idea of formal conversion is absurd and even irreligious, and now there is a real danger that many of these Tibetan children would be the hapless victims.

In the past we have been given subtle distortions of Tibetan thought. The remarkable Englishmen who visited Tibet, from Bogle to Gould – men like Sir Charles Bell – wholly responded to Tibet, as they might respond to the classical culture of Europe. Lesser men who did not know any better were merely interested in stressing the oddities and peculiarities of Tibetan beliefs, without adequate understanding or spiritual insight. A great deal was written about the ritual dances, about necromancy and polyandry and other such intriguing practices. No attempt was made to distinguish the crude and the vulgar, the debased and the distorted (which exist in every religious tradition) from the pure and the sublime aspects of Tibetan religion.

In his book, the Dalai Lama draws attention to the wholly false picture often given of "Lamaism" in Tibet, implying that Buddhist tradition in Tibet is something totally different from elsewhere. On the contrary, when they left India, the original and primeval Buddhist teachings took root in Tibet. This can be verified by reference to innumerable texts which have never left Tibetan soil until recently with the dramatic flight of the Dalai Lama. The Dalai Lama says in his book that no one today can say he really understands Buddhist philosophy unless he studies these Tibetan texts.

The Dalai Lama's book also clears up some other common misconceptions about Tibet. He readily concedes that there were social abuses in the old system, but refers to the programme of reform begun by the previous Dalai Lama and which he himself tried to continue. In any case, the existence of social abuses and pseudo-religious practices in Tibet does not lend any real justification for the Chinese conquest or for present attempts to Christianize Tibetan refugee children and alienate them from their traditional culture. If we are at all sensitive to the best in Tibetan tradition and recognize the importance of preserving its integrity intact, then we could do a real service to Tibet by raising our voices against the Westernization of Tibetan children.

Meanwhile, the Dalai Lama, characteristically, does not complain but looks ahead. For him there is still much to be done. Countless Tibetan refugees need practical assistance. The cause of Tibet must continue to be raised at the United Nations; it must secure the active support of an increasing number of people and their Governments. At the same time, he realizes that the suppression of religious life and thought in Tibet itself may result in a steady diffusion of Buddhist teaching throughout the world. In India itself, for the first time in many centuries, Hindu and Buddhist are drawing together, an event of great significance. It is as though Judaism and Christianity really drew together without people from one religion being converted to the other. It is as though for the first time Protestants were really prepared to learn from the Catholics, and Catholics prepared to learn from the Reformation. Of course, the renewal of the Hindu-Buddhist tradition is now only in its early, seminal phase, but it could eventually produce a rich harvest. The Dalai Lama himself may move about from one end of the country to the other, reaffirming once again, in the homeland of the Buddha, the simple and profound truths that he preached on Indian soil. The soul of Tibet will survive, and therefore we cannot despair of the survival of Tibet, in that ultimate sense.

But we dare not despair of the survival of Tibet even in the more worldly and ephemeral sense as long as Tibetan resistance continues and men respond to the claims of conscience, as long as we can still take a long view of history and smile at the inordinate pretensions of messianic systems, and as long as people retain their faith that truth must triumph and justice will prevail.

The Royal Society, London
June 13, 1962

Hermes, February 1976

ENLIGHTENMENT

> *The 'last vibration of the Seventh Eternity' was 'fore-ordained' – by no God in particular, but occurred in virtue of the eternal and changeless LAW which causes the great periods of Activity and Rest, called so graphically, and at the same time so poetically, the 'Days and Nights of Brahma.' The expansion 'from within without' of the Mother, called elsewhere the 'Waters of Space,' 'Universal Matrix,' etc., does not allude to an expansion from a small centre or focus, but, without reference to size or limitation or area, means the development of limitless subjectivity in to as limitless objectivity. 'The ever (to us) invisible and immaterial Substance present in eternity, threw its periodical shadow from its own plane into the lap of Maya.'*
>
> The Secret Doctrine, i 62-63

The transcendence of *maya*, the awakening of wisdom and the realization of immortality are three in one. Though they may be distinguished for the sake of understanding and therapeutic meditation, they are in truth but aspects of unified perfection. Like the triple hypostases of the *Atman*, they form a purely noumenal matrix hinting at the inconceivable ideal of full enlightenment. That enlightenment has no specific ground, is not a state and is no event. Tautologically, it is the realization of the Real. Philosophically, it is the consummation of *philos* in *sophia*, the two becoming one, the extinction of divisions between subject and object. Inaccessible through mere affirmation or even negation, it is the One Truth (SAT) beyond all illusion, ignorance and death. It may be approached only by following the small, old path, the path that begins and ends outside of self. One must first become the path to enter it, and then one must realize that one travels on that path "without moving".

Ultimately, there can be no true comprehension of enlightenment or of the path outside of enlightenment itself. Mortality cannot judge of immortality; *avidya* cannot conceive of *vidya*. The insubstantial self of *maya*vic matter cannot encompass the boundlessness of the Real. The shadow cannot comprehend the light that casts it. Whether understood in terms of the attraction and repulsion of *tanha* that constricts motivation and the will, or in terms of the delusion of the mind through dichotomies, the lesser and partial cannot comprehend the supreme and complete. Nonetheless, there is latent in every human being the precious seed of enlightenment, *bodhichitta*. Consubstantial with the highest planes of cosmic substance, it is the core of that consciousness perfected by *Buddhas* and *Bodhisattvas*. It is the immutable ground of immortality, inseparable from the One Life or the Rootless Root of all manifestation. To begin to understand the permanent possibility of enlightenment pervading manifested life, one must ponder the ontological status of that unmanifest wisdom, the possibility of which is envisaged by esoteric philosophy.

In the *Bhagavad Gita*, Lord Krishna tells Arjuna that there is no non-existence for that which is, and no existence for that which is not. If supreme and boundless unmanifest wisdom constitutes reality, there can be no non-existence of wisdom bound up with what are called illusion, ignorance and death. Similarly, if these three themselves are not reality, then they are nothing which can pass into non-existence with the awakening of wisdom. If unmanifest wisdom is without antecedent, it is also without residue. Typically, however, human beings conceive of enlightenment as some sort of real change – a contradiction in terms. Put crudely, they suppose either that eternal wisdom has somehow become real, or that the unreal realm of *maya* has somehow become non-existent. Too objective a mind will produce the first misconception, too subjective a turn of mind will produce the second. In either case, the theoretical and, what is the same thing, the practical possibility of enlightenment is obscured. This root imbalance or eccentricity in the soul's vestures and in human understanding is multiplied a myriad times, affecting every arena of mundane thought and action.

In order to ameliorate this condition, H.P. Blavatsky devoted considerable attention, in *The Secret Doctrine*, to the emerging phases of manifestation from the long night of *Pralaya*. Whilst these considerations are so abstract as to be of immediate interest only to the highest Adepts, they nevertheless have a direct relevance to all who seek to enter the path. If absolute abstract Space, unconditioned Consciousness and boundless Duration are the fundamental terms in the equation of manifestation, then they must also be the ultimate factors in any adequate conception of self-reference, self-regeneration and self-realization. Through meditation upon *Mulaprakriti* and *Prakriti, Parabrahm* and *Mahat*, boundless Duration and conditioned Time, the mind can be balanced and brought into proper orientation to the problem of Self and non-self. As this inner posture is steadied by devotion, entry onto the path will come through intuition and a strengthening of the heart.

Non-self has its roots in a process which H.P. Blavatsky characterized as "the development of limitless subjectivity into as limitless objectivity". Put more symbolically, in terms of *Mulaprakriti*,

> the ever (to us) invisible and immaterial Substance present in eternity, threw its periodical shadow from its own plane into the lap of *Maya*.

Ibid., i 62-63

Mulaprakriti is pre-cosmic Root Substance, the noumenal origin of all differentiations and types of matter – the latter term referring to the aggregate of objects of possible perception. *Mulaprakriti* is wholly noumenal and so subjective that it cannot remotely be imagined by the human mind through extrapolation from a world of phenomenal objects. Even the subtlest abstractions employed in the sciences, involving intra-atomic particles and fields, will not yield a conception of the abstractness of *Mulaprakriti*.

To be able to visualize *Mulaprakriti*, one must imagine the disappearance of all worlds, all planets and all galaxies, a dissolution so complete that no thing remains. When this negation is pushed to the fullest cosmic level, one must visualize in what may be called absolute abstract Space a primordial substratum or field. At that level of abstraction, space and substance mutually imply each other. This inconceivable degree of abstract homogeneity and limitless subjectivity is prior to all worlds and continues to be at the hidden root whilst all worlds manifest and are dissolved. Therefore, it is eternal. Having no reference to change, it is unchangeable and thus ever exists in eternity. *Mulaprakriti*, unmodified homogeneous *prima materia*, must not be confused with the objectivized conception of prime matter entertained by nineteenth century scientists, for it represents the most noumenal and primal conception of substance, beyond all objectivized universals. That it cannot be imagined is attested even by contemporary cosmology with its limited notion of beginnings and endings, or of one specific Big Bang. Other more audacious astronomers will not surrender to a belief in temporal finitude.

Once one can begin to conceive of *Mulaprakriti* as an invisible and immaterial substance present in eternity, and by definition unrelated to time, one must consider its relationship to matter in any possible system of worlds. In an objective world, even the most subtle abstract manifesting or manifested matter at the sub-atomic level is only a shadow. It is, in the words of the Commentaries, a shadow thrown from that homogeneous eternal realm into the lap of *maya*. One analogous approach is to think first of darkness and light, then of a series of reflections. But even such analogies are inadequate because they are based upon a conditioned view of space as characterized by extension, and of time as characterized by succession. Such assumptions, rooted in the illusion of a separative personal existence, cannot comprehend pure primal pre-cosmic *Mulaprakriti*. Such limiting conceptions obscure recondite questions in contemporary science about the reversibility of events. But they also obscure the Divine Darkness, which is only a metaphorical expression for this invisible and immaterial substance, that is mystically said to cast a periodical shadow. The casting of this shadow already assumes the emergence of a world of seeming objectivity divided into planes and rays. Even at the most primordial level of this assumed division into what are called the primary seven *Dhyan Chohans*, comparable to the Ah-Hi, there is the assumption of a kind of shadowy partial existence. And that shadowing continues, replicating itself a myriad times, so that on the densest possible plane of objective matter the one primal substance is shadowed by a dazzlingly complex panorama of forms, changing and interacting, scintillating in ceaseless transformation.

To gain an accurate conception of the ontological status of this boundless plane of seeming objectivity arisen from limitless subjectivity, absolute abstract Space, one must take account of the potency of ideation and intelligence in the unfolding of cosmic process. If one overlooks noetic intelligence and pursues only matter and substance, the immense realm of *prakriti*, one will derive the impression that all these forms of matter are ultimately shadowy by reference to *Mulaprakriti*, which is timeless, without immanence and involvement even in the vastest periods of time. It is beyond them; thus it has been called a veil upon the Absolute, a veil upon *Parabrahm*, almost indistinguishable from the Absolute. Just as the Absolute, if it is to be truly the Absolute, cannot enter any possible relationship with anything relative, so too *Mulaprakriti* cannot possibly be converted into anything else. It cannot possibly be related to any form of *prakriti*. This puzzling and challenging fact must be counterbalanced by similar considerations with regard to intelligence.

At the level of immaterial Root Substance, there must also be a pre-cosmic Ideation which is pure subjectivity, unconditioned, unmodified consciousness. This pure potential subjectivity is prior to any modified consciousness restricted by any object, by any relations between objects, or by any limited modes of self-reference. In gestating pure subjectivity, one comprehends that a totally negative field is ontologically prior to the act of negation. Again, one should ask what conceivable relationship there could be between this pure limitless subjectivity and the limitless realm of objective existence. In the abstruse metaphysics of the ancient Hindu schools, it is taught that the Absolute, *Parabrahm*, could be viewed as *nirguna* – attributeless. As soon as one predicates attributes of the Absolute, one has obscured the attributeless Absolute, *Nirguna Brahman*. To remain true to the pure thread of philosophic thought, one must withhold all qualifications and predications of the Absolute. One cannot even say that It was, It is or It will be.

What *Mulaprakriti* is to *prakriti* – primal Root Substance to noumenal matter – *Nirguna Brahman*, the attributeless Absolute, is to *Mahat* or cosmic mind. To gain any intuition of the profound meaning of this paradigmatic truth, one must meditate upon the early passages from the *Stanzas of Dzyan*, which characterize the long night of non-manifestation – *Maha Pralaya*.

> THE ETERNAL PARENT (Space), WRAPPED IN HER EVER INVISIBLE ROBES, HAD SLUMBERED ONCE AGAIN FOR SEVEN ETERNITIES.

TIME WAS NOT, FOR IT LAY ASLEEP IN THE INFINITE BOSOM OF DURATION.

UNIVERSAL MIND WAS NOT, FOR THERE WERE NO AH-HI TO CONTAIN IT.

These Stanzas attempt the virtually impossible task of characterizing an immense period of total non-manifestation, wherein matter, mind and time were not. Whilst these Stanzas have a vital significance for those at certain high levels of abstract meditation, striving after universal self-consciousness, they also have a great theoretical importance for human beings merely trying to emancipate themselves from fragmented consciousness in a world of objects.

The apprentice at meditation must begin by considering non-manifestation metaphysically. One must first conceive of the possibility, and then proceed to ponder further questions, which may be resolved through the instruction of the Stanzas. From total non-manifestation, where the Absolute is as much as during a period of manifestation, there is an anticipation of manifestation as a whole. Something analogous to this may be experienced in the early morning hours, in the passage from extreme darkness to a noumenal participation in the progressive dawn. Because embodied human beings are already subjects and objects, minds in forms, they can conceive of this process in two ways: by visualizing *Nirguna Brahman*, the attributeless Absolute, generating the possibility of universal mind, which in turn becomes *Mahat*, the cosmic mind of a particular system; or by visualizing *Mulaprakriti*, primordial pre-cosmic Substance, becoming the noumenon of matter in relation to a sphere of potential existence. We may move either from unlimited pre-cosmic Ideation or from unlimited pre-cosmic Substance through the most abstract sense of limit – limit in the most extreme degree applying to millions upon millions of years and to myriads of worlds within worlds.

The purpose of this profound meditation is to shatter the association of space with extension and of time with succession. These conceptions must be destroyed at the root, so that one may return to the deepest possible ground of pure potential universal awareness. At every point, there is, predictably, the risk that the deepening of consciousness may be arrested through identification with material forms, even the most subtle. But there is another and equally profound risk, the fundamental nature of which can be readily grasped by those who have spent some time with the Indian schools of philosophy, especially *Vedanta*. H.P. Blavatsky noted that:

> With some schools, *Mahat* is 'the first-born' of *Pradhana* (undifferentiated substance, or the periodical aspect of *Mulaprakriti*, the root of Nature), which (*Pradhana*) is called *Maya*, the Illusion.

Ibid., i 62

Unlike the various Vedantin doctrines, the esoteric teachings do not hold that *Mahat* is derived from the illusory or periodic aspect of *Mulaprakriti*. As H.P. Blavatsky explained, the Wisdom-Religion holds that

> while *Mulaprakriti*, the noumenon, is self-existing and without any origin – is, in short, parentless, *Anupadaka* (as one with Brahman) – *Prakriti*, its phenomenon, is periodical and no better than a phantasm of the former, so *Mahat*, with the Occultists, the first-born of *Gnana* (or *gnosis*) knowledge, wisdom or the *Logos* – is a phantasm reflected from the Absolute NIRGUNA (*Parabrahm*, the one reality, 'devoid of attributes and qualities'; see *Upanishads*); while with some Vedantins *Mahat* is a manifestation of *Prakriti*, or Matter.

Ibid., i 62

Because these idealistic schools of thought strongly stress the need for union between the individual *Jivatman* and the *Paramatman*, one with *Parabrahm*, they also seem to suggest that the whole world is an illusion, from that philosophical standpoint which sees even the cosmic mind – *Mahat* – as only an outgrowth or outcome of *prakriti*, or matter. Yet if it is only an outgrowth of matter, it becomes totally unreal. Earlier in *The Secret Doctrine*, H.P. Blavatsky discussed a similar divergence between the views of the *Yogachara* and *Madhyamika* schools of *Mahayana* Buddhism, concerning their understanding of the terms *Paramartha* and *Alaya*. Calling the *Yogachara*s the great spiritualists and the *Madhyamika*s the great nihilists, she again drew a distinction between too vehement idealism and the Teachings of

Theosophia or *Brahma Vak*.

If *Mahat* is prior to *prakriti*, one might be tempted to ask whether *Mahat* is prior to *Mulaprakriti*. But *Mahat* is to *Nirguna Brahman* as *prakriti* is to *Mulaprakriti*, which is *Anupadaka*. The precedence of *Mahat* to *prakriti* is the key; ideation and consciousness are prior to everything else, save the veil over *Parabrahm*. If an individual human being ardently longs to attain to universal self-consciousness, he or she must be able to reduce everything to its homogeneous essence, to see through the relative reality and unreality of the world, yet acknowledge that in the world of unreal time there is that which is consubstantial with the Absolute. In the language of *Ishopanishad*, it is erroneous to reject either the Transcendent or the Immanent. The Absolute is neither. One must come to sense the Transcendent in the Immanent, and, as a first step in meditation, the Immanent in the Transcendent. *Parabrahm* is neither Being nor Non-Being; IT IS BE-NESS.

To gain universal self-consciousness one has to experience the continuity of consciousness from the highest to the lowest, from the most boundless to the most limited. This is perhaps the hidden intent of *Vedanta*, all too often obscured by schools of idealism, which emphasize the subjective approach to metaphysics. Subjective idealists like Berkeley, phenomenalists, even German phenomenologists – all, like *Vedanta*, are fundamentally concerned with the distinction between Being and Becoming. All require a doctrine of *maya* which involves either saying that *maya* is a superimposition or that it is an unreal shadow. But whatever it is, it leaves intact the fundamental ground, and therefore one has to cancel everything out and go back to that fundamental ground to gain enlightenment. Unfortunately, this view could become a justification for those who want to become absorbed in the whole, negating everything, without gaining universal self-consciousness and coming back into the world with that self-consciousness intact. Yet, it is just this process which enshrines clues to the sacred mystery of incarnation, especially of the *Avatar*.

To convey something of the development of limitless objectivity out of limitless subjectivity, it is helpful to employ concepts like expansion and contraction. When talking at the most macrocosmic level of the unmanifest and the manifest, non-being and being, it would be better to avoid such terms. To understand the Stanzas when they speak of an expansion "from within without", it is necessary to purge the notion of expansion of any spatial reference. The entire range of mundane experience equally constrains the capacity to devise diagrams and models. For the expansion of the Stanzas is purely metaphysical and has no relation to objective space. It is best intimated by the lotus, which is phanerogamous, i.e., contains in its seed form the complete flower in miniature, just as an embryo develops into a human being. Because it is completely present in prototype, the unfoldment of the lotus is merely an elaboration of what is already present. This is the closest analogy to the unfoldment from the prototypic universal ideas in the cosmic mind into the world of many types and forms. But becoming accustomed to so lofty a conception is like acclimatizing oneself to the rarefied altitude of high mountains. Just as one must learn to breathe the thin air, while maintaining activity, so one must in meditation learn to give a sense of reality on the mental plane where there are no forms and beings but only Darkness. This cannot be done without purging all those notions that have been acquired through manifested existence in a world circumscribed by limited space and time.

Just as the cosmic lotus flowers in a space without extension, so too it flowers in a time without succession. Thus, the esoteric philosophy

> divides boundless duration into unconditionally eternal and universal Time and a conditioned one (*Khandakala*). One is the abstraction or noumenon of infinite time (*Kala*); the other its phenomenon appearing periodically, as the effect of *Mahat* (the Universal Intelligence limited by Manvantaric duration).
>
> *Ibid.*, i 62

These two different dimensions of time – *Kala* and *Khandakala* – stand to each other as *Parabrahm* and *Mulaprakriti* to *Mahat* and *prakriti*. It is possible to recognize that there is an unconditional, eternal and universal time that has nothing to do with clocks and chronometers. It is a time that has to do with consciousness, but not with embodied, differentiated and externalizing consciousness. When through meditation consciousness is deliberately turned inward, when it can do what Nature does when *Pralaya* comes, then it is possible to approach unconditional, eternal, universal time. But one must recognize that conditioned time is merely an effect of *Mahat* and a characteristic of *prakriti*. Boundless Duration is prior to *Mahat*, and therefore closer to *Mulaprakriti* and *Parabrahm*.

To understand this and to make it the basis of meditation, it is helpful to ponder upon the process of universal dissolution. The powerful mythic and poetic descriptions of the onset of the night of Pralaya in a variety of Indian texts can be made the basis of a purifying and meditative discipline. One can learn to experience within oneself the progress of universal dissolution, experiencing the destruction and absorption of the element of earth into water, the absorption of water into fire, of fire into air, and of air into ether –the rudimentary property of which is sound. Even that is dissolved into what may be called a seed of consciousness on the plane of *Mahat*, the primary property of which is Buddhi at the universal level. Even that must ultimately be transcended. All the elements are progressively gathered back into one element, and that is converted from a single universal field of sound through a root or germ of consciousness back into a field of pure ideation – and beyond. Hence the potency of A-U-M, merging back into the soundless OM. If one sees all manifestation as one vast golden egg of Brahmâ, in that luminous egg (*Hiranyagarbha*) the same process is ever taking place.

The Dawn of manifestation and the Twilight of the onset of *Pralaya* are not to be thought of as two points of sequential time separated by vast intervals. They are metaphysically fused in boundless duration as ceaseless creation – *Nitya Swarga* –and ceaseless dissolution – *Nitya Pralaya*. The individual who, through meditation upon these ideas, arouses intuition can reverse all that has happened since entering the mother's womb. Having experienced the shock of being thrown into the womb, and having progressively become involved through a series of identifications and limitations, human beings may be seen as fallen gods. Therefore, to overcome the bonds of illusion, ignorance and death, it is necessary to reverse this process, but not at the crude concretized level of those who talk of the primal scream and going back to the womb. It must be reversed cosmically, because nothing can ever be done fundamentally at the individual level unless it is understood cosmically.

This is the indispensable foundation of the Wisdom-Religion, of *Brahma Vidya*. As above, so below. As below, so above. In the below one must reach for the above; one must concern oneself with all humanity, on a metaphysical level, before any fundamental and irreversible change can be made in oneself. To understand this intuitively is to see that when one withdraws in meditation, at a steady and high level of abstraction, one is striving to experience the night of non-manifestation, where there are no worlds. To be able to do this is to empty and reabsorb all elements, dissolving everything elementally and at the level of ideation. To transcend the veils of conditioned existence whilst retaining full awareness is to realize the one primal Root Substance in boundless Duration. That is pure self-consciousness – *Atma Vidya*, one with the supreme attributeless unmanifest wisdom in *Parabrahm*.

> Say not that It is One, as there can be no second, nothing other than That. There is neither uniqueness nor commonality, neither entity nor non-entity; this secondless One is neither void nor plenum. How can I convey this supreme wisdom?
>
> Shri Shankaracharya

Hermes, March 1983

BUDDHA AND THE PATH TO ENLIGHTENMENT
I. Renunciation and Enlightenment

> *From sky to earth he looked, from earth to sky,*
> *As if his spirit sought in lonely flight*
> *Some far-off vision, linking this and that,*
> *Lost, past, but searchable, but seen, but known.*
>
> The Light of Asia
Sir Edwin Arnold

The *Dhammapada* is the laser-like quintessence of Buddha's luminous message to all humanity. Bridging eternity and time, the unmanifest and the manifest, thought and action, *theoria* and *praxis*, it is a highly potent *therapeia*, a catalytic agent of self-transformation, rooted in the realization of that essential unity which enshrines the meaning of events and relations in an ever-changing cosmos. Although the Pali, the Chinese and Tibetan Buddhist canons contain thousands of treatises which reveal myriad facets of Buddha's 'Diamond Soul', the *Dhammapada* is a preamble to all of them. It is a direct mode of transmission, succinct in style and fundamental in its content. Transparent and shimmering like the calm surface of the shining sea in contrast to the variegated contours of the diverse lands whose shores it touches, it has awesome oceanic depths, sheltering vast kingdoms of obscure species, in which every form of life finds its place, rhythm and balance, in which everything is inexplicably interconnected in a complex whole that teases and taunts the untapped potentials of human cognition. Its immense cleansing and restorative power conceals a hidden alchemy.

It teaches receptive seekers to free themselves without external props, without vicarious atonement or adventitious aids, through a self-chosen mode of purification which eludes the categories of behavioural psychology, utilitarian ethics and salvationist theology. It points to a radical rebirth, a programme of progressive self-initiation, becoming more than human, yet being in accord with all humanity, even in the most basic acts of daily life – rising in the dawn, rejoicing in bathing the body, in simple food, in sitting, thinking, meditating, speaking and working, and in preparing for sleep and death. The *Dhammapada* stands in relation to Gautama Buddha as the Gospels of John and Thomas stand in relation to Jesus Christ, for Ananda is like the beloved apostle John as well as the intuitive Thomas. Ananda walked with Buddha for twenty-five years and could recall the Master's words after his passing.

Although Buddha told his disciples that they should not blindly follow him or assume that they understood him, he so lived his life that it could serve as the paradigm and proof of the Path to Enlightenment. His life and his teaching were a seamless whole, the pristine expression of *Sanatana Dharma*, the Eternal Doctrine, the Ancient Way of the Noble Predecessors, the Tathagatas who have gone before. Whilst modern scholarship[1] has focussed on the details of Buddha's life, viewing recorded history as an accurate chronicle and providing a firm chronology of events, Buddhists have been sceptical of modern claims to explain the true significance of events by reference to their temporal order rather than to the mature thoughts and feelings of those who meaningfully participated in them. They have been even more concerned with Buddha's life as what the Tibetans call a *namtar*, the story of an exemplary Sage, which can help the intuitive to pursue the timeless track to illumination and emancipation. These traditional accounts, fusing fact with myth, do not reduce fidelity to truth to emasculated literalism.

Born early in the sixth century B.C., Siddhartha Gautama (Gotama) was the handsome and gifted son of King Shuddhodana, who ruled Kapilavastu, the small, prosperous kingdom of the Shakyas in northern India. According to tradition, Siddhartha's birth was heralded in a strange dream which came to his mother, Queen Maya. In it a snowy white elephant with six tusks approached the mother and

---

[1] A rare exception is A. Foucher's perceptive life of Buddha. "My task has been to sketch as close a likeness of Buddha as possible, but I have been careful not to neglect reflections from the Doctrine that have highlighted the face of its Founder."

pressed a lovely lotus to her side. The lotus entered her womb and became the embryo of the Buddha to be. When the time for birth drew near, Queen Maya followed the custom of her ancestors and set out on the short journey to her father's home. The pains of labour came upon her while she rested in an exquisite grove midway between her husband's and her father's abodes, and she delivered Siddhartha beneath a great sala tree. Though the baby was born easily and in good health, Queen Maya died seven days later. Her sister, Mahaprajapati, brought up the baby.

Since *maya* means 'illusion', the essential characteristic of the seven *prakritis* or planes of manifest existence, it is held to be hardly surprising that Queen Maya died seven days after Siddhartha's birth. The lotus symbolizes the architectonic paradigm of the cosmos, and the six tusks are its six primary powers or *shaktis*. The elephant itself is an emblem both of divine wisdom and its timely application in this world. Siddhartha was born between two homes, in the homeless state which is the mental perspective, and often the physical condition, of ordained monks or *bhikkhus*. Born away from his father's house and losing his mother shortly after birth, Buddha was indeed *anupadaka*, parentless. Thus his entire life as a homeless wanderer was prefigured in his birth. There is no reason to doubt the broad outlines of the traditional story, even if some of its symbolic elements were embellishments after the event. The legendary lives of Great Teachers are inimitably rich with allegorical significance that is readily enshrined in myth and sacred symbolism. About two centuries after Buddha's *Parinirvana*, the emperor Ashoka raised an inscribed stone pillar to mark Buddha's actual birthplace, and the striking pillar stands even today.

The court astrologers found Prince Siddhartha's horoscope enigmatic. Some thought it indicated that he would become a *Chakravartin*, an emperor who justly rules over many lands, but others, including Kaundinya, saw in it the cryptic lineaments of a consecrated life of renunciation and spiritual teaching. The *Sutta Nipata* tells of the *Rishi* Asita, who divined Buddha's birth and hastened to the palace to see him. Upon seeing the baby he wept, because he would not live long enough to hear Buddha's teaching. Siddhartha's father, King Shuddhodana, took due note of these discordant responses and sought to guide his son gently towards statesmanship. He initiated a plan of systematic study and royal training that provided Siddhartha with all the arts and sciences appropriate to a Kshatriya ruler, whilst screening him from those tragic experiences in life which turn the mind to profound and radical thoughts. So Prince Siddhartha grew up, blest in myriad ways, shielded from the unsettling facts of human misery which plunge so many into a state of utter helplessness. The prince's education was by no means easy, for he was subjected to a demanding intellectual discipline, mastering arts and letters, astronomy and mathematics; he was schooled in the kingly arts of diplomacy and warfare, learning to drive chariots, to handle deftly the spear and the bow, and gaining that combination of courage, stamina and magnanimity essential to statecraft; and he learnt the intricate etiquette which enables a man of high authority to set others at ease, to treat all with courtesy and correctness and to wield his gifts with grace and propriety.

While still rather young, Prince Siddhartha married his beautiful cousin Yashodhara, who gave him a son, Rahula. Established in a lavish court appropriate to a compliant Crown prince within the royal compound, Siddhartha took up the cloistered life of a future monarch. Traditional accounts of Buddha's life depict this formative period as a time of enjoyment, and even dalliance, perhaps to contrast it sharply with the rigorous and austere life to follow. Nonetheless, the allegorical *Jataka* stories seek to show that Buddha did not attain his astounding insight in a single life. He had spent many lifetimes learning to render the highest wisdom accessible to the awakened soul into skilful, compassionate action that could aid others without violating the subtle, interconnected balances of karma. Queen Maya's dream of the white elephant suggests that Buddha, like Krishna Avatar, chose to take up incarnate existence at a specific time for a specific purpose. The persisting discontent that hampered his princely life culminated in four critical events. Tradition testifies that Prince Siddhartha insisted upon investigating the world beyond the palace grounds and asked his faithful charioteer, Channa, to drive him through the city and into the countryside. On successive occasions he saw decrepitude, sickness, death and, finally, a homeless ascetic. Several chronicles show Siddhartha as wholly unprepared for these disturbing sights, for he had none of the defensive indifference that preserves the average person from collapsing under their cumulative impact.

Allegorically, they point to the receptive nature of a noble soul who combines *prajna* and *karuna*, insight and compassion, for whom the inexplicable, immense suffering of others became more urgent than his own concerns. He felt that the very core of cyclic existence is *duhkha* – suffering, pain and dissatisfaction – for all that lives must decay and die. Even if one could hide the inevitable end of each incarnate existence under a glittering veil of hedonistic distractions, ceaseless and chaotic change marks the filigree of the intricate veil itself and so reveals starkly that all things fade and vanish every moment. Since life and death are necessarily interrelated terms in a complex series of events, the prime fact of suffering is a powerful stimulus for altering and even transforming radically one's own consciousness. Siddhartha sensed that the only solution to omnipresent *duhkha* lay in that timeless realm beyond the vicissitudes of change, a realm so far beyond the familiar plane of the senses that only a fundamental metamorphosis of fragmented consciousness could experience it, a realm in which there could be no 'I' and 'you', 'mine' and 'thine'. If any such solution were at all possible, it must apply to all sentient beings and not to oneself alone.

Prince Siddhartha's Great Renunciation is poignantly depicted in his stealthily leaving his palace, exchanging his embroidered robes for the rags of a mendicant, turning his back with pained resolve on his regal destiny, family and wealth, friends and enjoyments. Yet his renunciation was deeper and more drastic than this, for he had dared to challenge the very basis of temporal existence, of all that the mortal mind craves in its desperate search for satisfaction, of all the heart's longings for lasting fulfilment. He was ready to face death in life, to confront the root cause of human misery and its permanent cure and emerge victorious in his uncharted quest, or lose everything in forsaking those closest to him. Tradition vindicates his sudden departure into a new life as motivated by a magnanimous resolve, an uncompromising sacrifice of everything for one single goal – the assured deliverance of humanity from the agonizing thraldom of a hypnotic spell which entices, enslaves, mocks and mutilates all human existence. Not once did he imagine he alone could save all others, but if he could chart the way, even as a trail-blazer marks a jungle track, some others might choose to pursue it courageously to its ultimate end. In pointing out the way by treading it, he would at least provide fresh choices for humanity, and thus testify to the possibility of redemption from bondage to worldly delusion.

Having renounced his life of luxury and even his princely name, Gautama crossed the Anoma River and made his way as a wandering ascetic to Rajagriha (now Rajgir), the capital of Magadha. His poise and charm attracted the attention of King Bimbisara, who was so captivated by his nobility of demeanour that, when he discovered his regal descent, he offered to share his kingdom with him. Gautama declined to take up the very trappings he had renounced, saying that he had no use for them in his quest for truth. He readily assented, however, to Bimbisara's wish that, should he be successful, he would return to Rajagriha and freely share his findings. He then journeyed across Magadha in search of any teachers who might guide him in his self-study. Though the generous responses of each one he met fell short of the goal he sought, he never reviled or ridiculed them, but rather gratefully accepted what they could give and then moved on. After his hard-won Enlightenment, he spoke of two of these teachers in discourses to his disciples. Arada Kalama, an esteemed thinker, had accepted him and freely taught him all he could. Gautama had not only mastered Arada Kalama's recondite philosophy, but also attained the high states of meditation fathomed by his teacher. The highest of these states was *akincannayatana*, the sphere of nothingness, which is called the third *arupa dhyana*, the stage in which consciousness is lifted beyond the realm of physical and mental forms. Despite the deep mystic state such a meditation induces, Gautama had pressed on. While staying with Udraka Ramaputra, he had entered the fourth *arupa dhyana*, called *nevasanna nasannayatana*, the sphere of neither perception nor non-perception.

Although Gautama had tasted the joys of exalted states of consciousness, he discerned a subtle temptation. To reach that level of meditative absorption, wherein even perception and its negation were swallowed up in pure consciousness, was still not to get to the root of noumenal reality. Whilst such sublime states can neither be articulated in ordinary language nor apprehended by ordinary consciousness, they are somewhat analogous to mistaking the manifest First Cause for the Ultimate Ground of All, or to mistaking the prime number 1 which initiates the number series for the primordial 0 presupposed by the entire system. Gautama, having gone as far in his fearless search for truth as he could with the willing assistance of others, now set out wholly on his own. Near the peaceful village of Senanigama, not far from Uruvela, Gautama joined five ascetics, including Kaundinya, one of those present at his birth who had seen in him a future Sage and Teacher. Together they attempted stringent forms of asceticism, as if one could so dominate and deny the body that it would be forced to yield up the hidden truth. One day, towards the end of the sixth year of these severe austerities, Gautama collapsed and came close to death. When he regained consciousness, he saw clearly that pitiless self-torment could no more release spiritual insight than thoughtless self-indulgence. A well-bred peasant girl, Sujata, noticed his emaciated condition and brought him a bowl of rice with milk. He ate with relish, restored his health and began to elucidate the Middle Way. Mistaking his fresh confidence for furtive abdication, the five ascetics who had hitherto followed his lead in asceticism were now shocked and hastily withdrew from his presence, leaving him alone to pursue his path.

Even though Buddha gave scattered hints about his solitary vigil in his subsequent discourses, it would be difficult to discern what actually transpired, for he had begun the steep ascent to summits of contemplation wherein the familiar contours and contents of consciousness are so radically altered that our conventional categories of thought and speech cannot possibly convey the ineffable experiences of inward Enlightenment. He had sat below an *Ashwattha* tree, now called a *bodhi* tree or *ficus religiosa*, and was totally resolved not to move until he had found the object of his single-minded quest. Apart from his unwavering resolve, his whole-hearted determination sprang from an inmost conviction that he had, at last, found the Way. As he persisted in his deepest meditation, Mara, the personification of severe impediments on the narrow pathway to truth, sought to distract him with his vast hordes of demonic tempters, ranging from hideous emblems of terror and torment to ethereal purveyors of ecstasy and enchanting reminiscence. Buddha calmly confronted and renounced all alike, calling upon *bhumi*, the earth, as his sole witness. According to the *Padhana Sutta*, Buddha once depicted Mara's array of distractions thus:

> Lust is your first army, and dislike for the higher life the second; the third is hunger and thirst, and the fourth craving; the fifth army consists of torpor and sloth, and the sixth is fear; the seventh is doubt, the eighth hypocrisy and obduracy; the ninth includes gain, praise, honour and glory; and the tenth is looking down on others whilst exalting self. Such are your armies, Mara, and none who are weak can resist them. Yet only by conquering them is bliss attained.

Buddha held that human suffering is so deeply rooted in spiritual ignorance that the two concepts are essentially psychological correlates. His graphic account of Mara's hosts suggests that *duhkha* and *avidya* may be seen as delusions on the mental plane, false expectations at the psychic level, physically painful and ethically pernicious. Summoning the six and ten *paramitas* or virtues as invaluable aids on the Path, Buddha's approach to Enlightenment instantiated the immense truth of the ancient axioms that clarity is therapeutic, cupidity is ignorance and virtue is knowledge.

In his climactic meditation Buddha cut through the myriad veils of mental rationalization to release the pristine light of universal, unconditional awareness beyond form, colour and limitation. This supreme transformation of consciousness, which shatters worlds, is sometimes conveyed through the recurrent temptations of Mara, vividly portrayed as magnetic personifications of the ten chief fetters which bind the unwary victim to the inexorable wheel of involuntary cyclic existence, the spell of *Samsara*. The first is *attavada*, which *The Voice of the Silence* calls "the great dire heresy of separateness" and which Sir Edwin Arnold depicted in *The Light of Asia* as

> The Sin of Self, who in the Universe
> As in a mirror sees her fond face shown,
> And, crying 'I', would have the world say 'I',
> And all things perish so if she endure.

The familiar egocentricity which deludes the personal self into seeing itself as the fixed centre around which the whole world revolves, and dramatizes reality in inverse proportion to the seeming distance from that imagined centre, can become on the spiritual Path the subterfuge that one is so much more perceptive than all others that one is no longer compatible with any of them. Even the goal of spiritual emancipation can be invoked on behalf of an expanded egoity which absorbs all around itself and thereby distorts everything in its sphere of awareness.

The second fetter is doubt, *vichikichcha*, which can become so deeply embedded in the *psyche* that one not merely mocks the very possibility of attaining Enlightenment but even the point of doing so, for if all is delusion, might not even the quest for freedom be delusive? In such a state of chronic doubt, the conception of partial knowledge can itself be subsumed under the category of abject ignorance by a sleight of hand which conceals the fact that ignorance and knowledge are relative terms, and even absolute knowledge is construed by the unenlightened chiefly through analogy. *Silabbataparamasa*, the third fetter, commonly assumes the cloak of faith in conventional religion, which restricts the sacred to a specific set of rituals based upon dogmatic beliefs. Even one's loftiest conceptions can hinder growth by excluding the hazards of progressive self-exploration. Furthermore, even when renouncing the lesser anchor for a plunge into the greater abyss, one may encounter new forms of *kamaraga*, sensory attraction which, together with buried memories, may suddenly pull against the upward path by stirring up forgotten fears and unsuspected longings. Even if one could set these aside, the force of craving can invert itself and focus upon the highest goal, becoming obsessional, ruthless, vampirical and strangely amoral.

If one managed to elude the deadly coils of *kamaraga*, the fetter of hostility and hate, *patigha*, may be harder to remove. Though one may seem to have moved beyond the polarity of attraction and repulsion which ensnares the unenlightened, one may experience intense disgust at the depravities of others and thus succumb to the familiar opposition that one had seemingly transcended. Then there is *ruparaga*, the craving for form, the longing for embodied life, sometimes assuming the unrealizable wish for physical immortality, and more often seeking its analogue in an imaginary paradise of endless enjoyment. A subtler temptation is *aruparaga*, the desire for formless goods, such as fame and glory or other alluring states of mind focussed upon immaterial ends. When the aspirant has freed himself from all these, then conceit (*mana*) and restlessness (*uddhachcha*) will manifest their most insidious aspects – the one turning inward to extol secondary accomplishments which hinder Enlightenment, and the other turning outward in shallow judgementalism towards other seekers. Thus the ten fetters comprise a tenacious chain which reinforces the common source, *avidya*, root ignorance. Only when all its aspects are dispelled is ignorance itself confronted in its naked hollowness, "the voidness of the seeming full", and when the entire chain is calmly analysed and stripped of its deceptive allure, it collapses utterly and pure awareness alone remains.

Hermes, May 1986

BUDDHA AND THE PATH TO ENLIGHTENMENT
II. The Message of Buddha

When in deep silent hours of thought
The Holy Sage to Truth attains,
Then is he free from joy and sorrow,
Released from Form and the Formless Realm.

Udanaa

The course of Buddha's prolonged vigil is often portrayed as a progressive ascent through a series of luminous states of being, rather like the gradual lifting of shrouds of darkness and the rapturous unveiling of the roseate dawn. Tradition testifies that in the first watch of the night he witnessed all his former incarnations and comprehended the poignant pilgrimage of humanity and the strenuous path of full emancipation. During the second watch, his spiritual insight, unbounded by space and untrammelled by time, expanded, opening the Divine Eye *(divya chakshu)*, which sees the inevitable dissolution of form and the involuntary rebirth of beings, yielding direct apprehension of the most difficult of themes, the intricate workings of the Law of Karma. During the third watch of the night, Buddha directed his attention to the invisible and visible worlds and grasped the immense implications of the Four Noble Truths, *chattari ariya sachchani* (Skt. *chatvari arya satyani*), the central core of all his subsequent teaching. Thus Buddha attained complete Enlightenment on the full moon night of *Vesakha* at the place which came to be known as Bodh Gaya.

If *shunyata* is initially apprehended as the "voidness of the seeming full", the radical negation of ignorance *(avidya)*, *shunyata* is then positively experienced as a boundless plenum, the "fullness of the seeming void". *Nirvana* is supreme bliss, *parama sukha*, utterly unconditioned, free from sickness *(aroga)*, free from fear *(abhaya)*, free from taint *(anashrava)*. It is pure joy *(shiva)*, deep peace *(shanta)* and calm assurance *(kshema)*, unsullied by ageing *(ajara)*, and untouched by death *(amata)*. *The Voice of the Silence* provides a memorable portrait of one who has attained perfect insight:

> He standeth now like a white pillar to the west, upon whose face the rising Sun of thought eternal poureth forth its first most glorious waves. His mind, like a becalmed and boundless ocean, spreadeth out in shoreless space. He holdeth life and death in his strong hand.

Buddha chose to set aside the joyous outcome of his complete Enlightenment. He deliberately postponed his entry into *Parinirvana*, the primordial source of all derivative states of consciousness on lesser planes of being – and so, from one point of view, severance from the variegated field of *maya*. He had initially vowed to find a solution to the problem of universal involvement in inexorable suffering. This meant that he had resolved from the first to translate the wisdom he gained, even if it be equivalent to the ultimate gnosis, into an accessible means which any honest seeker could employ in the quest for self-emancipation. So Buddha continued to contemplate under the Bodhi Tree for several weeks, crystallizing his insights into a compact, yet compelling, message that he could transmit to others. And he deeply pondered whether or not it was truly possible to convey his profound insights with sufficient clarity and urgency to inspire many to pursue the solitary path he had trod. It is said that, before his birth and after his Enlightenment, he reflected upon the lotus and likened its phases of growth to the human odyssey. Many lotuses under water are so entangled in the mire at the bottom of the pond that they cannot rise to the surface; analogously, many human beings are so submerged in ignorance that they would remain deaf to all alternatives. A few lotuses are already close to the light of the sun; such individuals need no counsel. But alas, there are those in the middle, desperately needing the assurance of sunlight and the hope of approaching its radiant warmth. For the sake of reaching as many of these as possible, Buddha rose from his meditation and returned to a world he had renounced, attempting the formidable task of communicating the possibility and promise of universal emancipation.

Buddha recalled with affection his original mentors, Arada Kalama and Udraka Ramaputra, but both had died since he left them to take up his austere life in the forest. He then proceeded to proclaim his message to the five ascetics who had once shared his severe asceticism and then been repelled by his sudden repudiation of their mode of life. He saw them at Isipatana (now called Sarnath) near Varanasi, but when they beheld him at a distance, they agreed amongst themselves to avoid him and to ignore his presence. As he calmly approached them, however, the serene beauty of his noble countenance, the lustrous aura of inner peace which shone around him and his transparent assurance compelled their attention. Declaring that he had discovered the means to Enlightenment and was now fully awakened (*samma sambuddha*), he proclaimed the Four Noble Truths. His first sermon has come down through the centuries, appropriately called the *Dhammachakka Pavattana Sutta (Setting in Motion the Wheel of Dharma)*.

The First Noble Truth is that all existence is enmeshed in suffering, *duhkha*. Whatsoever exists comes into being and must eventually pass away. Constant change is inescapable and entails much pain. Birth initiates suffering, growth means suffering, sickness and old age cause pain, and death brings sorrow. Psychologically, the past, present and future entail suffering, for recollection breeds remorse and anticipation engenders anxiety. Human consciousness is caught in a contest between inexplicable fear and ineradicable hope. Its imaginative capacity to visualize a better condition induces further pain, owing to the glaring gap between "what is" and "what might be". Suffering is indeed the concomitant of human existence and the piteous plight of all sentient creatures.

The Second Noble Truth is that all suffering has a basic cause (*samudaya*). If this were not so, there could be no means of release from the bondage of sensate existence. The entire assemblage of proximate causes of misery may be traced through a long chain of causation to a single source: *tanha* or *trishna*, "thirst". This continual thirst or deepseated craving for embodied existence is not simply the pure, objectless desire to be, which is *Nirvana*, for no impure desire can summon or penetrate that unqualified and unquantified state of peace. As all craving is for sentient life in manifest form – mental, physical, even spiritual – and form necessitates limitation, coming to be and passing away, so this craving is unceasing. The Third Noble Truth is that this ubiquitous cause, which initiates the entire chain of causation, can be countered, transcended and negated *(nirodha)*.

The Fourth Noble Truth affirms that the well-tested means by which all misery is ended is the Noble Eightfold Path *(atthangikamagga,* Skt. *ashtangikamarga)*. It is the *majjhima patipada,* the Middle Way between self-indulgence and self-mortification, neither of which is edifying. The eightfold series of interrelated stages of spiritual awakening leads to the fullness of freedom. It begins with *right perception and understanding,* a clear and firm grasp of the Four Noble Truths, combining mental discipline and open-textured conceptualization. *Right thought* is the deliberate resolve, the confident release of the volition, to follow the Eightfold Path to its farthest end. *Right speech* infuses non-violence, benevolence and harmony into the individual's most potent means of interaction with others, and also fosters tranquillity of thought and feeling. "Never a harsh truth", Buddha said, "and never a falsehood, however pleasing." *Right action* exemplifies conservation of energy, timeliness and economy, calming and cleansing the emotions. Although many Buddhists have drawn up diverse lists of prohibitions over the centuries, the basic principle of right action is that appropriation and expropriation are improper. Right action is facilitated in daily life by *right livelihood*. If action should not injure others, one's means of livelihood should not exploit anyone, and one's work in this world should contribute, however modestly, to universal well-being and welfare. *Right effort* would be marked by continuity of endeavour and thus conduce to the maintenance of *right mindfulness*, vigilant attention in regard to one's thoughts, feelings and acts, and their interaction with the intentions of others as well as the psycho-physical environment. *Right meditation* requires concentrated one pointedness at all times and regular periods of intense absorption in exalted states of consciousness.

The Four Noble Truths are starkly simple, yet far-reaching and profound. They subsume observable facts under broader laws of noetic psychology, fusing an acute awareness of the human condition with the testable promise of self-redemption and effective service of others. The Eightfold Path is formulated as a series of steps, but these are intertwined and recurrent stages of growth at greater levels of apprehension. Wisdom, *prajna*, commences and completes the journey, whilst righteous conduct, *shila*, becomes the stimulus as well as the outcome of deep meditation, *samadhi*, which in turn refines compassion, strengthens morality and ripens wisdom into a wholeness that makes one's breathing benevolent. Thus, one ascends a spiral stairway of being, returning to the same point at a greater elevation, but moving at an assured pace towards an ever-widening horizon. Eventually one is stripped of all one's fetters and effortlessly merges with the empyrean. "The dewdrop slips into the shining sea." This ideal of Buddhahood can be mirrored in mental states that precede complete Enlightenment.

The five ascetics who were fortunate to hear Buddha's first sermon readily accepted his message without reservation, for it gave coherence to their own experiments and endeavours. They became the earliest members of the *Sangha*, and thus honoured the Triple Gem *(triratna)* of Buddhist tradition. A few days after his first sermon Buddha delivered the *Anatta Lakkhana Sutta*, propounding the Doctrine of No-Self. What the ignorant individual mistakes as the self, the enduring and unchanging unity of a being or object, is a persisting illusion. A person, seemingly constituted of mind and body, is actually a mutable composite of *skandhas*, heaps or aggregates, which come together and coalesce, only to separate after a time. When they come together, the person or object comes into being as a seeming entity, and when they radically separate, death is said to have intervened. These volatile aggregates can be broadly categorized into five classes: *rupa* or form, *vedana*, feeling or sensation, *sanjna* or perception, *sanskara* or mental impulses, tendencies and predilections, and *vijnana* or sensory consciousness. Owing to the fact that these *skandhas* come together in a certain order, proportion and combination, one not only comes to believe that an impartite self is there, but also that this self is wholly unique and separate from all others. Eventual decay and death should show the living that such thoughts are delusive, but the illusion of a self is continually reinforced and consolidated by *tanha*, the craving for embodied existence and sensory indulgence, so that one may vainly imagine that this ever-changing self somehow survives the dissolution of the aggregates in some disembodied, ghostly reflection of the composite collection of *skandhas*.

If the Four Noble Truths are relatively easy to grasp at a preliminary level, however rich and recondite their fuller implications, Buddha's Doctrine of *Anatta*, No-self, is daunting and elusive even at higher levels of apprehension. This is partly because the apprehending mind which seeks to seize upon the doctrine and make sense of it is itself a constituent of the composite *skandhas*. A contrived illusion cannot construe itself as illusory any more than a dream can negate itself. Most modern scholars and, unfortunately, some nihilistic Buddhists have insisted that Buddha held that *anatta* implies the non-existence of any self whatsoever.[1] It is instead the explicit denial of the reality of any self-conceived in terms of the mutable *skandhas*. Whatever can be qualified, quantified, formalized or described cannot be the noumenal self. But if *Nirvana* is possible, that in oneself which can become Buddha is beyond quality and number, unformulatable and indescribable. It is what remains when everything is stripped away. It is that which experiences *Nirvana* because it is not essentially different from *Nirvana*.[2] And it can never be understood in terms of what comes into being, is composite and subject to measure, alteration and particularization. The five ascetics understood Buddha's meaning, for upon hearing it they became *arhants*, faithfully following him and disseminating his Teaching.

Buddha also taught the Doctrine of Dependent Origination, *patichchasamuppada* (Skt. *pratityasamutpada*), which displaces ordinary notions of causality as an explanation of the operative principle in the cycles of *Samsara*. Long before Hume, Buddha recognized that thinking of causation in terms of necessary connections between sequential events involved extraneous assumptions unwarranted by strict observation. He also saw that reducing macrocosmic causation to isolated generalizations derived from sensory or time-bound

---

[1] Quite apart from consequent philosophical difficulties in regard to the Law of Karma, moral retribution and moral striving, the *Maha Parinirvana Sutra* in the Chinese *Tripitaka* (ten times longer than any of its Hinayana counterparts) portrays Buddha as asserting that the Great Self, equated with *Nirvana*, is identical with the *Tathagata* and the Buddha-nature inherent in all beings. "Self" means the *Tathagatagarbha*.

[2] This is somewhat similar to the Socratic assertion in *Phaedo* that the immortal soul is like unto the *eidos*.

experience obscured the all-pervasive Law of Karma, or universal determination. He dispensed altogether with the idea of temporal causation and synthesized his profound insights in the powerful conception of Dependent Origination, wherein one condition or set of conditions is seen as arising out of some other condition or set, forming a chain which can account for the uninterrupted flow of phenomenal and transient existence. Such a bold leap recognizes and preserves the insight expressed in the doctrine of *skandhas*, whilst avoiding the problem of the self which deeply vexed Hume, Bellamy and others.

Every condition can be traced to some anticipatory condition, and for the sake of radical understanding Buddha started with the common condition of fundamental ignorance, *avijja (avidya)*. Ignorance or nescience gives rise to aggregates or compounds, including mental qualities, *sankharas (sanskaras)*, which in turn foster differentiated consciousness, *vinnana (vijnana)*. This consciousness induces name and form, *namarupa*, from which arise the senses and mind, *chalayatana (shadayatana)*, inducing contact, *phassa (sparsha)*. Contact induces responses to sense-objects, *vedana*, and these mental and emotional reactions generate craving or thirst for sensory experience, *tanha (trishna)*. This is persisting attachment, *upadana*, which directly produces coming into existence, *bhava*, which involves birth, *jati*, and consequently, *jaramarana*, ageing and death. Hence, suffering is a fact of embodied existence and not an adventitious or malign feature of life, for it is bound up with the ceaseless change of dependent origination which makes embodied existence possible.

During his stay in Varanasi, a wealthy youth joined the *Sangha* and his parents became Buddha's first lay followers who took refuge in the Triple Gem – *Buddha, Dharma* and *Sangha*. Soon enough, the basic codes for ordained monks and lay disciples were set down so that the prime requirements of cooperative effort were met and maintained. Although Buddha's many discourses provided extensive elaboration and suggested varied applications, the vital core of his message was conveyed in the first two sermons. When Buddha decided to go to Uruvela, he did not take all his monks with him. Rather, those who had become proficient were sent forth in every direction – "Let not two of you go by the same road", he said – to spread the gospel of hope. Encountering a group of ascetics on the road to Uruvela, he delivered the *Aditta Pariyaya Sutta,* the *Fire Sermon,* in which he likened the world and everything in it to a burning house. Since these ascetics already grasped a great deal about the nature of *Samsara,* they needed only to identify clearly the root cause of suffering. By showing how *tanha* or craving smoulders in all sentient existence, Buddha freed them from its spell and they gladly entered the *Sangha.*

Buddha then fulfilled his promise to King Bimbisara by journeying to Rajagriha, and the king gave his own park, Veluvana, to the *Sangha* as a monastic retreat. It was there that the two remarkable ascetics Shariputra and Maudgalyayana, who later became Buddha's outstanding disciples, first met their Teacher. Shariputra had come to Rajagriha to find Buddha because he had first heard of the Four Noble Truths from Ashvajit, one of the original disciples who had followed the injunction to take a different road and promulgate the *Dharma.* When King Shuddhodana, Buddha's earthly father, heard amazing stories about his visit to Rajagriha, he promptly sent a message entreating Buddha to return to Kapilavastu. As soon as Buddha and his disciples arrived in the capital city he had renounced, King Shuddhodana was shocked to see his son joining the other monks in the daily round of alms-seeking. Buddha expounded his teachings before the king and his court, and soon his father, Shuddhodana, his aunt, Mahaprajapati, who had raised Siddhartha as a child, his beloved former wife, Yashodhara, his half-brother, Nanda, and a few days later, his son, Rahula, became his followers. Ananda, a cousin who became Buddha's constant attendant and cheerful companion, interceded on behalf of women followers, and Buddha blest the formation of the bhikkhuni *Sangha,* the Order of nuns. Mahaprajapati and her friends became the first nuns of the *Sangha.*

After spending some time at Kapilavastu, Buddha received an invitation from Anathapindika, a rich banker of Shravasti, the capital city of Koshala. He had met Buddha at Rajagriha and became such a devoted follower that he donated the famous Jetavana Grove to the *Sangha.* Buddha moved to Jetavana, and it became the chief centre of his work for almost half a century. During that time monastic centres were established in most of the flourishing cities in the Gangetic plain – Varanasi, Rajagriha, Pataliputra, Vaishali, Kushinagara, Pava – as well as in numerous hamlets and villages, but most of Buddha's great discourses were delivered in the Jetavana Grove. Since no caste *(jati)* or social distinctions were recognized or tolerated in the *Sangha*, Buddha admitted male and female disciples from every sector of society. Although his initial converts were from affluent and cultured and even aristocratic families, all classes of seekers were welcomed into the *Sangha* without any predilection or prejudice. As several discourses in the *Dhammapada* show, Buddha was not primarily concerned with the external reform of the prevailing social order, for any social order can become corrupt in the absence of a vital spiritual and ethical foundation. His revolution was fundamental, and it included the radical redefinition of the very basis of social esteem, stressing the exemplary virtues and graces which were originally extolled in the *Vedas*, the epics and the forest hermitages of antiquity.

There were, of course, militant groups of orthodox individuals who were hostile to Buddha's message and monastic Order, and various desultory attempts were made to vilify him. The main focus of opposition was Devadatta, a jealous cousin who had grown up with Buddha. An ambitious and impetuous individual, Devadatta had found his own accomplishments eclipsed by Prince Siddhartha's rare gifts and excellences, and Devadatta had sadly succumbed to a competitive spirit in which he lost every encounter to a magnanimous man who knew nothing of rivalry in his own generous nature, though he was well aware of every human weakness that hinders the spiritual will. When Buddha returned to teach in Kapilavastu, Devadatta joined the *Sangha* but could not assimilate its redemptive spirit of unconditional, universal benevolence. After Buddha had already taught for three decades, Devadatta rashly sought to assume the leadership of the Order, invoking a principle of personal ascendancy which would have been repugnant to highly respected elders like Shariputra and Maudgalyayana. Just as the Teachings *(Dharma)* had been orally transmitted by Buddha, so too the monastic code *(vinaya)* had been evolved under his guidance, and he entrusted the ethical continuity of the *Sangha* to the entire fellowship of older and younger monks.

When Devadatta's sudden offer to "relieve" Buddha of the onerous task of guiding the *Sangha* and to tighten the rules was rejected, tradition suggests that he made three crafty attempts to assassinate his spiritual benefactor. The mad and drunken elephant he unleashed upon Buddha fell before the feet of the Master. The avalanche he diverted towards Buddha receded before his presence. And the hired assassin he dispatched into Buddha's vicinity was converted and entered the *Sangha*. Having repeatedly failed, Devadatta then fomented a schism in the *Sangha* by withdrawing with some disciples he had flattered, but Shariputra and Maudgalyayana went to each of them and won them back into the fold. Having exhausted every means of eliminating or undermining Buddha, Devadatta was eventually overcome by the accumulated karma of his lifelong animosity, fell gravely ill and died. One tradition declares that even whilst dying he sought out Buddha in order to beg his forgiveness, but that he perished before he could reach his Master. Nonetheless, this account suggests that Buddha knew of his belated remorse and announced his death to the monks around him, stating that a reconciliation had indeed occurred on the mental plane. Another account suggests that Devadatta lived after Buddha and died in a penitential state.

It would be impossible to reconstruct the details of Buddha's journeys back and forth across the Gangetic plain during the nearly fifty years that he taught. He freely taught in many places, and though each sermon was fresh and adapted skilfully to the mental faculties and predilections of his listeners, his main message was always the same: the Four Noble Truths provide the basis of proper understanding, the Noble Eightfold Path is the assured means to freedom, and the common conception of a separative self, "the great dire heresy of separateness", is a costly delusion. When he was about eighty years old, he set out on his last journey, travelling north from Rajagriha. Reaching Vaishali, he accepted a park donated to him by the courtesan Ambapali, but he spent the rainy season in a nearby village called Beluvagama. He fell ill and came close to death, but willed his own recovery in order to prepare his disciples for his imminent departure. Announcing to the assembled monks that he would die in three months, he left and continued on his journey. When he reached Pava he took up residence in the park of Chunda, a blacksmith who was a lay devotee.

Chunda invited Buddha and his monks to a meal at his house, and he prepared many delicacies for them. Amongst the dishes he set before the gathering was one called *sukaramaddava*. There are different interpretations of the nature of this dish, but it was most probably a sweetened concoction of local mushrooms called "pigs" feet", owing to their appearance. When Buddha was served the dish, he requested that it be given to him alone and that the uneaten portion be buried, since none but a *Tathagata* could assimilate it. Unknown to Chunda, the dish was poisonous, and Buddha saw it as the karmic indication for his departure from the world of men, upon which he had already deliberated. After this last meal, Buddha became ill and suffered acute pains. He at once set out for Kushinagara and, after resting twice on the way, he settled on a low couch between two *sala* trees which stood in Upavattana Park, belonging to the clan of Mallas. He asked Ananda to reassure Chunda that he need feel no remorse for the meal he offered Buddha and his companions. "There are two offerings of food", he explained, "which are of equal fruition, of equal outcome, exceeding in grandeur the fruition and result of any other offerings in food. Which two? The one partaken of by the *Tathagata* on becoming fully enlightened, in supreme, unsurpassed Enlightenment; and the one partaken of by the *Tathagata* on coming to pass into the state of *Nirvana* wherein the elements of clinging do not arise. By his deed has the venerable Chunda accumulated that which makes for long life, beauty, well-being, glory, heavenly rebirth and sovereignty."

The scene under the *sala* trees was one of intense sadness, but Buddha calmed the weeping Ananda by reminding him that separation must inevitably occur in transient existence. "Of that which is born, come to being, put together, and so is subject to dissolution, how can it be said that it must not depart?" The Mallas paid homage to Buddha, and a wandering ascetic named Subhadra listened to his instruction. Subhadra was the last direct disciple of Buddha to enter the *Sangha*. Buddha called upon his disciples to take the *Dharma* as their Master, for Buddha himself is ever present in it. They were to be guided by the monastic code *(vinaya)*, even though they could modify its minor precepts to suit changing conditions. Together, the *Dharma* and the discipline *(vinaya)* would meet all their needs. Calling on them to be lamps unto themselves, he enjoined them to seek the goal with diligence. Thus on the full moon day of *Vesakha* – the day of his birth and his Enlightenment – Buddha entered *Parinirvana*. His body was cremated and the ashes were divided into eight portions by a revered *brahmana* named Dona and taken to the centres where Buddha had taught, so that *stupas* could be erected to enshrine them. Recent excavations at a site identified by some archaeologists as Kapilavastu have revealed an ancient *stupa* which contains a casket of ashes on which is an inscription suggesting that they are a portion of the original division of relics. Despite their grief, monks and lay disciples joined together in holding great feasts to honour Buddha and the Teaching of universal peace, moral concord and full Enlightenment that he bequeathed to suffering humanity.

Hermes, June 1986

BUDDHA AND THE PATH TO ENLIGHTENMENT
III. The *Dharma* and the *Sangha*

The Path is one for all, the means to reach the goal must vary with the Pilgrims.

The Voice of the Silence

There is a time-honoured tale that soon after Buddha's passing an aged monk chastised the disciples for being heavy-hearted. Since Buddha had gone, the monks were now free to do as they liked, no longer being bound to follow the exacting discipline he established. Many of the other disciples were stunned by this remark, and they now realized how rapidly the *Sangha* could become corrupt in the absence of Buddha. They decided to gather as many monks as possible into a general council to review, confirm and renew their understanding of the Teaching and the monastic code. According to tradition, the first *sangiti* or recitation was held at Rajagriha within a year of Buddha's *Parinirvana*. Owing to his prodigious memory and constant companionship with Buddha, Ananda was chosen to recite all that he had heard of Buddha's words. He began each discourse with the humble statement *evam maya shrutam*, "Thus have I heard", the memorable opening of every Buddhist scripture of whatever school. When Ananda completed a recitation, others would add or correct from their own recollections, until the *sangiti* as a whole approved the contents. Similarly, the *vinaya* or discipline was reiterated by Upali and confirmed by the assembly. Since Buddha had insisted that people should be instructed in the *Dharma* in their own languages, there was considerable resistance to putting the scriptures in writing, though some evidence suggests that at least two short discourses were written out even in Buddha's lifetime.

A second *sangiti* is said to have been held at Vaishali some hundred years after the *Parinirvana*. By this time, diverse perspectives had emerged on a variety of issues. This comprehensive recital was convened by those monks who wished to preserve the purity of the Teaching, but their conservative stance precipitated the split they had sought to avoid. The monks who controlled the Council tried to be true to the transmitted Word of Buddha, which had been formulated by the first *sangiti*, and they were called *Sthaviras* for taking this stand. Another group of monks, who came to be known as *Mahasanghikas* – the Great Order – ventured with equal fervour to be faithful to the spirit of Buddha's Teaching. The First Council had endorsed only what all monks could recollect that they had heard Buddha utter, but he had spoken to many groups and individuals in different contexts, and numerous traditions survived indicating that his instructions were adapted to the spiritual and mental competence of his listeners. A large portion of Buddha's Teaching, the *Mahasanghikas* argued, could not be confirmed by all the monks present at the First Council, for only some of them had heard it directly. This made it no less valid, however. When the *Mahasanghika* standpoint won no support in the Second Council at Vaishali, its followers withdrew and compiled their own canon.

The *Mahasanghikas* were the forerunners of the *Mahayana* or Great Vehicle, whilst the *Sthaviras* were pioneers of a number of schools later called *Hinayana* or Little Vehicle, though today they are often called Theravada or Way of the Elders to avoid the somewhat pejorative connotation of *Hinayana*. History has confirmed the vital concerns of both standpoints. Theravada has avoided a wide range of excesses, but in recent times its phenomenological emphasis and its doctrinal rigidity have sometimes led to atheism and even nihilism. *Mahayana*, on the other hand, has saved itself from such destructive tendencies but has often been vulnerable to arid scholasticism, and Vajrayana, avoiding both these extremes, has been periodically diverted into fetishism and grey magic. As Buddha himself taught, the battle for Enlightenment cannot be won in cloistered academies or congregational assemblies. It must be fought by each one in the forum of his individual conscience and in the sanctuary of his inmost struggles and deepest meditations.

There is a story in the *Sanyutta Nikaya* which illumines the core of the earliest controversies. Once Buddha was with his disciples in the Simsapa Grove at Kosambi. He gathered up a handful of fallen *simsapa* leaves and said:

> "What do you think, *bhikkhus?* Which are more, these few *simsapa* leaves in my hand, or the other leaves in yonder Simsapa Grove?"

> "These leaves, which the Exalted One holds in his hand, are not many, and many more are those in the Simsapa Grove."

> "So also, *bhikkhus,* is that much more which I have learnt and have not told you, than that which I have told you. And why have I not told you? Because, *bhikkhus,* it would bring you no benefit; it does not conduce to progress in holiness; it does not lead to turning away from the earthly, to the conquest of desire, to cessation of the transitory, to peace, to knowledge, to illumination, to *Nirvana*. Therefore I have not declared it unto you."

Yet in another discourse Buddha promised: "If you walk according to my Teaching...you shall even in this present life apprehend the Truth and see it face to face."

The effort to adhere to the prescribed path of the *Dharma*, whilst remaining open to the vast range of Buddha's Word *(Buddhavachana)*, gradually led to a remarkable variety of views which in time emerged as divergent schools of thought. By the time of Emperor Ashoka, perhaps two and a half centuries after that of Buddha, a Third Council was held at Pataliputra to establish the canon, and it is here that the *Tripitaka* was finalized. Although it appears that the texts had been written down by this time, their exact form is unknown. Ashoka's son Mahinda, a monk in the *Sangha*, went to Sri Lanka with a complete canon. He was welcomed, and following the custom initiated by Buddha, the texts he brought were translated into Sinhalese. It was not until the Fourth Council (as it is called in the orthodox Pali tradition, even though several other councils had already met in North India) held at Anuradhapura in Sri Lanka in A.D. 1160 that monks of the Mahavihara edited the Pali canon in the form known today. Although the Pali scriptures are of indisputable antiquity, and despite fashionable views to the contrary, they have no greater claim to being the exact or pristine utterances of Buddha than do a number of other sacred texts, including some *Mahayana sutras*. However divergent and controversial Buddhist views later became, they all took as their common touchstone the Four Noble Truths and the life of Buddha, and so they combined abstruse debates over doctrinal matters with mutual toleration and genuine goodwill. Theravada, *Mahayana* and even Vajrayana schools flourished side by side for centuries in India, Sri Lanka and Southeast Asia.

As the gospel of Buddha spread into South India and Sri Lanka, eastwards to Southeast Asia, northwards into Bactria, Nepal, China, Japan and eventually Tibet, and westwards as far as Alexandria in Egypt, its formulations multiplied and took on many tints. Buddha's Teaching fused the highest metaphysical clarity with an exacting ethical and mental discipline, but the basic *Dharma* had to be rendered into the cultural idiom of remarkably diverse peoples, many of whom had no formal education and whose languages and dialects could not readily render some of Buddha's recondite doctrines. Unlike the Christian Church, which had a sufficiently homogeneous creed of salvation to ensure fidelity to dogma, the *Sangha* was always more concerned with conduct than with belief. Buddha taught and exemplified the Eightfold Path to Enlightenment and therapeutic means to self-emancipation, but no doctrines and beliefs, however ardently held, can ever be more than provisional aids on the aspirant's journey. In practice, this implied that those who sought to spread Buddha's Word must become skilled in means, *upaya*, and employ only those formulations or expressions which really touch the hearts of listeners, encouraging them to take the first step on the Noble Eightfold Path. As different schools and traditions emerged, Buddhist teachers – more or less or hardly enlightened – adapted their discourses to rectify recurrent tendencies to absolutize, concretize or obscure the compassionate core of the *Dharma*. Schools and sects became as distinct as the differing temperaments of human beings, and as flexible and fraternal as the original *Sangha*. By hearkening repeatedly to the Four Noble Truths, they could hold one another in considerable mutual respect even whilst freely disagreeing on specific formulations of the truth, all of which must ultimately be swept aside in the climactic experience of Enlightenment.

Some schools gradually emerged as uniquely transmitted traditions, owing to the comparative isolation of small groups of cloistered monks. Others arose out of specific disagreements over aspects of the monastic code, though the essentials of *vinaya* were never in serious dispute. Major differences were the unavoidable result of varying modes of conceptualization and of conveying the Teaching. Although Buddha seems to have spoken several Indic languages, including Maghadi, he must also have taught in the language of Koshala, the kingdom to which his own clan, the *Shakyas*, belonged. He insisted that monks and lay people learn the *Dharma* in their own languages, even though local tongues and dialects were not always capable of conveying his deepest thoughts. Thus there was no "official" language for the *Buddhavachana*, the Word of Buddha, and no single canonical set of texts emerged in the early years after his *Parinirvana*.[1] Ancient tradition asserts, however, that Buddha repeatedly referred to ten "inexpressibles", *avyakatavatthu* (Skt. *avyakritavastu*), for which language and conceptualization are inherently inadequate to provide definitive formulations. These include whether the world is eternal or not; whether it is finite in space or infinite; whether the Tathagata exists after death, does not exist after death, or both does and does not exist after death, or neither exists nor does not exist after death; and whether the soul is one with the body or different from it. Serious reflection on any of these metaphysical themes will soon show that a radical rethinking of familiar concepts is required even to begin to make sense of such thorny issues.

Starting with the earliest Council and the original recitation of Ananda and Upali, the *Sangha* rapidly recognized those who were reliable memorizers of the *sutras*, others who were trustworthy reciters

---

[1] An excellent and judicious examination of the language of Buddha and the problem of a canonical authority in relation to *Buddhavachana* is found in *The Eternal Legacy* by Sangharakshita, Tharpa Publications, London, 1985.

of the *vinaya* and a gifted few who were skilful commentators. Ancient chronicles testify that eighteen schools and myriad subdivisions had emerged in the *Sangha* within three centuries of the *Parinirvana*, and they can be distinguished in terms of the emphasis each gave to the *sutras*, the *vinaya* and the various commentaries. Of the schools nurtured by the *Sthaviras*, Theravada alone survives and so is often held to be of the greatest significance. It postulates a three-tiered universe, consisting of *kamadhatu, rupadhatu* and *arupadhatu* – the planes of desire, form and formlessness – in which time moves in vast cycles, each comprising four ages – *krita*, the Golden Age, *treta, dvapara* and *kali*, the Dark Age in which present humanity struggles. Each human being is potentially a Buddha, and he or she can move in that direction through righteous thinking, feeling, speech and action. All phenomenal existence, which encompasses everything outside *Nirvana*, is unstable and transient, enmeshed in the endless flux of instants or *Dharmas*. In order to tread the path to Enlightenment, it is essential to know the kinds of *Dharmas* which make up one's fleeting existence in embodied form, and so Theravada places great stress upon the complex doctrine of *skandhas* (Pali *khandhas)*, the vestures and avenues through which they operate and the basic elements of sensory experience. Though a careful and close analysis of these fundamental concepts presupposes an elaborate metaphysical framework, and has often been construed in predominantly psychological terms, its deeper purpose is to find the way to *Nirvana*, which necessarily reaches far beyond the range of critical metaphysics and analytical psychology.

Nirvana is *asankhata* (Skt. *asanskrita)*, wholly unconditioned, and therefore can neither come into being nor cease to be. As such, it cannot be linked to the formidable chain of dependent origination. No one in search of Enlightenment can cause it to come about; nonetheless, like the wind which dispels obscuring clouds, the progressive removal of ignorance through traversing the Noble Eightfold Path must eventually enable the Sun of Enlightenment to shine forth. This arduous process can be demarcated into four distinct stages. One who has "entered the stream" or decisively commenced that constant endeavour which leads to the terrace of Enlightenment is in the first stage. One whose course is irrevocable but incomplete has definitely entered the second stage of the "once returner" who has only one more birth before him. The third stage is only entered when one has drawn so close to Enlightenment that there neither need be nor will be any more rebirth. The *Arhant*, however, has fully attained freedom even in this life and is able to savour *Nirvana* whilst still in a body. All this naturally suggests that Buddhas appeared on earth long before Prince Siddhartha and that a series of Buddhas will appear thereafter. Specifically, *Theravadins* anticipate the advent of Metteya (known in Sanskrit as Maitreya), the healing Buddha of universal love who will inaugurate a new epoch in the world. His liberating message, like that of all Buddhas, will be the timeless truth *(Sanatana Dharma)*, yet wholly original in expression and fresh in its idiom.

As with thought and action, *Theravadin* meditation, *jhana* (Skt. *dhyana)*, also aims at purification. Starting with withdrawal from sensory indulgence, it moves swiftly to steadfast one-pointedness, *ekaggata* (Skt. *ekagrata)*, the firm foothold from which all emotion, attraction and reaction is removed, leaving the solitary meditator serenely detached from every aspect of the phenomenal world, even whilst remaining fully conscious and supremely alert. Such a purity of apprehension permits the aspirant to enter into the transcendental states of awareness which Buddha himself experienced beneath the *bodhi* tree. Entering the state characterized by infinite space, he moves on to a direct immediate experience of infinite consciousness, and still pushes on to a stage which can only be called Nothingness. Beyond that, however, there is an indescribable condition known as "neither perception nor non-perception", the lofty terrace from which the final leap into *Nirvana* is possible. Although each school has its own priorities and preferences in classifying and characterizing exalted states of consciousness, along with its own distinctive practices of meditation, the entire system set forth in *Theravadin* doctrine is the original basis of every type of Buddhist meditation, furthering insight or *vipassana* through mindfulness and bare attention.

If the *Sthaviras* focussed on the *suttas*, the *Sarvastivadins* emphasized the *abhidhamma* (Skt. *abhidharma)*, or abstruse philosophical doctrines. They held that everything exists only in the sense that it comes into contact with a cognizing agent. Anticipating the phenomenalist Bishop Berkeley in this way, they nonetheless answered the question "What exists?" rather differently: name and form, *namarupa*, alone exists, *rupa* being material and *nama* its nominal definition by a cognizing agent. There is no room here for any enduring self, *puggala* (Skt. *pudgala*). Though the *Sarvastivadins* faded from history, Vasubandhu ingeniously interpreted their basic philosophy in terms of the Sautrantika thesis that there is a continuum of psychic states, each instantaneous and of no intrinsic reality but entirely conditioned by the stronger impulse which gave rise to all of them, and thus laid the basis for the *Yogachara* or "Mind-Only" school. The *Dharmaguptakas* accepted the scriptures which have come down to the present in the Pali canon, but they added two other collections of texts. One of these, the *Bodhisattvapitaka*, stressed the sacrificial nature of Buddha's mission. Holding that an *Arhant* produces no karma, his willingness to remain in the world is only for the sake of helping others. The *Sammitiyas*, on the other hand, were troubled that an *Arhant* could become obscured whilst dealing with ignorant humanity, and they therefore stressed that generosity of every kind provides the surest means for protection and purification. Although only the *Theravadins* survive from these interrelated schools, their distant descendants took root in China and Japan, where they flourished many centuries after the tradition waned in India.

Like the *Sthaviras*, the *Mahasanghikas* are still represented today by their numerous offshoots. Although they looked to the life of Buddha as a pristine model for treading the Path, they ascribed to it immense metaphysical import, holding that Buddha is *lokottara*, transcendent, and indestructible. His entire message, *Buddhavachana*, is not limited by time and place but touches all beings, though they hear and understand it only in direct proportion to their individual purity. *Bodhisattvas* incarnate voluntarily out of compassion and remain amongst human beings as long as they choose – a hopeful teaching that is intimated in the *Maha Parinibbana Sutta* of the Pali canon. The *Lokottaravadins*, the descendants of the *Mahasanghikas*, taught that nothing in manifest existence is real, the sole reality being *shunyata*, which is twofold – the voidness of subjects and the voidness of objects. Thus Buddha, as he moved among men, was in truth an illusory if luminous appearance of a transcendent reality. Here the emphasis is shifted from the man who struggled to ultimate victory, to the transcendent being who cast a compelling series of sublime mental images on the screen of time for the instruction, edification and emancipation of humanity. Buddha is the perfected *Bodhisattva*, who assists, guides and benefits an ailing world from which he has nothing to gain.

The *Pudgalavadins* took the bold step of affirming the reality of the *pudgala* or self as the reincarnating but transcendent source of consciousness, a view somewhat reminiscent of certain Upanishadic suggestions concerning the *Atman*. This unorthodox and heretical-seeming standpoint led them to assert that intermediate states of consciousness and modes of being exist between death and rebirth. Such views as sprang from the *Mahasanghika* perspective formed the doctrinal basis of the *Mahayana* or Great Vehicle. *Mahayana* placed the self and the world on the same level, thus holding that both seem real to the self precisely because self and *Dharmas* – elements of existence – are inherently non-existent. Both are like empty space, characterized by *shunyata*, voidness. The removal of suffering cannot be seen in terms of some one individual escaping and evading the cycle of existences. Rather, the holy *Arhant*, though honoured, is superseded by the more exalted *Bodhisattva*, who sees no difference whatsoever between himself and any sentient creature and who ardently seeks the Enlightenment of all.

The *Bodhisattva* ideal, central to all *Mahayana* teaching, calls on all compassionate individuals to seek Enlightenment purely for the sake of the whole. Self-sacrifice is self-emancipation, for in truly giving up one's sensate and separative life, one who follows this all-demanding ideal attempts a progressive ascent through ten levels *(bhumis)* of spiritual attainment, which is made possible by cultivating and perfecting the ten *paramitas* or modes of purity in daily life. The first six stages constitute the strict prerequisites for the successful pursuit of the *Bodhisattva* Path. They are: *dana*, charity and loving kindness; *shila*, morality, "harmony in word and act" which mitigates and negates the formation of new karma; *kshanti*, "patience sweet, that nought can ruffle"; *virya*, unwavering vigour, courage and dauntless energy directed towards the goal; *dhyana*, deep daily meditation; and *prajna*, spiritual insight and wisdom. When these six *paramitas* are mastered, the *Bodhisattva* is fit for the seventh level, that of irreversibility, when the Buddha-nature manifests in him. He no longer struggles to purify himself, for the impulse to perfection now operates as the dynamic aspect of his own intrinsic nature and each subsequent stage is a rapid depletion of former karma, a radical dissolution of all limitations of consciousness and a resplendent dawning of that transcendental omniscience which is the Buddha-light. Thus *upaya*, skilfulness in action, leads to *pranidhana*, unshakeable resolution, and to *bala*, inward strength, culminating in the four transcendental *(arupa)* states of mental absorption *(jnana)*.

Mahayana elaborated the esoteric doctrine of the three bodies or modes of being, *trikaya*, of Buddha. Concern for proper attention to the physical body composed of the four elements, for the invisible mental body and for the hard-won body of Law, *Dharma*, is found both in the *Dhammapada* and the *Udanavarga*. When these powerful seed-ideas found their full fruition in *Mahayana* soil, the *trikaya* became three modes of existence. The *Dharmakaya* is ontologically prior to the others and the "highest". It is the quintessential nature of Buddha, identical in all Buddhas, absolutely unmanifest in itself, yet that upon which all manifestation is conditioned. "He who sees the *Dharma* sees me," Buddha once said, "he who sees me sees the *Dharma*." Here the open-textured conceptions of *Dharma* as the priceless Teaching of Righteousness and as the omnipresent operative principle of all existence (reminiscent of the rich Hindu concept of *Rita*) have been metaphysically fused into the fundamental idea that *Dharma* is the primordial reality out of which all manifestation must derive and into which all must dissolve. In the universe it is seen as Law; in sacred speech it is the Law-like Teaching, which is at once metaphysical and moral; in the human species it is the fully perfected Buddha. It is also the magnetic afflatus of the aspirant who has merged in consciousness with Absolute Truth, the Divine Wisdom that ensouls the cosmos.

The *Sambhogakaya* or body of bliss is sometimes portrayed as the glorious body of omniscience to which meditative consciousness can ascend. It is the celestial seat of supramundane understanding and supernal splendour. Arcane schools of initiation teach that the progressive awakening of consciousness requires a conscious transformation of every aspect of the human constitution. The *Sambhogakaya* is a noumenal vesture created by alchemical transmutation of the basic elements of existence. It serves as the supreme focus of universal insight *(prajna)*. It is wholly unconcerned with the world. The *Nirmanakaya*, sometimes thought of as the phenomenal body of a Buddha projected into *Samsara* through the power of illusion, is in the arcane schools the projection of the *Sambhogakaya* for the sake of contact with this world. *Trishna*, the thirst for embodied existence, has been utterly eradicated beyond recall. Nonetheless, the *Bodhisattva* can choose at will to renounce the total disconnection from the mundane world which he has fully earned, and he voluntarily continues to abide in a sensate world he does not need, cannot gain anything from and yet has freely vowed to serve. Seen in this soteriological context, the *Nirmanakaya* is the noumenal body which can be the powerful focus of universal intelligence and also the assumed vesture through which the *Bodhisattva* can aid humanity in its arduous search for Enlightenment. Although the *Nirmanakaya* is the "lowest" or least ethereal of the three bodies, it is ethically the most exalted to all votaries of the *Bodhisattva* ideal. Since the three *kayas* abide at the cosmic level of universal cognition, they can be viewed as formless bodies, spiritual vestures of omnidirectional states of universal consciousness. Since these remote states cannot be adequately characterized outside of their direct realization by the initiated Adept, the full meaning of the *trikaya* necessarily remains a sacred theme, an incommunicable secret of initiation.

All such esoteric doctrines presuppose the possibility of direct awareness that the transcendental states of consciousness discoverable in meditation have always been represented by divine beings constituted of the very essence of supernal awareness and noumenal substance. Just as *Dharmakaya* is beyond any hint or measure of conditionality, so too *Adibuddha*, the primordial reality, is beyond the seeming multiplicity of differentiated subjects. Just as everyday human consciousness manifests through permutations of the five *skandhas*, so the primeval Buddha emanates five cosmic *Dhyani Buddhas* (in some arcane accounts both are seven in number), who in turn manifest as fully realized cosmic *Bodhisattvas*. All spiritual activity in the phenomenal world is a manifestation and mirroring of their noetic thought and theurgic activity. The aspirant who has entered the stream that flows inexorably, though not automatically, towards the ocean of Enlightenment becomes an accredited member of one of these "Buddha families" on earth. He becomes part of the vital bridge between unenlightened human beings and a vast range of supermundane, celestial, supercelestial and utterly transcendental *consciousnesses*.[2] On the one hand, *Mahayana* envisages a great chain of being which corresponds to the broad continuum stretching from perfect wisdom to incorrigible ignorance. On the other hand, it sees the *Sangha* neither as a simple unit nor as a collection of differing schools and sects, but rather as a shining host of lineages which constitute a single "Buddha family". Thus in the *Mahayana* a variety of daring perspectives spring from concentrated devotion to one or another *sutra* or from the striking formulations of one or another esteemed Teacher. All are accommodated within a single sacred family in which there is benevolent non-interference and authentic mutual respect amongst its diverse members. The *trikaya* doctrine reaffirmed the immemorial sanctity and inviolable privacy of the *guru-chela* relationship and the *Guruparampara* transmission.

The *Madhyamika* school traces its origin to Nagarjuna, the brilliant philosopher and formidable dialectician who flourished in the late second century A.D. Taking Buddha's advocacy of the Middle Way between harmful extremes, between avid indulgence and austere asceticism, and between sterile intellectualization and suffocating mental torpor, Nagarjuna developed a rigorous dialectical logic by which he reduced every philosophical standpoint to an explosive set of contradictions. This did not lead to the closure of scepticism, as the less vigorously pursued pre-Socratic philosophies did, but rather to the elusive standpoint that neither existence nor non-existence can be

---

[2] Modern man, despite science fiction, has still to catch up with the awesome world of Leibnizian monadology or the calm recognition by the Victorian scientist T.H. Huxley that "there must be things in the universe whose intelligence is as much beyond ours as ours exceeds that of the black beetle, and who take an active part in the government of the natural order of things". He also said: "Without stepping beyond the analogy of that which is known, it is easy to people the cosmos with entities, in ascending scale until we reach something practically indistinguishable from omnipotence, omnipresence, and omniscience."

asserted of the world and of everything in it. The *Madhyamikas*, therefore, refused to affirm or deny any philosophical proposition. Nagarjuna sought to liberate the mind from its tendencies to cling to tidy or clever formulations of truth, because any truth short of *shunyata*, the voidness of reality, is inherently misleading. Relative truths are not like pieces of a puzzle, each of which incrementally adds to the complete design. They are plausible distortions of the truth and can seriously mislead the aspirant. They cannot be lightly or wholly repudiated, however, for they are all the seeker has, and so he must learn to use them as aids whilst remembering that they are neither accurate nor complete in themselves.

By the fifth century two views of Nagarjuna's work had emerged. The followers of Bhavaviveka thought that *Madhyamika* philosophy had a positive content, whilst those who subscribed to Buddhapalita's more severe interpretation said that every standpoint, including their own, could be reduced to absurdity, which fact alone, far more than any positively asserted doctrine, could lead to intuitive insight *(prajna)* and Enlightenment. Chandrakirti's remarkable defence of this latter standpoint deeply influenced Tibetan Buddhist traditions as well as those schools of thought that eventually culminated in Japan in Zen. Nagarjuna's dialectic revealed the *shunya* or emptiness of all discursive, worldly thought and its proliferating categories.

For the *Madhyamikas*, whatever can be conceptualized is therefore relative, and whatever is relative is *shunya*, empty. Since absolute inconceivable truth is also *shunya*, *shunyata* or the void is shared by both *Samsara* and *Nirvana*. Ultimately, *Nirvana* truly realized is *Samsara* properly understood. The fully realized *Bodhisattva*, the enlightened Buddha who renounces the *Dharmakaya* vesture to remain at the service of suffering beings, recognizes this radical transcendental equivalence. The *Arhant* and the *Pratyeka Buddha*, who look to their own redemption and realization, are elevated beyond any conventional description, but nonetheless do not fully realize or freely embody this highest truth. Thus for the *Madhyamikas*, the *Bodhisattva* ideal is the supreme wisdom, showing the unqualified unity of unfettered metaphysics and transcendent ethics, *theoria* and *praxis*, at the highest conceivable level.

Madhyamika thought rooted itself in the remarkable collection of *Mahayana sutras* known as the *Prajnaparamita* (or perfection of wisdom) literature. These *sutras*, from the one hundred thousand verses of *Shatasahasrika Prajnaparamita* to the terse *Heart Sutra* and the short *Vajrachchedika* (literally, "Diamond Cutter", but commonly called *Diamond Sutra),* share the same themes skilfully expounded at different lengths. According to these *sutras,* all *Dharmas* or elements of existence are *shunyata* or void. Although many human beings are terrified of voidness, as is shown by the instinctive dread of the dark and the unknown, this arises from a basic misunderstanding of *shunyata.* It is unchanging, deathless, unqualified reality. If one understands *shunyatashunyata,* the Voidness of the Void, one recognizes that it is not any "nothing" one knows or can imagine. Being truly unknown, there is no sufficient reason to dread it. Rather than entertain vague, ill-conceived and inchoate images of the imageless, one would do better to practise the *paramitas,* the dynamic virtues of the Noble Eightfold Path leading to the inestimable glory which the ignorant world calls *shunyata* solely because it is beyond its ken. The *Bodhisattva,* however, sees the plenitude of that Void as well as the emptiness of the phenomenal world, and so he labours in joy for the redemption of those who suffer from abject ignorance.

Madhyamika led almost effortlessly to the emergence of the *Yogachara* school, founded by Asanga and his younger brother, Vasubandhu, in the fifth century A.D. Sometimes called the "Mind-Only" or *Chittamatra* school, especially in China, it held that consciousness is the key to understanding reality and so quintessentially *is* reality. *Yogacharya* thought is based on the *Lankavatara Sutra,* wherein Buddha, abiding in a realm accessible only through the exercise of high spiritual powers, discoursed to Mahamati, chief of the *Bodhisattvas.* Adopting the "Mind-Only" standpoint, the *Lankavatara* provides a detailed metapsychology which explains the efficacy of treading the *paramita* Path. The consciousness of an incarnate human being reflects the architectonic range of consciousness itself. There are the six *vijnanas* consisting of the five senses and *manovijnana* – that aspect of mind which synthesizes them. *Manas* uses *manovijnana* to grasp the world, but it also knows, apart from the *vijnanas,* that there is something higher than itself. In this crucial respect, therefore, *Manas* is dual and hence the indispensable pivot upon which redemption and Enlightenment depend. *Chitta* is the storehouse of thoughts and deeds, a complete record of the progress of consciousness through time, and in exalted states of meditation it seeks to attune itself to *Alayavijnana*.

Alayaviynana is the universal storehouse, containing the seeds of all that has been and ever will be. It is neutral in that it contains every possibility of consciousness, but does not thrust forward any of them. Since it contains the seed of Enlightenment, it is also *Tathagatagarbha*, the womb of reality. It is *Atman*, the Self, but it is also devoid of individuality. *Manas* is the principle of individuation, whilst *Alayavijnana* is the principle of universality. Through ignorance and desire, *avidya* and *trishna*, *Manas* becomes entangled in things, conditions and states – all of which arise out of consciousness itself. It is somewhere conscious of *Alayavijnana*, however, and Enlightenment is the result of a "turning around of consciousness", *paravritti*, in which *Manas* detaches itself from involvement in *manovijnana* and beholds *Alayavijnana*. The seed of Enlightenment in the universal storehouse is guided by the gaze of *Manas*, and it will come to fruition through practice of the *paramitas*. Though *Alayavijnana*, being universal, has no distinct self, the fusion of *Manas* with *Alayaviynana* is the union of individuation and universality. This is the fully awakened, supreme Buddha, the farthest limit of noumenal reality which is neither one nor many, but which understands both.

In religious language, *Manas* ascends to *Alayavijnana* through *paravritti*, the turning upwards of consciousness. Metapsychologically, it does so through self-purification by cultivating the *paramitas*. As in all Buddhist thought, Buddhas can only point the way to Enlightenment, and the aspirant has to strive single-mindedly to attain it. The *Lankavatara*, however, gives a mystical dimension to this principle. *Buddhavachana*, the Word of Buddha, is his *adhishthana*, his sustaining power, his anchor in manifest existence. It is his call or summons in consciousness to Enlightenment, affirming its possibility and indicating the Path to it. Every dimension of Nature responds at some level to that powerful summons and is also supported by it. Below *Manas*, and so in the lower kingdoms, that call quickens the collective impulse towards individuation and the threshold of self-consciousness. In the human family it is the stirring summons to self-purification and conscious effort. Those who do their utmost to honour that call are mystically yoked to Buddha, which Shantideva memorably phrased as "joining the Buddha family". To enter a lineage is not simply to give allegiance to a school of thought: it is no less than to accept a sacred bond, to enter a mystic communion the fruition of which is Enlightenment.

If the *Prajnaparamita Sutras* point to *shunyata* as the hidden core of manifold existence and the *Lankavatara Sutra* provides the underpinnings for the journey to its realization, the *Avatansaka (Garland) Sutra*, of which the *Gandavyuha* comprises the last section, views the world from the threshold of reality. Delivered by the *Dhyani Buddha* Vairochana, it depicts the supreme abode of Buddhas as *Dharmadhatu*, the universal principle, the realm of pure perception. Beyond space and time, it abides without individuation, for it is *anabhasa*, shadowless, and admits of no distinctions. Human beings dwell in *lokadhatu*, the world of particulars conditioned by the senses, and for them *Dharmadhatu* defies both sensory experience and conventional logic. Yet its unconditioned luminosity suffuses *lokadhatu* at every point, for the two realms are reflective of each other. From the standpoint of *lokadhatu*, the entire manifest world arises all at once; all *Dharmas* are so inextricably dependent on one another that none could arise without all of them appearing. From the standpoint of *Dharmadhatu*, this is because of the mutual interconnection of all things. Each *Dharma* implicitly expresses all *Dharmas*, and all phenomena express *shunyata*, the Void, in its particularity.

Fa-Tsang, who spread *Avatansaka* teachings across China as the Third Patriarch of the Hua-yen school, explained the principle of mutual interpenetration to the Empress Tze-t'ien with the aid of a room filled with mirrors. Having arranged her enormous collection of mirrors so that they would catch the light of a single candle, he drew curtains over the window of the chamber. When he lit the candle, its light was caught and reflected back and forth amongst the mirrors, giving the impression of myriad candles where there was in fact only one. The single candle represented the *Dharmadhatu*, the mirrors stood for the particulars of the *lokadhatu*, and the reflected light the mutual interpenetration of all things. *Dharmadhatu* is causal to *lokadhatu* as well as its source and ultimate nature.

Since the two realms – the lofty abode of Buddha and the true home of *Bodhisattvas*, as well as the sense-bound world of unenlightened beings – are one, the *paramita* Path can be seen as the alchemical process of transmuting *lokadhatu* into *Dharmadhatu*. The *paramitas* are virtues on the level of ordinary thought and action, but when fully understood they are revealed as transcendental powers which bring the two realms together in consciousness. Just as Buddha is peerless wisdom, *prajna,* so too the Path which he set forth is pure compassion, *mahakaruna,* and the *paramitas* are jewelled facets of that adamantine compassion. As *Dharmadhatu* is present in every nook and corner of *lokadhatu,* so Buddha is within each being. The *Bodhisattva* Manjushri, embodiment of transcendental wisdom and supernal insight, is in each human being the sovereign principle of irreversibility, which makes possible that change of consciousness whereby *lokadhatu* becomes *Dharmadhatu*. The work of universal Enlightenment, implicit in Buddha's first vow in the palace at Kapilavastu and explicit in the *Bodhisattva* ideal, is the timely entrance of all awakened beings into the refulgent world of unshadowed light wherein all suffering, desire, space and time come to an end.

Hermes, July 1986

BUDDHA AND THE PATH TO ENLIGHTENMENT
IV. The Dhammapada and the Udanavarga

> *Let one's thoughts of boundless loving-kindness pervade the whole world, above, below, across, without obscuration, without hatred, without enmity.*
>
>

Sanyutta Nikaya, 150
Gautama Buddha

Myriad schools and far-flung traditions sprang from the fertile streams of Mahayana thought. They developed in their own distinctive way in Tibet, but in China, Korea and Japan they were deeply influenced by the Sthavira philosophy preserved in Theravadin teachings. Some schools incorporated potent ideas from Taoist alchemy and others emphasized the elimination of doubt by deep faith, giving rise to the Pure Land *(sukhavati)* schools. Yet others stressed meditation, *dhyana*, developing the Ch"an tradition which became Zen in Japan. However divergent the perspectives, they all readily recognized and consistently preached the fundamental importance of morality in thought, word and deed to any authentic progress on the Path to Enlightenment. In the *Shrimala Devi Sinha Nada Sutra*, Queen Shrimala summarizes the standpoint of all Buddhist schools when she addresses Buddha:

> World-honoured One, the embracing of the true *Dharma* is not different from the *paramitas;* the embracing of the true *Dharma* is the *paramitas*.

It is indeed significant that the *Dhammapada* has always been venerated as the finest expression of the ethical principles upon which all wise practice and compassionate therapy must be firmly based.

The *Dhammapada* is a remarkable collection of memorable utterances attributed to Buddha. Given the rich variety of meanings which can be ascribed to the *dhamma* and to *pada*, the title may be translated "The

Way of Virtue", "The Path of the Law", "The Foundation of Religion" and even "Utterances of Scriptures". Although the Pali version is best known today, partly because of its internal coherence and beautiful imagery, Chinese Buddhists have long preserved fine translations of four apparently different Sanskrit versions. The Tibetan canon did not include any version of the *Dhammapada per se*, though it contains two careful recensions of the Sanskrit *Udanavarga*, a similar collection of Buddha's words which contains many of the statements found in the *Dhammapada*. The *Dhammapada* was well known in some Tibetan monasteries where Prakrit versions were discovered in the 1930s.[1]

The Prakrit *Dhammapada* was discovered recorded on ancient prepared birch bark. Written in the Karosthi script, it is in the Prakrit dialect generally called Gandhari, after the Gandhara region where early Buddhist art and civilization flourished. The Gandhari *Dhammapada* has the distinction of being the oldest known Indian manuscript and the only text which survives in this language and script. Unfortunately, the *Dhampiya*, a Sinhalese version brought to Sri Lanka by Ashoka's son Mahinda, has been lost to history. Despite the destruction of most of the sacred texts belonging to groups and schools which did not survive into modern times, these varying recensions are sufficient to suggest that there may not have existed a single, original *Dhammapada* text. For example, although the Gandhari text is close to the Pali in length, its contents are on the whole more like the much longer *Udanavarga*. Whilst there are nearly identical verses which can be found in all surviving versions, yet they are ordered differently in each one. Rather than thinking in terms of a complete original of which others are supposed derivations, one might more profitably think of a *Dharmapadani* literature, a kind of scriptural text analogous to a *sutra* or a discourse, and see the surviving *Dhammapadas* as worthy examples of that kind of text cherished by different schools and traditions.

No one knows who first compiled any particular version of the *Dhammapada*. *Dharma*trata is traditionally credited with compiling the

---

[1] The Tibetan scholar Dge-'dun Chos-'pel knew of the Prakrit manuscript found in Tibet, but he proceeded to Ceylon (Sri Lanka) to work with the distinguished monk Reverend Dharmananda. With his guidance Chos-'pel translated the Pali *Dhammapada* into Tibetan.

Tibetan *Udanavarga,* consisting of about three hundred and seventy-five verses from the *Dhammapada* and a considerable portion of the *Udana*. Since *Dharmapadani* texts seem to have been widespread amongst early Buddhist schools, they clearly form a very early strain of the *Buddhavachana*. Unlike the *sutras* which are more or less extended disquisitions on some question or topic, and which all begin with the reverential expression *evam maya shrutam,* "Thus have I heard", indicating an oral recollection of an occasion on which Buddha taught, the *Dhammapada* seems to come closest to the direct speech of Buddha. Unlike the *Udana* or "breathing out", representing spontaneous utterances which arose from the depths of feeling occasioned by a particular event, the *Dhammapada* seems to consist of recurrent sayings which arose out of and apply to practical problems repeatedly found in everyday attempts to tread the Noble Eightfold Path. Whilst a *sutra* has an overarching unity of theme, standpoint or topic, and the *Udanavarga* is broadly arrayed into *vargas,* or sections according to subject, the *Dhammapada* exhibits shifting criteria of composition. Verses are grouped together because of shared characteristics (for example, *Yamaka,* "Twin Verses"), or because of shared metaphors and similes ("The Elephant", "The Thousands"), or because of a sustained theme ("The Brahmana"), and at least one canto has no explicit basis of any kind ("Miscellaneous"). All of this suggests that the *Dhammapada* consists of memorable utterances of Buddha on different occasions and in varied circumstances. Though they arose in particular contexts, they were hardly bound by them, and so several monks recalled these sayings as invaluable aids in many situations. Thus the *Dhammapada* is a sort of handbook or compendium of practical ethics, a comprehensible guide to the Path, which also provides much food for thought and contemplation.

Since the subtle differences in the surviving versions of the *Dhammapada* do not suggest conscious sectarian divergences, these ancient recensions are most probably the result of recording very early oral traditions which go back to Buddha himself. Without speculating as to how long these sayings were transmitted orally, it is reasonable to assume that the long-standing tradition of the *Sangha* preserved Buddha's Word without imposing any rigid structure upon it. Thus the Pali *Dhammapada* consists of four hundred and twenty-three verses arranged in twenty-six chapters, whereas one Chinese version has thirty-nine chapters. Comparing the twenty-six chapters in the Pali with the Chinese versions of the same, we find seventy-nine additional verses. The *Udanavarga* has around nine hundred and fifty verses in thirty-three chapters. Though the surviving Gandhari recension is incomplete, a careful examination of textual evidence suggests that it was originally about five hundred and forty verses in length. According to the oldest Buddhist traditions, the *Dhammapada* emerged from the First Council shortly after Buddha's *Parinirvana*, and Buddhaghosha, who wrote extensive commentaries on the Pali canon in the fifth century A.D., accepted this tradition. Some ancient histories date the writing down of sacred texts to the time of King Vattagamani (early first century B.C.). Since the verses of the *Dhammapada* were uttered on specific occasions, a commentary or *attakatha* appeared which provided stories about specific events which gave rise to one or more sayings. The Pali commentary on the *Dhammapada* (dubiously ascribed to Buddhaghosha) and its Chinese counterpart may have simply set down stories from the oral tradition which preserved echoes of original events.

The Pali *Dhammapada* cannot claim to be the canonical archetype of all *Dharmapadani* literature. Nonetheless, its forthright style and moving simplicity and beauty justly place it in the front ranks of Buddhist sacred literature. In addition, its aim, purpose and origin vindicate its rightful place among the sacred texts which constitute the spiritual heritage of humanity. Like the *Bhagavad Gita* or the *Gospel According to Thomas,* the Pali *Dhammapada* is readily accessible to any enquirer and also provides ample fare for the most ardent seekers and austere anchorites. It has the stamp of self-validating truth as well as the infectious common sense which transcends the constraints of time and place, sect and tradition, race and culture. Its ethical content is trustworthy and testable. In all these, the Pali *Dhammapada* can rightly claim to be *Buddhavachana*, the Word of Buddha. In the Pali canon it forms part of *Khuddaka Nikaya*, the *Collection of Shorter Texts*, which includes the *Udana* and the *Jataka* or previous lives of Buddha. The *Khuddaka Nikaya* belongs to the *Sutta Pitaka*, the second of the three "baskets" of instruction known as the *Tripitaka*. Generally, the *Vinaya Pitaka* addresses monastic discipline, the *Sutta Pitaka* deals with

Buddha's basic Teachings and the *Abhidhamma Pitaka* consists of philosophical reflections and psychological investigations. The *Dhammapada* shows, however, that these divisions are tentative and fluidic rather than rigid and exclusive, for it considers with equal ease the basic teachings, monastic discipline and open-textured philosophical problems. It can serve as a clear summation of all one needs to know to begin to tread the Noble Eightfold Path and also as a thought-provoking compendium of what one needs to recall at every step along the way.

Buddha inseparably fused two fundamental principles and made them the firm basis of daily practice – the priority of mind and the ultimacy of *Dharma*. Declaring that *The mind is the precursor of all propensities* (I.1), he taught that the tropism of the mind can enslave or emancipate, inducing perpetual discontent or progressive fulfilment. Seeking pleasure and shunning pain is wasted effort, for pleasure and pain intermix in unpredictable ways, and since their unstable admixture aggravates frustration and repeated disillusionment, no mere tinkering with external conditions can bring mental and moral strength. The tropism of the mind must be confronted and understood if it is to be changed significantly. One must come to see clearly that *If with a pure mind a person speaks or acts, happiness follows him even as his never-departing shadow* (I.2). Altering the habitual orientation or oscillation of consciousness demands wise restraint, a taste for temperance, increasing faith and cool perseverance, but at root it requires a fundamental rethinking of one's shallow relationship with a fast-moving world. *Hatred is never stilled through hatred in this world; by non-hatred alone is hatred stilled. This is the Eternal Law (sanantana dhamma)* (I.5). *Dharma* is not just religiosity as distinguished from other profane aspects of life, nor is it a remote ideal unrelated to the world of imperfect subjects and illusory objects. *Dharma* is the omnipresent normative order, the bedrock of the manifest universe. If this were not so, it would be difficult to grasp how ignorance, *avidya*, invariably leads to suffering rather than arbitrarily producing a variety of alterable results in *Samsara*. Given that *Dharma* is the fundamental anchor amidst the flux of fleeting existence, it follows that unrelieved ignorance leading to *tanha*, the desperate thirst for sensory consciousness, gives rise to a false sense of self which seeks to situate and shape the world around its unauthentic centre and thereby comes into continual conflict with *Dharma*, the common source of universal obligation.

The false "I" seeks to expropriate the regulatory function of *Dharma* in a cosmos of myriad subjects and objects. This tenacious yet precarious sense of self, regardless of the degree of refinement and versatility that might be brought to the notion, vainly seeks to be the invulnerable protagonist and judge in all situations. But such egocentrism ensures suffering of every sort and accumulated resentment. In utterly renouncing hatred, in letting go of all forms of selfish clinging and shallow judgementalism, one can begin to learn to live in concord with mutable things and volatile persons. The common tendency to expropriate is as infectious as ignorance itself, and Buddha showed how it can operate on many levels of consciousness. Even the most earnest aspirant can fall into the trap of substituting one sense of self for another and thereby delude himself into thinking that he has transcended the psychic core of ignorance, whereas he has only reinforced it. Buddha counselled all to be mindful, judicious and fully awake in every context and circumstance. The Middle Way is not a passive aloofness or a violent shrinking from extremes and excesses. It is a position of inner strength, enabling one to take a quantum jump in activity, being *vigorous, vigilant, pure in conduct, considerate, self-restrained, righteous and heedful* (II.4). *Mindfulness is the way to immortality* (II.1), and it requires rigorous mind-training on three levels. First of all, the mind must cease to identify with anything of a transient nature, or the entire panorama of shapes and forms, masks and veils. Secondly, it must repeatedly purify itself by a rigorous purgation of desires from all thoughts and feelings. And thirdly, it must turn to regular meditation, the unbroken contemplation of the highest ideals, which mirror *Dharma* and Buddha, its exalted and ever compassionate custodian. The mind thereby ceases to be the pathetic victim of divisive tendencies in which it cunningly participates, whilst refusing to learn the lessons of life. It can be redeemed by turning deeply within, discovering its inmost core, consubstantial with the Buddha-nature, capable of translucent awareness, uttermost lucidity, supreme calm and effortless serenity.

The mindful individual neither succumbs nor invades in a world of deceptive appearances. He does what should be done and attends appropriately to his needs and tasks, without interfering with others or becoming ineffectually involved in things. *Just as a bee gathers honey and flies away, without harming the colour or fragrance of the flower, even so the silent Sage moves about in the village* (IV.6). The fool is fascinated by the world and thinks he learns thereby, but the wise man is not fascinated, indulgent or afraid and so moves noiselessly through the world, ever reflecting upon universal *Dharma*, the *Tathagatas*, the sweetness and light radiating from the invisible pillars of the never-ending *Sangha*. Untouched by the fever and fret of those overcome by fascination and passion, the mindful individual who is ever heedful gains a magisterial, hidden tranquillity which is hinted in his healing words and timely acts. His unruffled mind mirrors the magnitude and lustre of the *Dharma*, and he magnanimously loosens the ties that bind others or himself to compulsive, cyclic existence. Subduing himself, he masters the world of delusion and frees others who are ready to be freed, whilst calmly brooding on the benediction of Buddha-like Enlightenment.

Whilst Buddha refrained from any form of spiritual utilitarianism, which invokes a course of action in the present with the inducement of some future compensation, he did not hesitate to speak hard truths. The psychological tension between mindfulness and heedlessness, the mental contest between insightful knowledge and insolent ignorance, and the emotional conflict between fragile loves and persisting hates are all mirroring manifestations of a continual metaphysical encounter between *Sat* and *asat*, light and shadow, universal good and partisan evil. In a universe rooted in and ruled by moral Law, neither ignorance nor folly, attraction nor revulsion, can be wholly separated from evil. *Avidya* is not the aboriginal condition of man which only a favoured few may overcome; pristine spiritual awareness is the inmost essence of humanity, which has been distorted and obscured by the accumulated sins and follies of all our ancestors. The Noble Eightfold Path of the true exemplars *(Aryas)* is the legacy of all the disinherited, to be claimed by those who dare to challenge the collective ignorance that compounds human misery and to meditate upon the compassionate Sages who have shown both how to see the world from the summit and to live in the world, making of themselves islands emitting rays of benevolence, truth and love. *Dharma* unites the standpoints of the seeker and the Sage, serving both as the initial awakening and the eventual Enlightenment, the means and the goal, the pathway and its consummation in the peace that passeth all human understanding.

The Path to Enlightenment is indeed arduous, but each step in a series of progressive awakenings both anticipates and hastens the goal. The converse is also painfully real. Each backsliding and every procrastination ensures imminent torments that foreshadow the eventual congregation and incurable, anguished aloneness of the self-doomed, witnessing the self-annihilation of the perversely cruel, the defiantly slothful, the irredeemably damned. Hence Buddha warned all and sundry that no one can evade the relentless workings of the Law of Karma. He urged his disciples to understand fully that violence, coercion and playing upon the fears of others will rebound not only upon all such evil-doers but also upon entire communities as well as the earthly *Sangha*.

Rules must be decisive, impartial and firm, but ever applied with wisdom and compassion. If each one is to rule himself, the same principles have to be applied to oneself as to others. *Irrigators lead the waters; fletchers bend the shafts; carpenters carve the wood; the truly virtuous control themselves* (X.17). They must look at the glaring facts of life, including the unpleasant fact of inevitable decay and death. Rather than fighting, fleeing or forgetting it, each one must meditate upon its universal significance. All must come to see that either one is the body, in which case the outcome is already known, or one is not, and so daily identification with transient things is disastrous. At the simplest level, mindfulness *(appamada)* is lucid yet vigorous thinking that must release the will to act appropriately, without any delay. Fear is a failure of nerve, impetuosity a failure of patience, violence is a failure of courage, hatred is a failure of understanding and procrastination is a failure of penance. Rather than taking the cowardly course of constructing a world-picture in which one is the victim of malign fate and human malice, one must dare to respect oneself and to risk much as an apprentice initiate who daily enacts the *Dharma* in this world.

Like Bhishma in the *Mahabharata*, Buddha taught that individual exertion is mightier than inexorable destiny. Karma is not unalterable fatalism, but rather the universal operation of *Dharma*, which implies the integrity as well as the intelligibility of Nature. To alter course, to turn around and to inaugurate a course of wisdom and light, one can benefit enormously by contemplating the Vow, the Compassion, the Renunciation and the Enlightenment of Buddha. Reverence for Buddha, reliance upon the *Dharma* (and, therefore, karma) and refuge in the true *Sangha* are invaluable aids in gaining clarity of mind, preserving continuity of effort, and regenerating oneself at all stages of the Path to Enlightenment. The universal benediction and unceasing radiance of the *trikaya* of Buddha can draw like a magnet anyone who truly seeks and strives to transmute the lead of his lower nature into resilient iron, reflecting the lustre of the "Diamond Soul" and the golden glow of the *Tathagatagarbha*, the sacred source of gestation of past and future Initiates. Even in the early stages, the constant outflow of gratitude for the life and message and presence of Buddha can spur one along the Path. Reverence, gratitude and devotion can reliably sustain one's faith and courage in emulating the Buddha Vow without hubris or hypocrisy. One becomes joyous, like Shantideva, that one can become worthy of belonging to the Buddha family without any wavering, or shadow of turning, in one's irrevocable fidelity to the Triple Gem.

Buddha compassionately drew repeated attention to the treacherous ways in which one can periodically obstruct the processes of assimilation, growth and self-transformation. Perverse inclinations towards subtler sensory pleasures, which lead one to condone self-indulgence, righteous-seeming indignation and lurking impurities of motivation, are especially dangerous; they can unbalance the mind, resulting in confusion and loss of control. Hence eternal vigilance is the price of spiritual freedom, whilst mistaking appearances for realities at any level of meditation, morality and conduct can undo the good and end in self-destruction. Age does not ensure wisdom, speech is not gnosis, mere silence does not make a Sage, and neither austerities nor rituals bring one closer to complete renunciation.

That wise man who, as if holding a balance, accepts the good and rejects the evil is indeed a Sage. He is a Sage by reason of this. He is deemed a Sage since he comprehends both worlds. (XIX.13-14)

Thus Buddha defined the righteous man, the ordained monk and the Sage in terms which exclude identification through external signs, names or forms. Outward forms can at best reflect inward graces, but they cannot cause them or serve as surrogates.

Internality is the crux, the criterion and the index of fundamental growth in apprehension, motivation and the strength of meditation. The outward arena may serve for self-testing and gaining insight into the interdependence, the integrity and predictability of karma. But the Eightfold Path must become an inward reality before it can yield visible results. To tread the Path means in time that one becomes the Path. One must ever recall that everything which has a beginning is inevitably characterized by suffering, impermanency and insubstantiality. Only inward harmony, outer timeliness and constancy in meditation can emancipate one: for increasing harmony in thought, word and deed dissolves the pain of honest self-examination; right action overcomes residues and their karmic accretions; and deep, daily meditation can dispel delusion as well as *tanha*, craving for embodied existence in the phenomenal realm.

The basic chain of dependent origination is conventionally presented in a sequential arrangement so that it can be initially understood, but the *Avatansaka Sutra* makes clear that it arises as a unified whole. Ignorance, pain, craving and form likewise arise together, and from one philosophical standpoint can be seen as sharing a single quality – that of non-enlightenment. The Triple Gem – Buddha, *Dharma* and *Sangha* – can release the triune force which removes the false spell of conditioned existence and induce an ever deeper insight into the unconditioned reality, the "Untrodden Land" of *Nirvana* (XXIII.4). Thus Buddha, freed from all conditions and forms, freed from collective ignorance and all craving, asked: *By what track can you trace that trackless Buddha?* (XIV.1). As the distilled essence of the *Buddhavachana*, the *Dhammapada* is replete with the *guru's* guidance in stripping away everything that leaves tracks, that taints the tranquil harmony of all things and thereby generates needless karma, reinforcing the inexorable cycle of involuntary rebirths. *Empty this boat, Buddha enjoined. Emptied, it will move lightly* (XXV. 10).

Buddha came to humanity neither to plead for personal salvation nor to promise any terrestrial or celestial paradise; he came to show, to vindicate and to re-enact the Path to Supreme Enlightenment and thereby to demonstrate the universal relevance, reality and attainability of Buddhahood. His message of hope and healing, inimitably expressed in myriad ways, enshrined in thousands of texts, resounds with a deathless reverberation throughout the *Dhammapada* and the *Udanavarga*. These proclaim what all the texts teach:

> Shun ignorance, and likewise shun illusion. Avert thy face from world deceptions: mistrust thy senses; they are false. But within thy body – the shrine of thy sensations – seek in the Impersonal for the "Eternal Man"; and having sought him out, look inward: thou art Buddha.
>
> The Voice of the Silence

Hermes, August 1986

THE DIAMOND SUTRA

In *The Voice of the Silence* we are told that the aspirant on the Secret Path must come to see the voidness of the seeming full, the fullness of the seeming void. At a first glance, this injunction seems to say no more than Samuel Butler's statement in his *Notebooks* that everything matters more than we think it does and at the same time nothing matters as much as we think it does. In fact, however, the student of Theosophy soon finds in his attempt to practise his self-chosen discipline, that impersonality, detachment and discrimination are profounder concepts and more elusive virtues than he had thought at the threshold of Theosophical study. *Ahamkara* or egotism is so deep-seated and so pervasive that the very struggle to overcome it seems to facilitate its expression in newer and subtler forms. Similarly, the continual effort to free ourselves from personal preconceptions in our perceptions of the realities around us and in our relationships seems to engender new and unnoticed presuppositions, fresh and unseen barriers to understanding. In order to see the central problem of the spiritual life more clearly, it would be worthwhile to ponder over the *Mahayana* classic, known as the *Diamond Cutter* or the *Diamond Sutra*.

The *Vajrachedika* (Diamond Cutter) is a small Sanskrit text belonging to the *Maha-Prajnaparamita* (Perfection of Transcendental Wisdom). It has been suggested that this text was first transmitted by Nagarjuna who lived in the second century, but this has been denied by some scholars who have declared it to be written down only in the fourth century. It is, however, definitely known that this subtle and profound discourse was first translated into Chinese by Kumarajiva about 400 A.D. and has been subsequently rendered into Chinese and more recently into English by several scholars. Although the supreme doctrine of Voidness is now accessible to all truth-seekers, it remains essentially esoteric and difficult to comprehend. Mere head-learning will not enable us to grasp the Heart-Doctrine, and the *Diamond Sutra* stresses that the state of transcendence over all conditioned consciousness cannot be visualized by purely intellectual means or in terms of categories applicable to our common modes of awareness.

The first and last requirement for the attainment of spiritual wisdom is to rid our consciousness and our conduct of our continual obsession with the idea of an ego-entity, a personality, the dire heresy of separateness and the derivative notions of individual progress, personal salvation and self-realization. In order to hinder the hindrances to ego-free meditation and awareness, the mind should be kept independent of any thoughts which arise within it; for, as long as the mind depends upon anything, it has no sure haven. We are urged not to become passive or nihilistic but rather to make our Manasic consciousness more universal and eventually Mahat-mic by freeing it from the compulsions, obsessions and tortuous rationalizations of Kama Manasic activity. This means in practice that we must become increasingly aware of the extent to which every single thought, feeling and judgment is conditioned by the limited context in which we experience it. The wider and more universal and more enduring the context, the easier it should be for us to prevent ourselves from becoming dependent upon and attached to it.

This requires regular meditation but also the adoption of an attitude of relaxed and well-meaning impersonality in all our activities and relationships. The more we do this, the more meaningful it becomes for us to consider, in any particular context of a personal thought or reaction, how a *Mahatma* or a *Bodhisattva* would react or view the matter in the same context. It is no doubt extremely difficult for our Manasic consciousness to adopt or even to visualize a Buddhic standpoint in any given situation, but this is precisely the object of our training and our daily discipline. We are told that if a *Bodhisattva* cherishes, even to the slightest extent, the idea of an ego-entity or personality, he is consequently not a *Bodhisattva*.

In the practice of this yoga, there must be, as the *Diamond Sutra* and the *Bhagavad Gita* make clear, no mental or emotional attachment to the results of our actions. In this system of *yoga*, the *Gita* points out, no effort is lost and even a little of this practice delivers a man from great risk. The *Diamond Sutra* warns us against even charitable acts performed with a view to attaining a spiritual benefit. A student of Theosophy must not give of his time, money and energy with any thought of personal result or recognition or even because he is urged to do so, but it must become second nature for him to do so in view of the fact that he has initially accepted that all his obligations are wholly self-determined. It is paradoxically true that the assumption of full personal responsibility is the beginning of impersonality, for by ceasing to concern ourselves with the responsibilities of others we are ready to see that all our freely self-chosen responsibilities flow solely from the potency and will-energy of the Higher Self or the Divine Triad which belongs to all and therefore to none.

In the *Diamond Sutra* the Buddha denies the reality of all predictable things, of the individual self as of all changing appearances, likewise of merit and demerit, even of liberation and non-liberation. In the ultimate analysis, no differentiation is at all possible between the primordially undifferentiated and the differentiated cosmos. However we conceive the idea of the One Reality or of transcendental wisdom, it is no more than a mental concept, "merely a name." If we make a hard-and-fast distinction between *Nirvana* and *Samsara*, the Goal and the Way, we fail to see that they are, for the mind of man, merely the ultimate pair of opposites, no less unreal than all lesser pairs of opposites, like ego and non-ego. Only on the plane of the unconditioned consciousness, which is beyond all pairs of opposites and all dichotomous thinking, do we realize the Truth because we become IT.

Similarly, it would be a mistake for us to become concerned about our present incarnation in relation to past and future lives. It is no doubt useful to reflect upon the workings of Karma in relation to our present or any other personality, but we must gain the "higher carelessness" that is based upon the awareness that "there is no passing away nor coming into existence." Again, we must not become self-conscious about helping in the liberation of all beings, for this thought is itself illusory in so far as it fails to take note of the fact that the notions of being and of liberation are purely relative. Above all, we must see that the attaining of Buddhahood is not the attaining of anything, but only the realization of what is eternally and indestructibly potential in every living creature. The Buddha and the non-Buddha are not different in kind; a Buddha knows and the non-Buddha does not know that he, like everyone else, is a Buddha. On attaining Buddhahood, nothing is either lost or gained; "look inward, thou *art* Buddha."

The continual stress of the *Diamond Sutra* is upon the attainment of true impersonality, the performance of every activity, including charity, without any attachment to appearances. It is necessary for us to persevere one-pointedly in this instruction.

Another lesson in the *Sutra* for students of Theosophy is the assertion that the *Tathagatas*, the Masters of Wisdom and of Compassion, cannot be recognized by any material characteristic. As long as we are concerned with personal and material characteristics, we remain deluded. Nor should we cling to particular formulations of the truth; so long as the mind is attached even to the teaching of the Good Law, it will cherish the idea of "I" and "Other." In order to enter the stream and become a *Srotapatti*, the disciple must pay no regard to form, sound, odour, taste, touch or any quality. A *Bodhisattva* is one who has developed a pure, lucid mind, not depending upon sound, flavour, touch, odour or any quality. The *Tathagata* is He who declares that which is true, that which is fundamental, that which is ultimate. A disciple who practises charity with a mind attached to formal notions is like unto a man groping sightless in the gloom, but a *Bodhisattva* who practices charity with a mind detached from any formal notions is like unto a man with open eyes in the radiant glory of the morning, to whom all kinds of objects are clearly visible. Thus, by perceiving the voidness of the seeming full, he participates in the fullness of the seeming void. The *Tathagata* is a signification implying all formulas for the attainment of Enlightenment and he is beyond them all. He is wholly devoid of any conception of separate selfhood and cannot be identified with any sect or any particular formulation of doctrine. He understands the manifold modes of mind of all living beings, like the Krishna of the 10th and 11th chapters of the *Gita*. All *Bodhisattvas* are insentient as to the rewards of Merit. "Because TATHAGATA has neither whence nor whither, therefore is He called Tathagata."

The Buddha tells Subhuti:

> Who sees Me by form,
> Who seeks Me in sound.
> Perverted are his footsteps upon the Way;
> For he cannot perceive the Tathagata.

The *Diamond Sutra* has sometimes been misunderstood to be a plea for a world-denying and inert standpoint. It was actually meant as a dynamite to the complacency of formal believers and self-righteous coteries. At the time when the *Sutra* was written down, there were many Buddhists who had become as smug and yet as anxious for personal advancement in spiritual life as the Brahmins to whom the Buddha came with a profoundly relevant message.

Students of Theosophy, too, fall prey to the cosiness of complacency and the curse of anxiety. The message of the *Diamond Sutra* has been reiterated with pertinent clarity by Judge and Crosbie in their letters to those who came to them for counsel. Though we are not separate from anything, we are surrounded by appearances that seem to make us separate, and we are urged by Judge to proceed to state and accept mentally that we are all these illusions. If we are anxious, we raise a barrier against progress, by perturbation and straining harshly. No matter where we are, the same spirit pervades all and is accessible. "What need, then, to change places?" Again, we are told: "Now, then, is there not many a cubic inch of your own body which is entitled to know and to be the Truth in greater measure than now? And yet you grieve for the ignorance of so many other human beings!" Resignation, we are told, is the sure, true, and royal road. "The lesson intended by the Karma of your present life is *the higher patience*.... Insist on carelessness. Assert to yourself that it is not of the slightest consequence what you were yesterday, but in every moment strive for that moment; the results will follow of themselves." The higher carelessness that we are asked to cultivate is in reality a calm reliance on the law, and a doing of our own duty, checking ourselves by a periodic examination and purification of our motives. As we begin to rely on the Higher Self – the Buddha-nature – little by little new ideals and thought-forms will drive out the old ones as this is the eternal process.

Similarly, Crosbie warns against the danger of thinking too much of oneself, one's present conditions and prospects. We have to acquire greater control over our thoughts, the power of direction, the exercise of deliberation at all times. "Get the point of view of the One who is doing the leading and hold to it." No one can clear another's sight. "We try to free *ourselves* from *something*. Is not this the attitude of separateness?" We forget that "The One *sees* All." We have power over nothing but the "is." "We" are the One Self and there is nothing but the One Self. Masters cannot interfere with Karma. The Egoic perceptions on this plane are limited by all personal claims. "Impersonality isn't talking; it isn't silence; it isn't insinuation; it isn't repulsion; it isn't negation." It means becoming "less doctrinal and more *human*." Is that not the central message of the *Diamond Sutra*?

> It is not the individual and determined purpose of attaining *Nirvana* – the culmination of all knowledge and absolute wisdom, which is after all only an exalted and glorious selfishness – but the self-sacrificing pursuit of the best means to lead on the right path our neighbour, to cause to benefit by it as many of our fellow creatures as we possibly can, which constitutes the true Theosophist.
>
> The Maha Chohan

Hermes, January 1975

THE FLUTE OF KRISHNA

Hear, O son of Pritha, bow with heart fixed on me, practising meditation, and taking me as thy refuge, thou shalt know me completely.

Sri Krishna

Any person who seeks the supernal radiance of the Invisible Sun, the ceaseless vibration of the *Logos* ensouling the Fraternity of Enlightened Seers, must abide at all times with heart fixed upon the object of his devotion. He must be worthy of that total devotion, continually practising meditation, returning his mind whenever possible to its favourite subject of contemplation, the one *Guru* that he has chosen, the embodiment of the *Logos* that is the noumenal force behind the whole of life. Only then can he truly say that he has found the Krishna-Christos within himself. Only then does he activate and arouse, by his realization of the *Logos* in the cosmos, the spirit which moves and animates every single atom and molecule, endowing each with that vortical motion which maintains it for a time in the world of manifestation, thereby enabling it to have life in a form under law. To do this he must take Krishna as his refuge. He must have total trust and faith in the chosen one, the *Ishtaguru*.

In every case he has chosen Krishna. Suppose he was a very sincere disciple, for example, like John, deeply devoted, when writing the Gospel, to the memory of Jesus, Christ will write for him. Everyone is provided for, everyone is protected, everyone is helped. But those alone who embody Krishna's precepts will know Him completely. They alone will be instructed fully in this knowledge and in this realization, having learned which, there remains nothing else to be known. Clearly, this is an unattainable ideal for the average person in our time and in our culture. He cannot possibly expect suddenly to achieve that continuity of consciousness, that ceaseless contemplation, that total devotion, and above all, that unwavering and absolute allegiance to the one shelter and source chosen. He will not attain to this knowledge in this lifetime. He will not hear the pure strains of the flute of Krishna.

Nonetheless, there is hope for every human being. Every human being does in some moments experience the simple joys of daily life known to the great masses of mankind. No wonder that Krishna, the eighth *Avatar* of Vishnu, is the favoured incarnation among the common folk in India. No wonder the *Gita* spoke so powerfully to Thoreau and Bellamy in America, to Wilkins and Warren Hastings among the early Englishmen in India, and to Schlegel and Goethe and many others in Germany. No wonder, then, all over the world men have sat at the lotus feet of the Teacher, in any form, for the sake of true help. Anyone who has ever leafed through the sacred pages of the Song of the Lord has benefited, whether he turns to the translation by William Quan Judge which is mantramic, or the translation by Christopher Isherwood which is poetic and beautiful, or the many other translations that have been composed over the last century. Even more richly blessed are those who have been privileged to study that magnificent, unexcelled and supremely illuminating commentary recorded by Shankaracharya for those who are ready for the deeper mysteries of the *Gita*.

Whoever ponders the *Gita* over a long period of time is deeply stirred. It is sadly significant that Mahatma Gandhi, as also his assassin, appealed to the same scripture. He who died by the bullet of Godse reverenced the *Gita* as his mother, and he who slew Gandhi had deluded himself into thinking that he was obeying the injunctions of the *Gita*. In general, there is a very real sense in which a dedicated few hear Krishna's flute in tones that are sublimely different from the modes in which many others hear it. As long as there are as many ways to God as the breaths of the children of men – in the words of the *Koran* – while at the same time each man is lit up by the same light, so long will each choose his own path according to his own state of consciousness, his wants, his intentions and his goals. Everyone is included in the benediction of Krishna, in accordance with the karma of his "line of life's meditation."

This is a difficult doctrine to understand. There are no distinctions in it between the saved and the damned. In this doctrine the only elect are those who are self-elected, in the manner of Krishna, by the profundity of their overwhelming concern and continual sacrifice. Those who comprehend *Adhiyajna*, the supreme sacrifice, share in its celebration.

Everyone must, in his own way, find the *Logos* within and light up the lamp of true spiritual discernment. In this fundamental sense, all human beings are provided for and the important thing for anyone is not where he is but how he can do better.

All beginnings are seminal and are immensely significant. If a person really wishes to listen to the sound of the divine flute, he must understand the dialogue within his own consciousness which is like the interplay between flute and harp in the great concerto of Mozart. It occurs between the divine promptings within himself and the less rhythmic breathing of his lower self. Through it, he can become self-consciously capable of appreciating the flute. Among people who go to a concert there are those who are merely awed by what takes place. There are those who have some understanding of the music that is played. Others have some knowledge of the skill involved in using instruments and the immense deliberation and meditation behind masters of music in manifestation. Then there are those very few individuals who intensely love the music and, in Eliot's phrase, have heard it so deeply that it is not heard at all, who have become the music while the music lasts. They love the musicians so much that they are one with them, going beyond all the cacophony of inaudible sounds in the heads of the members of the audience. The function of the greatest music is in pointing to that which is unuttered on the physical plane, but which is a ceaseless utterance in eternity.

Any man who hears the rumbling of a thunder cloud, the roar of the ocean, or the rush of the winds above a holy place, is truly blessed, because of the sacred undertaking to which the whole of nature has been consecrated under Karma. Anyone who goes anywhere and is responsive to the F-note of nature – the keynote of Beethoven's *Pastoral Symphony* – the one sound into which all sounds are resolved, even if he hears it only in the still hours of dawn, hears the song of the flute. Anyone who then consecrates himself to the service of the unity of all men and women, has chosen a great undertaking. He feels the pulse of light, the "core of the unuttered" – in the words of Shelley. With Wordsworth, he hears the "still, sad music of humanity." And, hearing these, he may also, in favoured moments, in the season of spring, hear the nightingale "warbling its native woodnotes wild." We might say that the message and meaning of the incarnation of Krishna, over five thousand and seventy-five years ago, was to bring into the lives of men the beauty, the vital relevance and the abundant hope of the eternal rhythm of the cosmos.

There is a critical sense in which our ability to hear the flute is a function of our receptivity, and receptivity requires spiritual knowledge. The Heart Doctrine springs from the heart and lights up the mind. It also involves all aspects of our lives. If, with our whole being, whether intermittently or continuously, we can sift within the stillness and solitude of our inmost calm, only then can we feel the presence, hear the sound, and share the divine joy of the dance of the *Logos*. A person is deeply fortunate to have earned the opportunity to make such a consecration and, through devotion, to move in the mighty current of meditation sustained by those who are the perpetual servants of the *Logos*.

Tragically, most men do not grasp the universal significance of the benediction of Krishna and mistake the great magnanimity of the cosmos for an endorsement of their personal misconceptions and partial insights. But even they are provided for. Those who worship the lesser gods choose terrestrial things. They chase after shadows. They pursue secondary emanations. Some worship money, which comes from the elementals who preside over money, compounded out of the thought-elementals of all human beings focused upon the precious metals. They obtain what they crave. Some extol the pleasures of the body and think they seek Venus Aphrodite. They cling to secondary emanations, evanescent pleasures, for the sake of forgetfulness and momentary extinction. They also secure the object of their quest. Some woo the promiscuous goddess of fame, who courts different men and women on diverse occasions. They gain their object one way or the other, if not in this life, then in some future incarnation. Everyone in the progress of time receives such objects of imperfect devotion.

Some are truly fortunate, under karma, to be prevented from securing the objects of their devotion in this life because in previous lives they took a decision that they do not want them again, however tempting they appeared. What comes to the personality as a setback is a bonus from the past, a current from the Higher Self which protects. Thereby they are saved from endless repetitions and compulsive re-enactments of the mistakes of previous lives.

There are also those who, with simplicity, propitiate by means of *mantrams*, chanting in the streets. They do not know what they really want. At some level they love Krishna. At another level, they wish to reach out to other human beings. Though all of this is sincerely meant, they often mistake the chanting, the dining together, and various monastic practices for some kind of short cut to Krishna. This mistake is only possible if one does not study the *Bhagavad Gita*. Alas, there are also teachers who are very earnest but who, because of their own limitations, underestimate other human beings and say that there can be a substitute for *dhyana*, meditation upon the living words of Krishna. There is none.

No man can fully comprehend the *Bhagavad Gita* the first time he reads it, nor indeed, even if he reads it every day for the whole of his life. There are Hindus who merely take one stanza and chant it endlessly. This helps, though it cannot substitute for a study of all eighteen chapters. People often turn to the *Gita* only in times of distress. They get solace, but it is transitory. There are others who learn the whole of the *Bhagavad Gita* by heart in Sanskrit and intone it repeatedly. This may help as well, depending upon their state of consciousness. If they are thinking only of themselves, they have thereby blocked the inner channel to the divine flame concealed within and they cannot light the lamp of the heart. They cannot erect the throne upon which alone Krishna can preside with regal glory. There are still others who invoke Krishna at festivals, for the sake of getting a child, or for the sake of the means of livelihood that will enable the family to go through another year in times of trouble. There are those who invoke Krishna for the sake of consecrating the simple little book children use in learning the alphabet. There are those who at certain times of the year exchange gifts for the sake of bringing a little joy into the hearts of each other. Innumerable are the ways in which human beings seek to become worthy of a relationship with Krishna, the Divine Lover, the eternal darling of every *gopi*, the supreme guardian of each devotee.

During the sad prelude to the *Mahabharata* war, every effort had been made by Krishna, by myriad devices, to avoid a carnage that became increasingly inevitable. This was due to the demonic will of one man – Duryodhana – and the weaknesses, compromises and corruptions of other men, coupled with the fear of taking decisions which could avoid what many knew would be a catastrophe. When all attempts failed, Krishna made a speech in the court of the blind King Dhritarashtra, father of all the sons who were now going to be arrayed on two sides in the arena of confrontation. Krishna was known as a child as a prankster and as a young man as a flute player who charmed the milkmaids. In his manhood he was first involved in the slaying of demons, but also advised the court of King Dhritarashtra. At the critical point, he came to the king and said, in one of the greatest speeches in the *Mahabharata*, "For the sake of a village, an individual may have to be sacrificed; for the sake of a nation, a village; for the sake of the world, a nation; for the sake of the universe, a world." The whole must prevail, not the part. Then he appealed to the king to avoid the horrors of war. He said, "Bind that man." For the sake of the demonic will, the insatiable insecurity, the endless egotism of one man who was sick, so many people could not suffer. It became clear to the whole court that this was not idle talk, but the king himself was too weak, too exhausted, to be able to take such a painful decision at that moment. A definite choice would have been impossible for him, given his habit of shilly-shallying.

Krishna, knowing that the battle was unavoidable, went to Duryodhana and asked him to choose between himself and his finely trained warriors. Duryodhana scowled and said, "I can use all these people, but what can I do with you, one person? What can you do that is crucial?" So he chose the armies. Krishna went to each and every person and said, "You can have one gift, but only one. Choose what you want and you shall have it." And, of course, many only chose some paltry and ephemeral object of sense-desire from the great marketplace of the world. Arjuna alone was left with the option of either choosing or not choosing, accepting or not accepting, Krishna as his sole companion.

Arjuna chose Krishna as his charioteer without really knowing why. Hence the questions raised by him in the *Bhagavad Gita*. Arjuna was so filled with doubt that he simply could not understand the implications of his choice or the meaning of the war until, in the ninth chapter, Krishna addressed him, saying, "Unto thee who findeth no fault, I shall now make known this most mysterious wisdom." Krishna then gave to Arjuna a vision of the universal mystery because Arjuna had become unconditional in his devotion. Krishna does not do this for everyone, but because he excludes none and loves each and all, he can give each one something. Therefore, we are told, "Those who devote themselves to the gods go to the gods; the worshippers of the *pitris* go to the *pitris*; those who worship the evil spirits go to them, and my worshippers come to me." He says of those who worship him silently and secretly, as the Self of all creatures and manifested in any form and no form, as well as in the form of their chosen precepts, that they, "knowing me to be the *Adhibhuta*, the *Adhidaivata* and the *Adhiyajna*, know me also at the time of death."

So inexhaustible is the joy of the *Gita*, that any person, even late in life or after many tragic failures along the path, may turn to it and hear the regenerating rhythms and authentic accents of universal Wisdom. Even if a person were to see that his whole life was meaningless and without importance to a single living being, still, in making his obeisance to Krishna, he will find that he is not excluded from the boundless generosity of the *Logos*. Divine men, like Krishna and Buddha, and those of their tribe – the race of deathless kings, perfected beings, immortals from the Isle of the Blessed who move among men in many disguises – can help each and every man according to the manner of his devotion. "In whatever way," says Krishna, "men worship me, in that way shall I assist them." The flute of Krishna sings of unconditional love and infallible help. The limits are only set by those who ask in relation to what they are ready to receive. This is the priceless teaching, replete with boundless joy and timeless relevance for every honest and humble seeker, for each blessed devotee.

Hermes, February 1977

THE FIRE OF SELFHOOD

Manu...comes from the root "man", to think, hence a thinker". It is from this Sanskrit word very likely that sprang the Latin "mens", mind, the Egyptian "Menes", the "Master-Mind; the Pythagorean Monas, or conscious "thinking unit", mind also, and even our "Manas" or mind, the fifth principle in man. Hence these shadows are called amanasa, "mindless".

With the Brahmins the Pitris are very sacred, because they are the Progenitors, or ancestors of men – the first Manushya on this Earth – and offerings are made to them by the Brahmin when a son is born unto him. They are more honoured and their ritual is more important than the worship of the gods. May we not now search for a philosophical meaning in this dual group of progenitors? The Pitris being divided into seven classes, we have here the mystic number again. Nearly all the Puranas agree that three of these are arupa, formless, while four are corporeal; the former being intellectual and spiritual, the latter material and devoid of intellect. Esoterically, it is the Asuras who form the first three classes of Pitris – "born in the body of night" – whereas the other four were produced from the body of twilight.

The Secret Doctrine, ii 91

The mythical and metaphorical language of the *Stanzas of Dzyan* portrays the complex evolution of Nature and Man within the sevenfold framework of space, duration and motion. *The Secret Doctrine* traces a triple scheme of development – spiritual, intellectual and material – spanning seven planes of existence, from the highest, ever overbrooding and uninvolved, to the lowest, grossest and most ephemeral plane. Divine and mundane human nature are alike derived from the essences of each of these seven planes. The vast cycling theatre of human evolution, termed in *Gupta Vidya* "the earth chain of globes", exists on the four lowest planes of cosmic existence. Of this chain the fourth or grossest globe is the familiar physical earth. Generally, human beings have little or no awareness either of those worlds or of those aspects of themselves which exist on higher and subtler planes of the earth chain. Even less do they know the three formless planes of the septenary cosmos, *arupa* worlds that lie beyond the entire earth chain and beyond the ken of all beings except the greatest Adepts. Yet there is in every human being a set of latent centres that can be awakened and then attuned to these highest spheres of cosmic existence. These seats or centres, hidden in the subtlest vesture that belongs to the highest states of consciousness, must first be aroused through appropriate modes of concentration and activity. Even though this awakening must take place on a subtle plane – from the standpoint of the physical senses – it nonetheless must take place within a field of substance, because everything in consciousness corresponds to substance. The seven planes of consciousness in the cosmos correspond to seven meta-senses and seven planes of matter. The great mystery of human self-existence is that each human being is directly endowed with this sacred potential by the *Agnishwatha Pitris*, the solar ancestors who infused the current of *Manas* in the Third Root Race.

The master-key to the awakening of the higher centres of consciousness is the conception of selfhood actively entertained by a human being. One's conception of selfhood determines one's concepts of time, causality and energy and thereby the limits of one's potential sphere of action in any given lifetime. It also establishes the relative boundaries of aspiration connected with the ideas of perfection and imperfection. There is between a soul's quality of perfection and the ideational fuel used to light the flame of awareness an intimate and organic indivisible connection in the cosmogony and meta-psychology of *Gupta Vidya*. Perfection in awareness at any level derives from the burning away of imperfect materials belonging to lower realms. This process of self-purification through the use of mental fire is the central mode of human evolution both over the past eighteen million years and on into the millions upon millions of years that will make up the future of humanity. It is the archetypal process by which extraordinary beings gain the highest levels of perfection possible in the human form. Masters in the application of this Teaching, they become masters of the spheres of existence.

To understand how this works, one must first see that all perceptions at all times are affected by conceptions, which are in turn determined by past sense-impressions and sensations or by chaotic memories of past sensations and impressions. In a sense, present perceptions are partly an extrapolation from habit and memory, focussed in the form of expectations, wishes and hopes towards an as yet unrealized future. Even if these seem to be satisfied, this is usually through the present activity of fantasy and fancy. These masses of perceptions generate certain broader thought forms which have specific affinities with elements and aspects of the astral body. Once they become lodged there, they may lie latent, available for further karmic expression in future time. They become the elements, hidden or manifest, that are crucial in times of precipitation of karma and also in the transfer of consciousness from one set of karmic variables to another. Thus the possibility of transcending one set of states of awareness and entering into a higher set depends upon changes in the interior mental and psychic environment as well as in external karmic circumstances. These interior circumstances have an objective and substantial existence in the inner constitution of each human being, and have a great deal to do with an individual's ability or inability to govern thought and feeling.

Owing to the chaotic nature of experience, the conceptions formed within most minds are loose and nebulous. These indefinite reflections of past activity and habit, of memory and sensation, are projected upon the present, dulling perceptions and impressions. One effect of this is a general imprecision in human speech and communication, a persistent inability to convey or grasp ideas. Awkward and painful as the resulting mess of miscommunication may be, it is merely the effect of a more fundamental fragmentation that takes place in the notion of selfhood. Through making the desire principle the primary criterion of all experience, through judging everything in terms of whether it feels pleasant or unpleasant, is good or bad in terms of the personal emotional nature, one shatters the concept of selfhood into a myriad of pieces. One destroys any clear, coherent and stable conception of the self. When this happens – and it is the common condition of many in the world today – people become creatures rather than creators. They become enslaved by the temporal process.

Sometimes human beings can gain an ephemeral sense of freedom through a desperate kind of ego assertion, a self-destructive forgetting of obligations and an abject immersion in the temporal present. This is not authentic freedom, however, and has nothing to do with the eternal present. It is a state of illusion, a compounding of confusions, and a further fragmentation of the conception of selfhood. Nothing in this sort of nihilistic escapism alters the fact that there is a ceaseless and essential beating of the temporal process upon everything in the astral form. This not only quickens the ageing process but also in time destroys brain cells, making it harder and harder to effect a radical shift in one's life. Hence many souls, throughout an entire lifetime, can hardly make effective and enduring changes in their natures.

This is true for vast numbers of human beings all over the world. Although living in the Fifth Root Race, they are part of it only in one sense – they are passively coexisting with the opportunities for growth that are available in the Fifth Root Race. But essentially, they are dominated by the fourth principle of the Fourth Round, the principle of *kama* or desire. This legacy of the Atlantean Fourth Root Race may take a variety of forms, ranging from instinct and relatively harmless indulgence to stronger manifestations of desire and emotion working through and corrupting the feeling nature. There is no specifically human and proper basis of selfhood to be found in the principle of desire. Through desire it is impossible to generate the principles of continuity of consciousness, autonomy of awareness and creativity of choice. Insofar as human beings remain immersed in the diffuse effluvia of the desire principle, they have not really begun to individuate. Were they to interrogate themselves honestly in the court of their own conscience about what exactly they have chosen, they would be at a loss to know how to answer.

By and large, they have drifted into circumstances or else have exploited choices that are inherent in institutions and arise out of collective karma. Seldom understanding these institutions, much less being able to create or regenerate them, they cannot take credit for any authenticity or originality of choice: they have simply come to play out certain roles in institutional contexts. Even in what is called "personal life", most people's choices are in fact made by their parents or their friends, and do not even reflect any unique or original line of personal preference. In all of this it is difficult to recognize even the simulacrum of an autonomous human being who is a self-determining agent, capable of deep deliberation and of making conscious changes in himself or his environment. Yet, at this point in evolution, it should be the prerogative of every human being to exercise the capacity to abstract from the emotions of the feeling nature, to abstract from the physical and astral forms, to abstract from the runaway and indulgent mind, and thereby to make definitive changes in the inner vestures.

This broad retardation of the development of the human race, which led one of the *Mahatma*s to remark that humanity had not changed much in a million years, is truly the result of a misalliance between human beings and the lower *Pitris* during the Fourth Root Race. As *The Secret Doctrine* explains, the lunar (or *Barhishad*) *Pitris*, which gave to humanity its astro-ethereal and physical vestures, did not endow humanity with the active power of Manasic self-consciousness.

> They *would* not, simply because they *could* not, give to man that sacred spark which burns and expands into the flower of human reason and self-consciousness, for they had it not to give. This was left to that class of *Devas* who became symbolised in Greece under the name of Prometheus, to those who had nought to do with the physical body, yet everything with the purely spiritual man.
>
> *Ibid.*, 95

By misdirecting the power of self-consciousness to intensify and exaggerate the experience of the kamic principle in relation to form, both physical and astral, the Fourth Root Race damaged and deformed the conception of human selfhood that it transmitted to posterity. This is reflected in the general confusion of desire and will, passion and feeling, cerebration and thought, sensation and knowledge. The integrity of the lower kingdoms of Nature, acting through instinct, has been inverted into the automaton-like compulsion of passive human beings self-enslaved by kama manas. This submission of human consciousness to the hosts of sub-human creative agencies in Nature has cut humanity off from the hosts of its higher creators and so from its own higher powers of creativity.

> Each class of Creators endows man with what it has to give: the one builds his external form; the other gives him its essence, which later on becomes the Human *Higher Self* owing to the

personal exertion of the individual; but they could not make men as they were themselves – perfect, because sinless; sinless, because having only the first, pale shadowy outlines of attributes, and these all perfect – from the human standpoint – white, pure and cold as the virgin snow. Where there is no struggle, there is no merit. Humanity, "of the Earth earthy", was not destined to be created by the angels of the first divine Breath: therefore they are said to *have refused* to do so, and man had to be formed by more material creators, who, in their turn, could give only what they had in their own natures, and no more. Subservient to eternal law, the pure gods could only project out of themselves *shadowy* men, a little less ethereal and spiritual, less *divine and perfect* than themselves – shadows still. The first humanity, therefore, was a pale copy of its progenitors; too material, even in its ethereality, to be a hierarchy of gods; too spiritual and pure to be MEN, endowed as it is with every *negative (Nirguna)* perfection. Perfection, to be fully such, must be born out of imperfection, the *incorruptible* must grow out of the corruptible, having the latter as its vehicle and basis and contrast.

Ibid.

Active autonomy and deliberate self-perfection are the hallmarks of authentic human growth. Instead of exemplifying these Manasic characteristics, most human beings are in the condition of those caught in the lowest realm portrayed in Plato's Divided Line. Their consciousness is ensnared by images, punctuated now and again by borrowed opinions taken from the twilight realm of the astral light. To rise above this level, one must first emulate the most individuated human beings below the level of spiritual initiation. One must begin to be a human being in the true sense of the term – a man like Socrates or Gandhi or Thoreau, or like many others – who has, through the quality of his life, added lustre to the definition of being human. Such heroic lives show an intensity irradiated with a deep sense of humour. Next to such exemplars, most people cannot really be said to be truly alive. To recognize this enormous gap, however, does not necessitate falling into despair or guilt, reactions which are themselves only a further extension of the passivity of *kama manas*. Authentic Manasic human life consists of a considerable amount of sifting, an active cooperation with the life-process.

The more one sifts experience and oneself, gleaning what is meaningful and real, what is right and good, out of a chaotic mixture of thoughts, emotions, sensations and experiences, the more one is capable of recognizing how this sifting process itself works throughout all life. In effect, one begins to recognize the logic of karma. An individual who begins to do this, instead of merely taking his cues from other human beings, becomes much more solitary than human beings in general. At the same time, however, he grows much more conscious of the cosmic framework within which that solitude is strongly supported. By trying to understand something about universal laws and trends that apply to all humanity, to the course of history, to the karma of the earth or an age, a nation or a race, one can become aware of the sifting process that takes place in Nature on different planes. Through this subtle awareness, one can become involved in checking one's own sifting of oneself periodically against the constant sifting of karma. Thus an individual's life can become a boundless expanse of continuous learning, affording repeated discoveries, all of which occur around the fluctuating and expanding boundaries of the concept of selfhood.

This steady tropism towards growth in self-consciousness and an expanding sense of selfhood is characteristic of individuals who represent a kind of steadfastness in relation to a centre. They are capable of continual exertion towards perfection because they are deeply centered. Having passed through the fires of suffering and trial, temptation and error, they have emerged from the ashes of their own errors, much stronger and with a much greater sharpening of the centre of their own consciousness. This toughness makes them better able to experience a series of ever-expanding boundaries to selfhood, while at the same time becoming intuitively aware of the vast circle that indefinitely encompasses the upward strivings of all beings. Whether that vast circle is taken to refer to all of humanity or to the earth, or to human beings at any given time, or even ultimately to the cosmos as a whole, it is the sense of that greater circle that gives to each individuating human being a universal basis for individual consciousness. The ability to connect one's individual striving towards perfection with the calm depths of universal selfhood strengthens continuity of consciousness, the power of individual choice and the capacity to stay steadfast within that line of commitment. At the same time, the essential principle of transcendence inherent in the concept of universal selfhood gives flexibility and resilience to the individual, assuring him of a continuous willingness to learn from the process of sifting that continues forever in the world and the self.

One could find no finer exemplar, in the present century, of this continuous process of sifting than *Mahatma* Gandhi. From the dawn to the dusk of his incarnation, over a period of sixty years, his letters and speeches, his essays and articles, reveal a continuous stream of reflections that embody a consistency and constancy around a central commitment. Throughout his life, he sharpened his fundamental sense of selfhood through vigilant attention to opportunity, to responsibility and to the initiative that belongs to an individual human being. He also constantly made the subtlest possible rearrangements in the application and expression, the articulation and communication, of seminal conceptions like truth and non-violence. He was testing continually his inward sense of what it is that karma indicates, how it operates, and whether *dharma* is fulfilled. This painstaking sifting of experience and heroic determination to move forward is characteristic of human beings who have found their centre.

That inward centre is in *Manas*, because *Manas* alone is capable of a universal and impersonal standpoint. Once one's consciousness is anchored in that centre, it is possible to reflect that focus within lower *manas* through discipline, and so create a reliable conception of one's relationship to the world and a coordinate ability to act with increasing correctness and constant self-correction in the process of activity itself. This can only come about when one is able to draw a firm line between the essential centre within *Manas* – rarely expressed except in the intimations of the mystical language of sacred texts – and the shifting centre of activity in the personality, which is constantly involved in interaction and manifestation.

The ability to make the fire of *Manas* the firm centre of one's engagement in the world of form is the basis of *Karma Yoga*. Through it one can exemplify individual strength, remaining all the while invulnerable to the buffetings of fate and ordinary circumstance, which arise under karma and stem, it seems, from the outside world. Such a *yogin* preserves intact a fundamental concept of selfhood. He remains indifferent to pressures from the temporal stream, so inwardly detached that he can use every opportunity available under karma to the fullest. He fills up time as creatively as possible, and so generates a greater continuity of attention on the highest ideals, as well as a greater reliance on higher causality. In his interactions he is shifted away from ephemeral rearrangements of external human circumstances and towards fundamental changes in human consciousness. He is ever aware of the depth and level of awareness of the beings around him. He draws upon the bountiful energy of the *Atman*, focussed through *Buddhi Manas*, and is ready for any task of self-conscious cooperation with essential human nature. Individuating human beings centered in *Manas* will derive far more from life than their kamically obscured peers, be at once much busier and much more relaxed. Through concentration upon essentials, they will be filled with far more energy, yet make the fewest possible demands on their body and physical senses.

If such an individual were privileged to enter the Path that leads towards enlightenment, then he or she would be able to enjoy access to the exalted ideal of the *Dhyani*, the *Jivanmukta*, the *Bodhisattva* and the *Mahatma*. Such perfected beings represent in principle a total mastery of fundamental tenets and truths in relation to the logic of manifestation and in reference to spirit, matter and energy. Such beings are ultimately karmaless. They are totally uninvolved in the process of change and becoming. Though in one sense they have bodies – even material bodies at times – and so resemble human beings, it would be more appropriate to regard them as divine. The difference between them and the very finest examples of humanity in history is such an immeasurable difference of degree that it is tantamount to a difference of kind. Such perfected beings are the *alpha* and *omega* of human selfhood; they lie beyond all the categories of discursive thought. To approach them in the mind through meditation, however, is to approach them in reality, and every aspirant along the Path is encouraged to meditate upon the galaxy of Buddhas and *Bodhisattvas*, kindling awareness of them into a living power in life.

To meditate upon the *Mahatmas* is to bring about a fundamental transformation in one's conception of selfhood. But to do this through meditation involves not merely a withdrawal and abstraction from the world, but also a certain proficiency, if not reasonable mastery, over all one's obligations. One cannot wholeheartedly withdraw from the narrow self if one is thus attempting to run away from one's commitments. Any attempt to default morally only perpetuates the problem of a shrunken conception of selfhood. One needs more than a mere rearrangement of thought forms. One must cross fundamental barriers, philosophic and metaphysical, which lie between the unconditioned and the conditioned. This is because the higher vestures, though they are like formless breaths, are yet composed of intellectual substance. Hence, what is ordinarily understood as moral responsibility must first be perfected in the individual and then transmuted into a meta-ethical stance. The Taoist Sage, the *Jivanmukta* or the Buddha have no responsibilities in the ordinary sense. They have become so totally united to the One that is beyond all manifestation that they have also mastered a stern sense of universal necessity in relation to every thought, feeling and act. In one sense, they are continuously responsive, yet in another they have no specific responsibility. Even the devoted disciple can hardly begin to imagine the state of consciousness of such a being who has transcended all confining conceptions of selfhood and realized the self-existent ground of the highest individuation.

This difficulty in conceiving of the highest possible selfhood and individuation has direct consequences for one's capacity to act for the sake of one's ideals. When people think of time, they ordinarily think in terms of periodicity and succession. Thus, when they think of causality, they think in terms of conceptual differences between cause and effect, even if they are able to discern chains of causation. The seeming necessity of these conceptual divisions also forces the mind to think of energy in terms of units and rates of flow. Even if one attempts to think of energy in its most metaphysical sense, one assumes that energy must itself have its own approaches and its own discreet momentum. Captive to the illusion of successive time, one imposes units of division upon causality and energy. On the other hand, when one thinks in terms of selfhood at any level, however illusory or fragile, there is some degree of integration involved. That is partly because of the systematic elusiveness of the term "I". The moment, however, one speaks of "I" in terms of one's experience of likes and dislikes, satisfactions and dissatisfactions, connected with the experience of *kama* in time, one imagines an entity which is fragmented and conceptually subordinate to time. Typically, one conceives of selfhood as a sentient being, who has feelings and emotions, who savours pleasures and dreads pain. Whilst something unitary is implicit in the notion of selfhood, and is existentially carried forth by the ubiquitous nature of the sense of "I", this intuition of unity is blocked at every turn through attachment to temporality and form. This predicament is characteristic not only of all ordinary human thought and language, but also of all human experience, both social and individual. Thus the attempts of individuals to embody the principles of human unity and brotherhood are continually subject to truncation and disappointment.

Rather than see this as the result of some external fate or cruelty of Nature, much less the result of some original sinfulness in human nature, one must come to recognize that this frustration of human ideals arises from a foreshortened vision of selfhood. Whether put in terms of a restoration of the Golden Age, or of the realization of universal brotherhood or of the establishment of peace and goodwill among men, the ideal of human unity must be reached through diversity. The resolution of the human riddle of the many and the One depends upon the ability to take hold of categories that involve minute and sometimes extremely refined series of complex divisions. These must be given full value in consciousness and mastered, seen in relation to the One. One's concepts of time, causality and energy must be determined from within without by that which is essentially unitary. To attempt the reverse, to seek unity out of differentiated time, causes and effects and quanta of energy on the plane of form, is impossible.

Under karma each human being is capable of a certain degree of self-determination, from within without, of the concepts of time, causality and energy. This level may be connected with an X-factor, through which a set of ratios is established and a certain field of dynamic equilibrium is maintained. At whatever level, this equilibrium could be thought of as the individual's capacity to assimilate diverse experience through a steady commitment to an ideal. The crucial X-factor determining the individual's capacity to assimilate meaning from experience could be thought of as something like a reality coefficient within the conception of selfhood. Any individual's conception of selfhood is not, therefore, merely unitary to a greater or lesser degree in a logical or conceptual sense. Ontological unity itself works as a kind of meta-cause through one's conception of selfhood, affecting one's experience of time, of causation and of energy.

The potential presence of the Self or *Atman* in one's conception of selfhood is the basis for all meditation *(dhyana)* upon the identity of *Brahman* and *Atman*. In *Gupta Vidya* cosmogony and psychology are coextensive. The seven states of consciousness and planes of matter in the cosmos are inseparable from the seven principles in man. It is through these principles that the self-conscious task of connecting together all the aspects of manifestation must be carried out, not on behalf of any narrow sense of self, but out of a sense of being the Self of all. The process of realizing the One is the same as that of understanding and mastering the operation of the reality principle in the constitution of Man. Through the Manasic fire of self-consciousness, human beings may realize the perfect unity and correspondence of the Self and the All, fusing together *Atma Vidya* and *Brahma Vidya*. The very capacity to preserve, purify and perfect the sense of selfhood is the gift of the highest *arupa Pitris* who endowed humanity with *Manas* over eighteen million years ago.

> That class of the "Fire *Dhyanis*", which we identify on undeniable grounds with the *Agnishwattas*, is called in our school the "Heart" of the Dhyan-Chohanic Body; and it is said to have incarnated in the third race of men and made them perfect. The esoteric Mystagogy speaks of the mysterious relation existing between the hebdomadic essence or substance of this angelic Heart and that of man, whose every physical organ, and psychic, and spiritual function, is a reflection, so to say, a copy on the terrestrial plane of the model or prototype *above*.
>
> *Ibid.,* 91-92

To learn to live from above below, seeing all life from the standpoint of primordial and unbroken unity, is to awaken the power of noetic action. One must overcome the fragmentary sense of psychic selfhood through a ceaseless application of the Heart Doctrine, a continual sifting of experience through meditation and self-correction, continually cleaving to an intuition of the divine Presence within. Maintaining a sense of hope and possibility inspired by the paradigm of the Sage, individuals can learn to make a conscious and deliberate change, over a period of time, in their root conception of selfhood and so in their conceptions of time, causality and energy. As they do this, they will withdraw allegiance – and a sense of reality – from an entire class of perceptions and impressions. Then, after a period of transition, they will be able to endow a much higher class of perceptions with reality. This is both difficult and elusive. To change one's sphere of perception is not like changing one's clothes. That is why monasticism has failed over the last several thousand years and is no longer a viable option. Simply changing external circumstances helps in no way to bring about a fundamental breakthrough in thinking. At this point in human civilization, it is necessary to gain a good grasp of the metaphysics that is relevant to making true *metanoia* possible in human life and consciousness. Then, if one is so blest as to come into a sacred relationship as a disciple to a true *Guru*, one will be able to take full advantage of it so as to effect a radical and irreversible change in consciousness for the benefit of all beings.

Hermes, November 1984

THE SEVENTH IMPULSION: 1963–2000

The great and peaceful ones live regenerating the world like the coming of the spring; having crossed the ocean of embodied existence themselves, they freely aid all others who seek to cross it. The very essence and inherent will of Mahatmas is to remove the suffering of others, just as the ambrosia-rayed moon of itself cools the earth heated by the intense rays of the sun.

Shankaracharya

A night of superstition, dogma and degradation descended upon the West for a millennium between the politically prudent "conversion" of Constantine and the initiation of the Seven Century Plan. In 1357 a ray of Amitabha, the Buddha of Boundless Time and Infinite Light, appeared in Tibet as the Adept-Teacher Tsong-kha-pa. To purify, preserve and promulgate the Wisdom-Religion, he founded the Gelukpa Order, the third Dalai Lama of which was recognized as a manifestation of Avalokiteswara, "the divine SELF perceived by Self." Tenzin Gyatso, the present Dalai Lama, is the fourteenth incarnation. Tsong-kha-pa initiated a series of seven impulsions to prepare the world through mental and spiritual revitalization to be ready to participate in the formation of the distant sixth sub-race. In the last quarter of each century of the Seven Century Plan, an emissary from the Brotherhood of *Bodhisattvas* works in the West to further spiritual enlightenment and the continuity of collective growth.

In the fourteenth century two "supreme Pontiffs" were elected to the papal chair, and the resulting "great schism" cast doubt on the claims of the church to absolute spiritual and temporal authority. John Wycliffe (1320–1384) began preparing the ground for a reawakening of Manas by translating the *Bible* into English and teaching that transubstantiation and papal authority are superstitions. His disciples, the Lollards, showed in their lives the way of simple devotion and charity. Pico della Mirandola (1463–1494) led the Second Impulsion by introducing the *Qabbalah* to the West, deciphering the philosophical alphabet of the Hermetic teachings, and by founding human dignity upon the freedom to germinate and nourish some selection of the vast variety of seeds of possibility in plastic human nature. Paracelsus provided the transition to the sixteenth-century cycle by teaching that "everything is the product of one universal creative effort; the Microcosm and man are one." The luminous triad of Giordano Bruno (1548–1600), Robert Fludd (1575–1637) and Jacob Boehme (1575–1624) first used the term "theosophy" in modern times. The doctrine of Paracelsus of sevenfold cosmic and human correlations was given a firm metaphysical foundation and fearless exemplification by Bruno. Fludd explained to a surprised Europe that the ancient Mysteries which preserved these doctrines had not perished with classical Greece, but flourished in the East and in secret groups in the West. For the first time in the Seven Century Plan, the central idea that Adepts worked behind the scenes to improve the human condition was intimated. Boehme demonstrated that spiritual intuition was possible, thereby giving crucial evidence for the existence of Adepts, though he made no claim for himself.

In 1675 the Rosicrucian *Instructions* were issued. Disciples who wished to serve humanity were invited to prepare quietly the ground for the public work of the Movement. In the Fifth Impulsion there arose "four heroic characters who formed a Cross of Occult Light in the eighteenth-century sky" – Saint Germain, whose life is as mysterious as his overbrooding work in history; Louis Claude de Saint-Martin (1743–1803), who purified Masonry and coined the spiritual motto "Liberty, Equality, Fraternity," distorted by the violent passions of the French revolution; Cagliostro, who offered true Masons knowledge of the Lodge of *Mahatmas*; and Franz Anton Mesmer (1734–1815), who unified the physical, mental and spiritual principles of magnetism into a single therapeutic doctrine and practice.

The Sixth Impulsion witnessed the incarnation of the enigmatic being called Helena Petrovna Blavatsky (1831–1891). Boldly announcing that she was an agent of the Great Lodge, she outlined the fundamental teachings of the Wisdom-Religion even before she founded the Theosophical Society with her associate Henry Steel Olcott and her disciple William Quan Judge. Defining true magic as divine wisdom, she identified science and theology, "the Montecchi and Capuletti of the nineteenth century," as the enemies of occultism, offering *Isis Unveiled* (1877) as evidence for her ideas and *The Secret Doctrine* (1888) as explanation of the philosophy of theosophy. Braving the painful, though sacred, duty of openly naming the *Mahatmas* who are behind the Movement, she demonstrated the grandeur of the theosophical system and the danger of playing with its Fohatic fire. In expounding the fundamentals of *theosophia* and the basic principles of oriental *philosophia*, she pointed to the underlying roots of all individual and collective progress. Her travels from Russia to America, from India to England, cast powerful magnetic links across the world, so that the Mahatmic vibration could be tapped globally.

When H.P. Blavatsky departed on the completion of her task, W.Q. Judge continued her work in the spirit she had selflessly embodied.

> "Her aim was to elevate the race. Her method was to deal with the mind of the century as she found it, by trying to lead it on step by step; to seek out and educate a few who, appreciating the majesty of the Secret Science and devoted to "the great orphan Humanity," could carry on her work with zeal and wisdom; to found a Society whose efforts – however small itself might be – would inject into the thought of the day the ideas, the doctrines, the nomenclature of the Wisdom Religion, so that when the next century shall have seen its 75th year the new messenger coming again into the world would find the Society still at work, the ideas sown broadcast, and thus to make easy the task which for her since 1875 was so difficult and so encompassed with obstacles in the very paucity of the language – obstacles harder than all else to work against."

He reminded his readers that while "at the close of each century a spiritual movement is made in the world by the *Mahatmas*," they do not wholly withdraw their current. Rather the seeds sown are allowed to germinate.

Our destiny is to continue the wide work of the past in affecting literature and thought throughout the world, while our ranks see many changing quantities but always holding those who remain true to the programme and refuse to become dogmatic or to give up common-sense in theosophy. Thus we will wait for the new messenger, striving to keep the organization alive that he may use it and have the great opportunity H.P.B. outlines when she says, "Think how much one, to whom such an opportunity is given, could accomplish."

As the sun simultaneously passed across the Galactic Equator and the sacred asterism Punarvarsu, the Aquarian Age began its turn as the solar month in the Great Year. Astraea, the goddess of justice, descends toward the Pit, and Aldebaran, "the eye of the Bull," surveys earth from Meru. Into this complex, chaotic and crucial period the Seventh Impulsion is sent. When speaking of this age H.P. Blavatsky warned that psychologists would have their work cut out for them, many accounts will be settled between the races and that the twentieth century would be the last of its name. The forms and traditions, the beliefs and languages which inspired Piscean man over two millennia ago are dead and decaying. Those who cling to form rather than looking to the Spiritual Sun find themselves torn asunder by the collapse of familiar patterns. Riddled with self-doubt and insecurity, not sufficiently resolute in vision to see the soft golden hues of spiritual light among the flashing beams of *maya,* many are easy prey for doomsayers, negators and cynics, and crisis becomes a mode of living. Robert Crosbie founded the United Lodge of Theosophists in 1909 to continue the Work and preserve the foundations of the coming cycle, and B.P. Wadia carried the light of U.L.T. around the world.

Into this contrasting scene of daring and despair the Magus-Teacher of the Seventh Impulsion descends. The *Guru* alone determines when, where and how he will represent himself, the levels of language he will use, the modes of teaching he will adopt, and the speed and obviousness with which he will spell out the nature of the culminating Impulsion. His work involves the *sutratmic* synthesis of the Seven Century Plan. His duty is to nothing less than the whole of humanity, and as the Voice of *Vajradhara,* the Diamond Soul, every word he speaks will be a full account of himself. His teaching will be pure *theosophia* and his expression of it will be as fresh and vivifying as are those of every *Guru* when first delivered.

The Seven Century Plan is intimately connected with the 2500-year cycle of the Buddha, and the 5000-year cycle with which Krishna inaugurated *Kali Yuga.* Robert Crosbie said that Krishna "was an administrator, while Buddha was ethical intelligence." Vinoba Bhave has reiterated that Krishna was the incarnation of pure love, the Buddha of oceanic compassion. The synthesis of the "royal art" and the science of living, of unconditional love and unerring compassion, sets the archetype for the Aquarian Man: one whose head can feel and whose heart is intelligent, "like twins upon a line" while the star which is his goal burns overhead. The New Teacher will lay down the invisible lines which are the parameters of human development for the next 2000 years.

We have the privilege of being among those who enter a New Cycle under the Seven Century Plan, bringing together East and West so fully that the distinction will fade into history. The golden impulse initiated by Krishna, Buddha and Shankara in the East, and by Pythagoras, Plato and Christ in the West, will be carried forth into the civilization of the future. Those who strive to make theosophy by any name a living power in their lives, one-pointed in consciousness, calm and deliberate in action, may have the sacred privilege of recognizing and serving the Magus-Teacher of the Seventh Impulsion. Those who prepare themselves in the secret sanctuary of their hearts by letting go of all conditions and renouncing all wish for personal gain, may have the thrice-great privilege of working with the *Guru* for the regeneration of humanity.

Retrospective insight into the 1875 Cycle and intuitive readiness for 1975 are indissolubly wedded, with no danger of divorce in a marriage by mutual assent. The Wheel of the Good Law moves swiftly on, and those who are willing to drive out the worthless husks of feverish speculation, psychic excitement and unholy curiosity must seek the golden grain of self-validating truth in the mathematically precise marking of "the celestial dial" on the Solar Clock. 14 x 7 years and 7 months after the birth of "H.P.B.," as well as 3 x 9 years and 9 months after the Aquarian Age commenced, when the disc of the Sun crossed the galactic equator and entered the constellation of *Punarvarsu* (Pollux), an event took place on earth, under the aegis of the asterism *Punarvarsu*, containing the key to the 1975 Cycle. This says everything and nothing, in the time-honoured code language of the Wise Men of the East.

Hermes, November 1975

THE VIGIL NIGHT OF HUMANITY

If the Higher Mind-Entity the permanent and the immortal – is of the divine homogeneous essence of "Alaya-Akasa," or Mahat, – its reflection, the Personal Mind, is, as a temporary Principle," of the Substance of the Astral Light. As a pure ray of the "Son of the Universal Mind," it could perform no functions in the body, and would remain powerless over the turbulent organs of Matter. Thus, while its inner constitution is Manasic, its "body," or rather functioning essence, is heterogeneous, and leavened with the Astral Light, the lowest element of Ether. It is a part of the mission of the Manasic Ray, to get gradually rid of the blind, deceptive element which, though it makes of it an active spiritual entity on this plane, still brings it into so close contact with matter as to entirely becloud its divine nature and stultify its intuitions.

H. P. Blavatsky

The poet Tennyson said: "Ring out the old, ring in the new." There is, at this point in the history of human evolution, a tremendous and unprecedented golden opportunity. Its origin is not in outward forms and institutions, but in consciousness itself; its promise is rooted in a radical restructuring of the ratios in human consciousness between the unmanifest and manifest. Since this revolution arises within the very principle of Manasic self-consciousness, it can be neither understood nor entered through tellurian conceptions of human history or egoity below the fourth plane. Yet, everywhere, men and women of moral courage can glimpse this subtle transformation through the intimations of awakened intuition, and can authentically respond to the noumenal initiatives of our time. Each may uncover within himself the resources to contribute to the humanity of the future and the selfless strength to take those decisions which will assure participation in that humanity at the moment of death. Humanity now finds itself somewhat past the mid-point of a cycle initiated in the climacteric year of this century, and which will extend through a Mahabharatan re-enactment up until its closing years.

Before the dawning of the new order of the ages, in which the relations of nations will be changed significantly, humanity will witness the dismantling of the old structures. The clarion call has been sounded and it will be maintained continuously until all the obsolete megaliths that wallow in the debris of the past and the humbug of history, and until all the appalling vicissitudes of the Karma of Israel over two thousand years, will come to an end, and end not with a bang but a whimper. It is the solemn duty of those who have had the sacred privilege of entering the presence of the New Cycle to draw apart, in the words of St. Paul, from the multitudes of fatalists and to insert themselves into the whole human family. This is not easy, for everyone is a victim of his own karma over millions of years. All this karma may be strangely brought together in a concentrated form in a single lifetime, through a process which defies analysis and baffles imitation, and which can only be glimpsed intermittently, in hints and whispers, until the moment of death, when the immortal soul lays down its garment and gains, at last, some inkling of the hidden meaning of human life.

One of the long-standing problems with the western world, especially over the past two hundred and fifty years, has been its baseless assumption that the entire world owes it an explanation. The many owe no explanation to the few, and above all, there is no explanation owed to the ignorant and uninitiated by the Society of Sages. Krishna owes no one any explanation. If this is understood, it will become clear that human beings have assumed needless burdens of false knowledge. Through a mistaken conception of knowledge they assume that what they repeat below the fourth plane they truly know, because they have failed to grasp the crucial distinction between "knowing how" and "knowing that". Reading a textbook on carpentry does not ensure that one can become a carpenter. A cookbook does not make a chef. If this is true of carpentry and cooking, of music and mathematics, it is even more true of spiritual wisdom. The mere fact of repeating words below the fourth plane does not admit the soul of man to the stream of search. No one becomes a mountain climber by dreaming about it, or by exchanging images and fantasies with others. The truth can only be known by testing and training one's *psyche*, and this cannot be done without first asking *who* is really testing and training the *psyche*. If a human being were merely one of the six specialized principles of human nature, it would be impossible to engage in self-redemption.

All the principles of man are derivatives and reflections, on different planes of substance, of One Life, One Light and One Energy. When a human being ascends above the fourth plane and becomes immortal, living in the instrument but in the name of the music, inhabiting the vessel but in the name of the Light, remaining in the mask but in the name of the Nameless, he has become attuned to humanity at large. Anyone at any time can become more attentive to the vast milling crowds of human souls, who, though they may wander in the dark and sometimes tumble in the dust, come together in the dusk. As souls, all withdraw into deep sleep and come closer to the Divine within, finding in "nature's second course" the nourishment and strength which enables them to arise the next day and continue with courage their pilgrimage. To become attentive to the cry of the human race, to become responsive to the immemorial march of all human souls on this vast and uncharted pilgrimage, is also to come closer to Krishna within, and to comprehend the affirmation: "I am seated in the hearts of all beings and from me comes knowledge and memory and loss of both."

There is that facet of the *Logos* which is karma, the complex interaction of all life-atoms below the fourth plane in the great wheel of life, as the Buddha called it. All of these participate at different rates and with different degrees of semi-unconsciousness – partial, imperfect self-consciousness – in the long pilgrimage. Therefore, human beings generally do not know who they are, where they are or what goal they seek. This threefold ignorance is an integral part of the human enterprise. In the modern world, those who failed spiritually, being unable to maintain even minimal standards of what it is to be human, developed theories based upon the corruption of consciousness to apply to most human beings, who, however imperfect, are not warped in the essential intuitions of the heart. It is the tragedy of man and of human history that the monstrous necromancy and extreme sickness of so few should have imposed so great and so intolerable a burden upon large masses of human beings. This is the fault of modern miseducation, rooted in false ideas of human life, which asserts the quaint dogma – for which there is no evidence and never will be – that the human being is the body, that there is only one life, that this is a universe without moral law, that everything is chaos and without meaning, and that by counting the heads of the mindless, by collating the opinions of cerebrating machines, there is an accredited basis for either Truth or Equality or Freedom. There is none, and therefore the ritual of democracy has failed. All the deceptive tokenism that resulted from the eighteenth century revolution has evaporated.

Each human being is a Monad or individual, a ray of the Divine, immortal in essence, yet only potentially so as an incarnated ray working in vestures that are evidently mortal. These vestures, ever changing and evanescent, compel every human being to interact with all the seven kingdoms of nature. There is not an animal, not a plant or mineral, not a star or galaxy or planet, which does not feel every subterranean influence in nature. Therefore, all human beings are brought together in a vast solidarity of being in which breathe millions upon millions of centres of light in all the variegated kingdoms of nature. In finding itself, humanity must rediscover its ontological basis in the entire cosmic scheme. Five million years ago in Atlantis, human beings sought the mystery fires but then, alas, degraded them. They sought thaumaturgic powers at the expense of the majority of mankind. They exploited vestal virgins and the theurgic traditions of their wiser ancestors. They generated the intoxicating idea of individual perfection, for which exclusiveness there is no cosmic provision in the grand scheme of evolution. There is not a human being on earth who could truly ascend above the planes without coming into a compassionate relationship with all life. The true Teaching, which has always existed in the world, guarded in sanctuaries around the globe, reminds us that no one can ever make any real spiritual progress except on behalf of all humanity.

No one can separate himself from the meanest and most wretched of the earth. As soon as human beings utter the sacred sound of the AUM, yet harbour selfish thoughts and intentions, consolidating them and presuming to judge harshly a single being (let alone those who have played such sacrificial roles throughout eighteen million years), they are warped and self-condemned. They cannot hope to benefit at the moment of death from the regenerative compassion of the

Bodhisattvas. It is in blind ignorance that human beings perform these extraordinary antics, becoming mere mediumistic entities, collections of diseased and distorted life-atoms, brought together by a pathetic preoccupation with personal failure. The very idea is false. It is false at the very root. There can be no solace for the individual except in the context of universal enlightenment, universal progress and universal welfare. Any human being not threatened by the fact that other human souls exist, not disturbed by the fact that humanity is on the march, can receive help, but only in proportion under law and provided that he does not ask for any more than he deserves and not at the expense of any other being.

Thus, when the *Avataric* affirmation of Krishna is made and humanity is given its warning, this is done with a calm indifference to the opinions of individuals but with an unqualified insistence upon the simple proposition that the whole is greater than the part, that the tree is greater than the branch, that the mighty forest is greater than any individual tree. That eternal principle is the enduring basis of the custodianship of the sacred Mysteries amongst the Brotherhood of *Bodhisattvas*, who serve Krishna faithfully in ceaseless and effortless devotion, without let or hindrance, "without variableness or shadow of turning". This principle has been assiduously upheld without exception in every ancient nation and civilization of the earth, and it will not be forgotten in the future. The doors of the Mystery Temples must remain forever sealed, except to those whose Buddhic intuition resonates to the larger vision, the deeper purpose of all humanity.

> All ancient nations knew this. But though all had their Mysteries and their Hierophants, not all could be equally taught the great metaphysical doctrine; and while a few elect received such truths at their initiation, the masses were allowed to approach them with the greatest caution and only within the farthest limits of fact. "From the DIVINE ALL proceeded Amun, the Divine Wisdom...give it not to the unworthy," says a Book of Hermes. Paul, the *"wise Master-Builder,"* "but echoes Thoth-Hermes when telling the Corinthians "We speak Wisdom among them that are perfect (the initiated)...*divine* Wisdom in a MYSTERY, even the *hidden* Wisdom.
>
> H. P. Blavatsky

The golden tones of the humanity of the future have already begun to ring out around the globe, and have been greeted with gladness in the hearts of myriads of unknown human beings in every land. For those who have not yet felt it fully, or only intermittently within themselves, the problem is tunnel vision, an inability to see beyond and outside the narrow horizon of one's own myopic perception. This tunnel vision is a great obstacle to each and every one who wishes to come out of the multitude, especially in this extremely visual culture, descended from the peasants of the earth. In narrowness and instantaneity there is no basis for growth and enlightenment. The eyes and ears are proverbial liars. Rather, one must learn to use the eye of mind, to awaken the eye of the soul. Above all, in mystic meditation one must draw within one's own sanctuary in one's inmost heart, because only there can one come closer to the *Logos* in the Cosmos, closer to the living god in every man, woman and child on this earth. Many people are ready for this, now more than ever. But there are also, alas, some who are part of the sickness of the past.

Each human being, as a self-determining agent, is responsible for the opportunities and obstacles of his own making. Therefore, each must learn that to wish all human beings well means to hope that everyone may become a friend of the best in himself, may draw apart from the snake of separateness and the slime of selfishness, and emerge from the pit of ignorance, learning instead to use the senses and organs, and especially the sacred organ of the *Logos* called the tongue, on behalf of universal good. Yet, one cannot learn to affirm the authentic accents of human brotherhood all at once. Those who have made resolves to do so should not expect that they are abruptly going to become new people. At the same time, new beginnings are indeed possible.

All human beings know that they have had many opportunities to make some small difference to the quality of their life and consciousness. It is possible to make a much greater difference in the presence of the *Guru* and the Divine Wisdom, especially if one makes use of every opportunity, in the dawn and at twilight, at midday and perhaps even at midnight. Everyone can find some few moments during the day to devote himself to the sacred purpose of self-regeneration. That is the critical message of meta-psychology. And that is why the opportunity is given to various individuals, though they may be ignorant of the *ABCs* of the *Sanatana Dharma,* to do that which over a hundred years very few could do effectively, to study the *Gupta Vidya* – the Secret Doctrine – in a way that provides the basis for meditation. When the teachings are meditated upon daily, in conjunction with the use of *bija sutras* (*mantrams* given for the sake of creating a current that may be carried throughout the day), together with self-correction, hope is awakened. Regardless of the gravity effect from the past, individuals may make a new beginning; the more that beginning is made on behalf of all that lives, the more that beginning will become a holy resolve. It will be blessed by all the gods and guardians of the globe, and by the *Avatar* of the age.

This has nothing to do with nineteenth century rituals and Victorian habits, with slavish adherence to calendars and clocks. No one need labour under false burdens of expectation and regret bolstered by pseudo-psychological theories of human nature. These are but the rationalizations and residues of the failure of individuals to sort out their own lives, to see and acknowledge the nature of their obligations, needs and wants. Today, all over the globe, more courageous men and women than ever before are preparing themselves to become true learners and have already sensed and saluted in their hearts the coming of the *Avatar*. Seeing beyond roles and discerning the principles of meta-psychology within their own experience, by honest and voluntary work they are making their own modest but genuine contributions to the whole, thus inserting themselves into the humanity of the future and quietly unravelling the spiritual promise glimpsed in the vigil night of meditation.

The quintessential meaning of the contemporary revolution in human self-awareness is contained in the meta-psychological teachings that are the basis of *Buddhi Yoga*. The moral diversity human beings exhibit, ranging from pure compassion to abject selfishness, is to be understood in terms of the distinction between human individuality and its transitory mask, the personality. The tendency of the outward character is determined by the inward polarity of *Manas*. As H.P. Blavatsky explains:

> The mind is dual in its potentiality: it is physical and metaphysical. The higher part of the mind is connected with the

spiritual soul or Buddhi, the lower with the animal soul, the Kama principle. There are persons who never think with the higher faculties of their mind at all; those who do so are the minority and are thus, in a way, *beyond,* if not above, the average of human kind. These will think even upon ordinary matters on that *higher* plane.

H. P. Blavatsky

The faculty of the mind that predominates in any given lifetime is a function of all the past thoughts and feelings of the Monad in its varied incarnations over millions of years. The selection of the life-atoms that constitute the mortal vestures proceeds under strict law, rooted in the metaphysical unity beyond the cosmos and apportioning the elements to the vestures according to the individual's acknowledgement, or denial, of that unity. When, over a course of lives, an individual has neglected the development of the higher faculties of *Manas,* the noumenal potential of spiritual consciousness becomes obscured by the thick encrustation of life-atoms impressed with selfishness.

> This is why it is so very difficult for a materialist – the metaphysical portion of whose brain is almost atrophied – to raise himself, or for one who is naturally spiritually minded, to descend to the level of the matter-of-fact vulgar thought. Optimism and pessimism depend on it also in a large measure.

H. P. Blavatsky

If one's thinking is noetic, based upon that which is larger and more universal, and if, in this light, one considers calmly the lower and that which is lesser, one will be an optimistic person, glad that there are billions of human beings in the world, happy that children are being born, and above all, eager to greet the future. If, on the other hand, one is amongst those unfortunate people who have made pernicious alliances with the dark side of the moon, coming under its shadow through preoccupation with one's own shadow, one is *in extremis.* For such, no matter how many years of physical life may remain, it is, in fact, too late. At the moment of death, they will find that they have wasted their lives. Through meditation upon the shadow, through fascination with excreta, they have become afraid of the light. No one else has done this to them. They have excluded themselves from the school of human evolution and are unable to move onward with the awesome pilgrimage of humanity.

There are many such people in the world today, and, owing to their own selfishness, they are experiencing an extreme form of psychological terror. They, along with their inordinate selfishness, must and will disappear. Like *rakshasa* ghouls of the graveyard, they will make a great deal of noise before they are finished, but disappear they will because it is too late in Manasic evolution for abnormal selfishness. All human beings are, of course, concerned with survival and self-preservation to some degree, but there is a world of difference between this furtive selfishness and frenetic ego sickness. Ego sickness is abnormal selfishness; it has already created by the power of thought the very avenging demons which will destroy it. These *incubi* and *succubi* pursue the abnormally selfish in sleep and in waking life, all the time, until these dark monsters – created out of greed, out of fear of being wrong and making a fresh start, out of fear of the facts of spiritual life, out of exploitation of the patience and kindness, the generosity and magnanimity of others – surround their creator and close in for the kill.

This is no mere figure of speech, though it was graphically illustrated by Aldous Huxley in *The Devils of Loudon*. It is not merely a possibility, but a grave fact in the metaphysical realms of human existence beyond the veil of physical life. It is rooted in the capacity of Manasic thought-energy to disturb and impress the atoms of the astral light. Drawing from the science of optics, accessible in a crude form to her readers in the nineteenth century, H.P. Blavatsky explains:

> ...the rays of thought have the same potentiality for producing forms in the astral atmosphere as the sunrays have with regard to a lens. Every thought so evolved with energy from the brain, creates *nolens volens* a shape.
>
> H. P. Blavatsky

One may have the illusion of free will, but this production of astral forms through the power of thought proceeds involuntarily. In the case of an ordinary human being, both this form and the process of its formation are entirely unconscious. One simply does not know what one has done. By contrast, however, in the case of an Adept, who chooses each thought with a beneficent and well-directed motive, the mental emanation can be sent forth with enough of his will and intelligence to accomplish his purpose. The Adept needs no visible media, no complex computer or elaborate postal service. He can instantly transmit a thought over millions of miles. Thus, all Adepts are in immediate and effortless communication with each other, and Adepts in the Army of the Voice are able to take orders from their Chief, who transmits the will of the *Avatar* instantly to agents all over the globe, who thereby know what exactly they have to do.

Whilst this instant alertness to the Light of the *Logos* and the Voice of Vach will not be earned by humanity as a whole until future Rounds, the moment has come for men and women everywhere to choose between love of the Light and morbid slavery to shadows. The logic of Manasic evolution implies a division between forms fostered by astral attachment and vestures evolved through altruistic meditation. Each alternation of day and night, each cycle of birth, death and reincarnation, each pulse-beat and each breath taken is a living moment of choice, a link in the endless chain of potential spiritual growth. With every mental exhalation, one emanates into the common atmosphere either fresh blessings for all or the foul snares of one's future bondage. As the Monad's karma accumulates over the *aeons*, it does so amidst the vastly larger totals affecting the entire race, which are continuously adjusted by the *Lipikas* under the impersonal guidance of the laws of invisible Nature. It is the unwavering will of the *Logos* that every sentient atom of life shall realize its ultimate unity with the One Life, and become thereby an active centre of beneficent light-energy, consecrated to the law of sacrifice – the law of its own being.

Manasic humanity today is at a moment like the dawn of Venus, filled with the promise of a future wherein societies and civilizations founded upon the sacrificial love of wisdom will flourish. Every dawn dispels the shadows of the night; they are wise in their time who learn to love the light they cannot yet see in its fullness, whose harbinger they can recognize in the bright messenger of the dawn. In a few brief hours on the clock of human evolution, the Sun of Truth will arise for all who are courageous enough to turn towards the East, and mankind will rediscover itself. Having chosen the noetic light of *Buddhi* within, it will find itself in the company and service of the Servants of the *Logos*, and engaged in the compassionate travail of the true City of Man.

Hermes, March 1982

AQUARIAN CIVILIZATION

> *Our races ... have sprung from divine races, by whatever name they are called ... Every nation has either the seven and ten Rishis-Manus and Prajapatis ... One and all have been derived from the primitive Dhyan-Chohans of the Esoteric doctrine, or the "Builders" of the Stanzas. From Manu, Thot-Hermes, Oannes-Dagon, and Edris-Enoch, down to Plato and Panadores, all tell us of seven divine Dynasties, of seven Lemurian, and seven Atlantean divisions of the Earth; of the seven primitive and dual gods who descend from their celestial abode and reign on Earth, teaching mankind Astronomy, Architecture, and all the other sciences that have come down to us. These Beings appear first as "gods" and Creators; then they merge in nascent man, to finally emerge as "divine-Kings and Rulers." ... There were five Hermes – or rather one, who appeared – as some Manus and Rishis did in several different characters ... But under whichever of these characters, he is always credited with having transferred all the sciences from latent to active potency, i.e., with having been the first to teach magic to Egypt and to Greece, before the days of Magna Graecia, and when the Greeks were not even Hellenes.*
>
> The Secret Doctrine, ii 365-367

To take the entire subject of cosmic hierarchies at the human level to its sublime heights, one must start with the momentous recognition that many of the "gods" of the ancient theogonies belonged to the First Race of humanity. Human beings in that First Race were gods or *devas*, and in the Second Race they were demi-gods – celestial spirits still too ethereal to occupy the human form that was being gestated by the lunar *Pitris*. Then, in the Third Race, with the lighting-up of *Manas* and the incarnation of the *Manasaputras* into human form, humanity underwent an evolution which passed through several stages. Beginning with the androgynous and bisexual, it proceeded through the protracted dual-sexed epoch of the human race. There was the legendary era of great heroes and giants. The seven divine dynasties were thereafter to be found in the Third Race and again in the Fourth Race, the Lemurian and Atlantean periods. Instructing humanity in diverse arts and sciences, they laid the primeval foundations of human culture and civilization around the globe.

   Within this broad framework, the extraordinarily evocative power of the name and presence of Hermes is especially relevant to the 1975 Cycle and to the civilization of the future. Hermes is a generic name, associated with potent thought, and linked to Mercury-Buddha – a *Dhyani* – as well as with multiple incarnations in the history of humanity. As the god Hermes-Thot, he is the pristine archetype of Initiators in ancient Egypt, where he was revered as Hermes Trismegistus, a name applying to an entire lineage of Initiators. This solar line of spiritual Teachers can be traced back to Shiva as Dakshinamurti, the Initiator of Initiates. The hoary tradition which holds that Hermes taught all sciences to the nascent Mediterranean civilization suggests that he instructed those ready for divine theurgy. The arcane sciences transferred by Hermes from latent to active potency collectively constitute divine *gnosis*, a precise and comprehensive knowledge of the complex laws governing the seven kingdoms of nature. These laws encompass the planes of matter, both visible and invisible, the planes from which noumenal prototypes become precipitated or projected into the phenomenal realm. Science in its essence is concerned with primary causes and is rooted in a mature apprehension of noetic consciousness. This is the true and noble meaning of science, *vidya* in the old sense, which was mysteriously intimated by the *Mahatmas* to European civilization in the seventeenth and eighteenth centuries to counteract the corruption of creedal religion.

   Modern science is a recent flower, emerging sporadically after the Renaissance, and, in particular, after Giordano Bruno's activities in Germany and his historic visit to Oxford. The Royal Society was founded by heretical and courageous clergymen, men like the Warden of Wadham, who recognized that Aristotelian scholasticism was throttling the growth of human thought, that theology had become nothing more than a corrosive word-game. Together with bold patrons in the discreetly pagan aristocracy, these pioneering heretics founded a small club in London which they called the Royal Society. It was concerned from the beginning with the systematic support of all earnest experimental investigation into the natural world. In this, its purest sense, early modern science is one of the minor contributions of the Brotherhood of *Bodhisattvas* to the post-Renaissance world. Yet, in the context of the ancient meaning of science, it is a limited thing indeed, shadowy and modest. Originally, "science" referred to a system of laws capable of application by human consciousness to what later came to be cherished by a few reticent brotherhoods as true magic or divine wisdom. Magic is an exact and definite knowledge of the noumenal laws of invisible nature. Through the proper use of that carefully transmitted knowledge, one can affect the rates of growth and primary structures of energy on the Akashic and astral planes, and so affect conditions and combinations on the physical plane. Modern science, through its neglect of the primacy of consciousness, can hardly approach such a universal synthesis, fusing meta-geometry, meta-biology and meta-psychology.

In the ancient and archetypal view of noetic magic, there is a summoning from latency to active potency of arcane knowledge that was originally impressed in the imperishable soul-memory of all humanity. Going all the way back to the middle of the Third Root Race, when self-consciousness had been attained, human beings were in astral vestures that were capable of effortless and benevolent use of the spiritual senses. Human beings, therefore, through their intuitive knowledge of the correlations of sound, colour and number, were able to communicate effortlessly. In that Golden Age, shrouded in the myths and mists of antiquity, they showed spontaneous reverence to Magus-Teachers, Hierophant-Adepts moving openly among human beings, teaching in fabled "concord groves" all over the earth. Seated under banyan trees (varieties of *ficus religiosa*), they bestowed divine wisdom upon those who were ready to learn. In that idyllic time the vast human inheritance of spiritual wisdom and scientific magic was assimilated into the *karana sharira*, the permanent vesture of the Monad. It is in that inmost vesture, which is the container of all soul-memories, that the original wisdom and theurgy of humanity lie latent to this day.

It is suggestive and significant that contemporary physicists, like Roger Jones, have come to see that a great deal of what is known in particle physics and quantum mechanics points to a necessary transcendence of conventional space and time. This is strikingly reminiscent of the recondite concept of the *karana sharira*. A few intuitive scientists find the idea of such a causal field or morphogenetic matrix intensely meaningful because it intimates modes of action that are independent of many of the restrictions that hold in ordinary space and time. Because it allows for what would appear from a physical standpoint to be simultaneous transmission, it suggests the operation of laws very different from those applicable to the objective-seeming world of disparate material entities. Hence, it may have application or relevance to some of the energy fields and the "broken symmetry" that pertain to fundamental particles. Considered in relation to noetic consciousness and benevolent magic, the significance of the *karana sharira* is that it is the ground of the latent knowledge called to active potency by Hermes.

Hermes is the paradigm of the oldest sacred tradition, going back a million years ago to India *(Bharata Dwipa)*. There, among the Initiates, the basis was laid in all the Mystery Schools for the Manasic development of the seminal civilizations of the Fifth Race. When the most creative minds of the Aquarian Age gain a sufficient knowledge of Sanskrit, they will come to see that all latter-day sciences are but pale and poor fragments compared with the systematic ontology and epistemology of *Brahma Vidya, Theosophia* or *Dzyan*. With reference to astronomy, to physics, physiology and to chemistry, to the mathematical and geometrical sciences, even to mechanics, transmission devices and aerial transport, the lost knowledge of the ancients was overwhelming. Some of this knowledge, still accessible through scattered texts, is being slowly recovered today by remarkable young scholars like David Pingree, who has dedicated his life to the translation of available Sanskrit texts in astronomy. This is only one small field within a vast body of information, but by the end of the century many such texts should be accessible to those who can effectively use them.

The constructive use of such knowledge requires the timely initiation of a global Pythagorean Academy, so that at the right time those who have the requisite spiritual and intellectual qualifications will be able to participate in the highest level of path-breaking investigation. All of this harks back to that which was in the beginning, to that which was taught to sub-races such as the Egyptian and Greek by the mysterious Hermes-Thot – Hermes Trismegistus. Just as it was before the days of *Magna Graecia*, the work of Hermes is to summon from latency to activity the innate knowledge of benevolent magic inherent in the *karana sharira*.

The foreshortened view of the emergence and growth of civilization which has characterized the last two hundred years is rooted in a habit of mind extending back over a period of some two thousand years, but nonetheless a minor incident in human evolution. Historians tend to focus upon the material aspects of civilization and cultures, to become obsessed with power and violence; yet since a nation's spiritual decline accompanies its material ascent, such a truncated approach can only distort the truth and mislead the unwary. Any attempt to account for this messianic history of recent millennia must begin fundamentally with a recognition that many human souls were badly scarred in decadent Atlantis, and, having lost the Third Eye, were left merely with an external sense of power connected to a crude conception of energy which still mesmerizes them through awe of tangible bigness and gross strength.

This is reminiscent of Plato's memorable reference to the contest between the Gods and the Giants. Whilst such events go back far beyond even the declining period of Egyptian dynasties, it does not, after all, characterize the entire million-year history of the Fifth Root Race. Certainly, such a shrunken perspective does little or no justice to the more than eighteen million years of human existence on this globe, or to the immeasurable reservoir of soul-memories garnered in the earliest golden ages. Every major culture reflects, to some degree, these finest and persistent intuitions in human beings. That is what gives many people a kind of reverence, however confused, before the Native Americans and other so-called "primitive" peoples. Even if many of these cultures have lost their spiritual knowledge, and so have fallen to the mercy of inferior races, these same Monads may yet recover and re-enact their wisdom in future civilizations.

This process has recurred again and again. It was played out before the days of *Magna Graecia* in events that were encapsulated by Herodotus in his brief work, *Euterpe*. Therein he acknowledged the debt of gratitude that the Greeks owed to the grand Egyptian civilization which preceded it. This is even more explicit in Plato, who made Socrates speak of Solon, and the great Egyptian teachers of Sais, next to whom the Greeks were as little children. Yet whilst the reverence of Herodotus for predecessors was genuine, and expressed with almost religious awe, he also wrote that more familiar kind of historical narrative through which he is known as the "Father of History". In an often overlooked passage, he commended the Persians for their exemplary bravery and sense of truth, which, he said, were lacking among the Greeks. The courage to tell the truth and stand by it, the sense of the sacredness of a man's word of honour – these, he thought, were virtues that the Greeks could learn from the ancient Persians.

At the same time, however, Herodotus, in dealing with the Persian legal system, began to generate some of the snobbery that long prevailed among Athenians when they contemplated their *polis* and its democratic institutions. Through dramatized contrasts with the corrupt despotism of Persian institutions, Herodotus managed to compress, and devalue, the scope and successive phases of Persian civilization. In virtually every subsequent account of the supposed history of ancient civilizations, this same compression is found compounded. It arises because of decadence and the disappearance from active human memory of the greatest epochs of antiquity. This has led to the extraordinary and confusing conclusion that all the collective knowledge of the human race can somehow be made readily available to the common man. Some even insist that the less one knows, the more one has a right to demand all and sundry information.

This puny standpoint is seriously threatened by the fact that the seminal periods of human evolution are hidden and secret, and yet span millions of years which are inaccessible except through initiation. The profoundest truths were never written about in popular chronicles. They were available only in glyphs and symbols, in monuments, in secret libraries in central Asia and elsewhere. They were not for the eyes of curious crowds. In any event, even ordinary people in more mature cultures have a natural reticence about spiritual wisdom. Just as, in old age, those beset by a sense of failure, a fear of death and a feeling of audience deprivation seek refuge in reminiscence, so too cultures grow infatuated with telling their inflated history only after they have begun to decay. They become compulsively autobiographical, repeatedly retelling their life story. The truly creative, mindful of the enormous potency of mathematical and spiritual knowledge, are careful to protect that knowledge. They will make it available to those who can use it constructively; but they will keep it away from those who may abuse it, delude others and harm themselves.

Seen from this perspective, one can begin to appreciate the sense in which much of modern science is based upon the half-baked occult secrets of the semi-esoteric groups that persisted from the days of the early Church Fathers to the Renaissance. Whilst it may come as a surprise to post-colonial Europeans, it is still held by the Ashanti elders that had they been more careful with their accumulated wisdom, modern science and medicine could have avoided their premature and amoral growth. What such wise elders knew, and what was intuited by Pauwels and Bergier – the authors of *The Morning of the Magicians* – is that what is presently extolled as modern science is significantly based upon the scattered and leaked secrets of medieval and ancient classical knowledge.

The disappearance of alchemy and the authentic occult arts is inseparable from the karmic record of those souls who were not capable of handling theurgic teaching and practical knowledge in relation to the various secret sciences. But something of that tradition remained – in the Platonic Academy, which lasted for nine hundred years, among the early Muslims in Cordoba, and through them, among their pupils in Italy and France. At about the same time, out of small beginnings in a few houses the University of Oxford was born. All these communities struggled towards an understanding of the seven sciences – the *trivium* and *quadrivium*. Respect for these sciences is the origin of what were once sacred terms – bachelor of arts and master of arts. These were degrees going back to old initiations, carrying memories of earlier times. Then they became attached to universities which, since the twelfth century, have helped to bring knowledge to thousands of people who would otherwise have had no access to it. Until Wycliffe, for example, no one who was poor or ignorant of Latin could read the *Bible*.

This breaking down of the closed circle connected with knowledge in general, and sacred texts in particular, is not yet complete. It is thus a vital part of the present climactic Cycle: over the coming decades Sanskrit and Greek will be simplified and taught so that anyone may acquire them. Languages will be rescued from the grammarians. For so-called experts, who have never penetrated the inner meanings of ancient texts, nonetheless manage to discourage the spiritual enquirer from learning the language. At a certain level, this renaissance in ancient languages will be part of the Hermetic work of the 1975 Cycle.

To understand the work of Hermes at a more fundamental level in relation to civilization, one must begin to generate a conception of the cosmic hierarchies in Nature and in Man which unites the spiritual with the physical, and both of these with the moral and the political. This fundamental recognition of the relationship of the celestial and the terrestrial must be forged through a living link in the psychological realm. That link is Man. Only through the rediscovery within human nature of all orders of being from the gods to the elementals can there be a recovery of the continuity of the Great Chain of Being from the highest to the lowest. All hierarchies – from the *Dhyanis* through the *danavas* and *daityas*, to the *devas* or gods, the *devatas* and elementals – are represented within the individual human being. The five middle principles of human nature, leaving out of consideration the *Atman* and the physical body, are the direct gift and transmitted essence of the six-fold *Dhyani Buddhas*. That is why even *kama manas* is in essence sacred. It is lent to human beings to show them how to connect and how to discriminate.

If this is difficult to perceive, it is because all of these intermediate principles have been polluted, all have been abused on behalf of the shadowy self, of egotism and separatism. Human beings of the past, like little children in the present, showed an innate confidence that comes from knowing oneself as a ray of the Divine. They recognized themselves as immortal souls, centres of consciousness capable of expansion and contraction, of diffusion and concentration. Thus they could regard the body as an instrument, to be used by the soul as a horse by its rider. The mind is a necessary and useful tool of the soul, but it must be regularly cleansed. A person who senses this does not identify with his clothes in the spiritual and philosophical sense.

Instead, he is always turned inward through meditation, and upward through aspiration; he is forever rising heavenward towards the invisible cosmos. It becomes natural for him to start with the cosmic and come down to the human, to descend from *Hiranyagarbha* – the luminous golden egg of Brahmâ – to the recognition of one's own egg, from *Mahat,* or cosmic mind, to *Manas,* his small share in cosmic ideation. Descending from the universal to the particular is essential to the Hermetic method.

Modernity, by contrast, stands on its head, tries to move upward, and thus severs off the umbilical connection between man and cosmos. This approach, antithetical to the spiritual nature of man, had to be corrected by the Copernican revolution, which clarified the relation of the earth and the sun. But while the contemporaries of Copernicus thought they were discovering new truths, they were, in fact, only recovering the ancient laws of Pythagorean wisdom. If a sense of the right relationship of heaven and earth is to be restored, the sort of reorientation and recentering that has taken place in astronomy must take place psychologically and metaphysically. This can be attempted in many ways. Ordinary people could, for example, develop skill in consulting the *I-Ching.* They would not be able to use it for precise prediction, for that mysterious science requires a great deal of reverence. But by simply considering the *I-Ching,* they will be reminded that there are seasons, and continuous connections between heaven and earth.

A recognition of the correspondences between the celestial and terrestrial is the beginning of wisdom. The fear of God is not the beginning of wisdom. Wisdom is attainable only through love of the gods and recognition of their immanence within the human temple. The realization of human nature as a living psychological link between the celestial and the terrestrial will come about only through meditation and contemplation in the highest sense. Through the awakening of Buddhic feeling, one may feel close to the stars and to the galaxy. But one will also feel close to that which corresponds to *Akasha* within the astral brain and spiritual heart, and also within the *karana sharira.* Without this therapeutic and creative feeling, true learning and science can never progress. A few pioneers have recognized that for three centuries now science has been a mutilated victim of methodological dogmatism. This has led to a mechanistic reductionism, often trumpeted only because people are not good at mathematics. When they are lacking in mathematics in the highest sense, they become addicted to the habit of tinkering with jars and lamps. Owing to the delusion that has shadowed the diffusion of science, the tremendous integrity of the highest mathematical method has been inaccessible to the majority of practitioners, who have become like Shaw's barbarians. They resemble the civilized savage, who, upon switching on the light, thinks he knows about electricity.

Fortunately, this adolescent state of science is coming to an end. Yet although many people now recognize that science must deal with consciousness, most scientists are still encumbered by a philosophically narrow view of sense-data, sense-experience and inductive logic. As a result, pioneering researchers who want to elevate consciousness have difficulty in doing so. They must meditate, consult maps of consciousness, employ philosophical criteria, if they are to make any genuine progress. In the Aquarian academies of the future, they will have to submit themselves to certain rigorous tests. They will have to prove that they have the powers, not just of concentration, but also of directing consciousness towards universally constructive connections and correlations. This will involve both analogy and correspondence, intuition and mathematics; it will draw upon meta-sciences as yet only dimly formulated. In general, what is required is a conception of mind correlated with a conception of matter, both of which exist on many levels. Different planes of matter corresponding to different states of mind are richly interconnected with each other in different sets and subsets, systems and subsystems, as well as supersystems. All of this has application to the arrangement of atoms and molecules, but also to what lies beyond what are presently called atomic and subatomic particles. These are but ghostly shadows of the invisible atoms in which inheres the eternal motion of the *Atman* and which may be spoken of as the *Atma-Buddhi-Manas* of the atom.

Science will not truly advance unless it goes beyond the mere analysis of physical matter, the mundane tricks which for a while bewitched hordes of ex-peasants coming out of villages. It was advantageous to have a little vulgar technology in the age of the automobile, the steam-engine and the electric motor. It was comforting to share in a collective sense of automatic progress. But that time is over. The present aim must be to transcend the mere classification of matter which characterizes, for example, most of modern medicine, and instead to determine critical and relevant factors through theoretical and experiential knowledge of general and universal laws. This capacity must extend not only over the realm of physical phenomena, but also over psychological and moral life, and the social and political realms of human existence. Ultimately, this capacity will derive from strong foundations in spiritual self-awareness that can only be laid through a fundamental inner change. One might say this decisive change will require not merely framing the Hippocratic Oath but directly experiencing a reverence for life and truth. Early in the century such a spirit blessed the scientific academies of Germany, Switzerland and England.

Since 1914, however, much of this has been lost in the tumultuous rush after more technology and mere techniques. That is why the shining example of Mahatma Gandhi is so important to everyone who is authentically concerned with the disinterested pursuit of pure truth, while secure in its indifference to worldly concerns. The celestial was joined to the terrestrial in the West in certain monastic and intellectual communities, but since that connection was lost, to recover it requires something far more fundamental – a discriminating knowledge of metaphysics strong enough to broaden all one's categories and to deepen one's insights.

The radical regeneration of civilization and the restoration of a golden age can ultimately only be understood in relation to the descent of the gods. The golden age is eternally associated with Shiva Saturn and the hosts of the *Kumaras*, whilst its terrestrial incarnation is inseparable from the incarnation of divine dynasties and king-hierophants. Thus, Thot-Hermes was the secretary of King Saturn presiding over the pre-dynastic Golden Age. Plato, in the *Statesman*, speaks of the Golden Age as a time of universal well-being wherein all basic needs were fulfilled. This dream continually recurs in myth and literature, for example, in the vision of Gonzalo in *The Tempest*. But it is more than a dream. It is a recollection of reality. It refers not just to the Third Root Race, but also to certain recurring moments in human evolution. The time of Rama, a million years ago, was the last great

Golden Age. It was possible then for Divine Instructors to move openly among ordinary human beings. As kingship was sacred, rulers in that age could exemplify benevolent magic, exercising a just and compassionate custodianship over their close-knit communities. In the age of Shiva-Saturn, the cooperative hierarchies of human relationships mirrored the cosmic hierarchies of invisible nature.

However, as Plato recognized in the *Statesman*, once the Age of Zeus began, it was no longer possible for Divine Instructors to come openly into the world. Here Plato is referring to the beginning of *Kali Yuga* five thousand and eighty-four years ago. It is a familiar characteristic of the Iron Age that human beings must rely on rules to restrain their weaknesses and vices. But it is also well known that all rules can be manipulated and that in rule-governed systems oligarchy and inequality work continuously. The pervasive recognition that rule-governed societies are only dim reflections of some higher ideal is itself evidence that one cannot extinguish from the human heart an innate sense of devotion to true Teachers, *Gurus* and ethical leaders. One of the crucial contributions of the 1975 Cycle has been to awaken soul-memories in many peoples around the world. This had to be done before the beginning of the present Cycle, because no one can benefit from it until he or she has first been shown how to learn and to respect Teachers. Because all of this was significantly accomplished before 1975, many people are now more open and willing to function in environments that are precursors of the secular monasteries of the future, spiritual centres profoundly hospitable to learning and to oral instruction by true Teachers.

This was wisely anticipated by Damodar K. Mavalankar in the nineteenth century, who understood that the Theosophical Movement has essentially one object and no other. As a natural logician, Mavalankar knew that what he understood, others would also understand, namely, that if *Mahatmas* and Adepts can move freely among human beings, any one of them can solve myriads of persisting problems among myriads of responsive human beings. One need only open the door to the free movement of such enlightened beings. This could not have been attempted during the last Cycle; if anything it was retarded, first by ignorant misuse of the Teachings, and later by abject cowardice. The lifeless thought-forms, crippled images and paranoid vestiges of the old Cycle must be bypassed in the progressive initiation of the Aquarian *sanghas*, the academies and the lodges of the future. As this Pythagorean fusion attains fruition during the next century, there will around the globe be widespread hospitality to the wisdom and necessity of acceptance of the *Guruparampara* Chain. There will be a willingness to learn, which can draw upon the natural reciprocity and self-validating strength of the relationship between teacher and taught. Like a deep and loving relationship between a parent and a child, this cannot be manipulated by a third party. Its reciprocity arises within the unique context of a particular karmic field, and points to the timeless ideal of the *Guru-chela* relationship.

This universal Aquarian diffusion of the true ideal of spiritual science and lifelong learning will enable human beings to awaken a vibrant sense of universal justice, universal compassion and universal concord. It will enable people to learn anew how to think, how to speak and how to contribute fearlessly yet appropriately to the collective fund of human wisdom: how to evoke benevolent spirits. If one employs harsh words, or even gentle words in a harsh manner, one will attract negative elementals. These, over time, accumulate, blocking the capacity to question or to formulate truths. But, by purifying words, speech and the aura around words and by cleansing one's motivation, one's tone of voice and one's movements, one can reorient oneself and so draw finer elementals into one's sphere. Through this elevation of the orbit of one's consciousness, one may become more benevolent and more magnanimous, while at the same time learning to use potent knowledge with more deliberation, courage and compassion.

The regeneration of global civilization through such a tapping of the inward spiritual resources of humanity is the enigmatic Hermetic and Avataric function exemplified by Hermes-Thot. It is the sacred function central to every Mystery School in recorded and unrecorded history. It goes back directly to Dakshinamurti, the Initiator of Initiates, and it has never been absent from the earth. It has been self-evidently crucial when the beginnings of civilizations were laid in different parts of the world. To make it now a vital part of a universal outlook in the dawning Aquarian Age, where there is more freedom from competitiveness and more openness to universal truths, could lead to a new kind of soul-etiquette. Founded upon the principle of drawing the larger circle, there could be the elaboration of a new code of relationship between human beings which would be more hospitable to the profoundly paradigmatic teachings of the *Upanishad*, "Sit down near me and let me whisper in your ear." This is the ancient Platonic-Upanishadic method, born with the human race, perpetually nourishing it, and recognized by the noblest precursors of the Aquarian Age.

Hermes, December 1983

INDEX

A

abhidharma · 234
Absolute · 125, 132, 140, 150, 201, 202, 204, 205, 234
absolute values · 55, 67
Adibuddha · 234
Agnishwatha Pitris · 280
ahimsa · 1, 2, 9, 11, 12, 13, 14, 15, 16, 31, 45, 55, 56, 57, 66, 67, 69, 113, 116, 140, 174, 175, 179, 180, 181, 182, 193
ahimsa as a policy · 14
akincannayatana · 215
Alaya · 204, 299
Alayavijnana · 234
anahata · 98, 124
ananda · 95, 107
Ananda · 210, 228, 231, 233, 234
anarchy · 31, 38, 73
Anasakti · 13, 16, 27, 68, 72, 113
anasakti yoga · 27, 68, 72
Anatta · 224, 225
Anatta Lakkhana Sutta · 224
anekantavada · 3
antaskarana · 23
Anupadaka · 204, 211
aparigraha · 47, 87, 178
Aquarian Age · 296, 298, 313, 323
Arhant · 226, 234
Arjuna · 29, 97, 101, 103, 104, 105, 106, 107, 108, 198, 277
arupa dhyana · 215
arupa Pitris · 291
aruparaga · 218
Aryas · 259
asat · 259

ashram · 16, 22, 27, 50
Ashram Observances in Action · 50
Ashwattha tree · 216
atheist · 5, 119
Atlantis · 302, 314
Atma Vidya · 208, 290
Atman · 27, 29, 96, 108, 125, 127, 147, 176, 197, 234, 287, 290, 317, 320
attavada · 68, 217
attraction and repulsion · 105, 198, 218
AUM · 96, 101, 124, 302
Avatar · 30, 108, 205, 213, 272, 305, 308
avidya · 164, 171, 177, 197, 216, 218, 220, 227, 234, 257

B

B.P. Wadia · 296
Barhishad Pitris · 148, 283
Bhagavad Gita · 95, 118, 275
bhakti · 101, 105, 107, 108, 112, 118
bhikkhus · 211, 234
Bible · 117, 293, 317
Big Bang · 200
binding oath · 7
bodhi tree · 216, 234
bodhichitta · 23, 198
Bodhisattva · 122, 123, 128, 131, 132, 190, 234, 265, 267, 287
Bodhisattva ideal · 234
Bodhisattva Path · 234
Bodhisattvas · 96, 105, 130, 198, 234, 268, 288, 293, 303, 312
Bolshevism · 47, 50
bondage · 58, 65, 114, 214, 223, 308
boundless Duration · 199, 206, 208
Brahma Vak · 133, 204
Brahma Vidya · 208, 290, 313
Brahman · 168, 179, 204, 290
Buddha · 1, 3, 19, 23, 25, 100, 118, 120, 128, 140, 146, 174, 176, 181, 190, 192, 196, 209, 210, 211, 212, 215, 216, 217, 220, 221, 222, 223, 224, 225, 226, 227, 228, 229, 230, 231, 233, 234, 237, 252, 253, 254, 255, 256, 257, 258, 259, 260, 261, 262, 263,266, 267, 268, 269, 277, 288, 293, 297, 301, 311

Buddha families · 234
Buddhahood · 224, 262, 267
Buddhas · 1, iii, 96, 105, 122, 132, 191, 198, 234, 288, 317
Buddha's Word · 234, 255
Buddhavachana · 234, 237, 254, 256, 262
Buddhi · 28, 94, 95, 97, 99, 101, 102, 103, 104, 105, 107, 108, 124, 125, 126, 127, 128, 131, 136, 137, 147, 148, 149, 207, 287, 306, 309, 320
Buddhi Yoga · 1, ii, iii, 9, 28, 94, 95, 97, 99, 101, 102, 103, 104, 105, 107, 108, 306

C

calm assurance · 221
capitalist system · 46
ceaseless contemplation · 105, 107, 271
charity · 13, 150, 157, 172, 173, 191, 234, 267, 293
charkha · 68
chattari ariya sachchani · 220
Chitta · 234
chittashuddhi · 106
Christ · 19, 25, 27, 120, 145, 174, 210, 271, 297
Christos · 271
civil disobedience · 61
civil resistance · 59, 60
class war · 52
Collection of Shorter Texts · 256
collective welfare · 70, 190
common good · 6, 39, 62, 90
communism · 19, 44, 45, 46, 48, 49, 50, 51, 52, 72, 82, 114, 178, 190
Communist Manifesto · 45
communists · 30, 33, 38, 40, 48, 51
compassion · 25, 26, 73, 95, 96, 121, 147, 148, 149, 164, 174, 190, 191, 193, 213, 224, 234, 260, 297, 303, 306, 322
conatus · 98, 99
conceit · 218
concentration of wealth · 70
concord · 9, 19, 69, 232, 257, 312, 322
conditioned Time · 199
Conscience · 8

Constructive Programme · 27, 31, 32, 33, 34, 36, 40, 62, 68, 72
continence · 16
Copernican revolution · 318
cosmic hierarchies · 310, 317, 321
cosmic interdependence · 2
cosmic order · 8, 11
courage · 77, 162

D

Dakshinamurti · 311, 323
Dalai Lama · 184, 185, 186, 188, 189, 190, 193, 195, 293
dana · 234
daridranarayan · 72
Dark Age · 234
Darwinian theory of evolution · 188
deep peace · 221
Dependent Origination · 226
determinism · 186
Devadatta · 229
devotion · 95, 97, 103, 105, 107, 108, 118, 150, 168, 174, 179, 199, 234, 261, 271, 274, 275, 277, 293, 303, 321
Dhammapada · 2, 209, 210, 229, 234, 252, 253, 254, 255, 262
dharma · 6, 8, 16, 28, 37, 47, 68, 70, 107, 119, 286
Dharma · 6, 145, 222, 227, 228, 229, 231, 233, 234, 252, 256, 257, 258, 259, 260, 262, 305
Dharmadhatu · 234
Dharmaguptakas · 234
Dharmakaya · 234
Dharmas · 234
Dhritarashtra · 276
dhyana · 105, 107, 234, 252, 275, 290
Dhyani · 122, 123, 234, 287, 311, 317
Dhyani Buddhas · 234
Dhyanis · 7

96, 106, 291, 317
Diamond Soul · 143, 209, 260, 297
Diamond Sutra · 234, 264, 265, 266, 267, 268, 269

dispassion · 106
Divine Darkness · 96, 129, 131, 133, 200
divine dialectic · 100, 108
Divine discontent · 6
Divine Eye · 220
Divine Instructors · 321
Divine Triad · 266
divine truth · 9
divya chakshu · 220
Dnyaneshwar · 28
Doctrine of Dependent Origination · 226
Doctrine of No-Self · 224
duhkha · 213, 216, 222
duragraha · 60
Duryodhana · 276

E

egotism · 4, 12, 94, 123, 129, 147, 176, 264, 276, 318
Eightfold Path to Enlightenment · 234
ekagrata · 234
emancipation · 5, 6, 94, 113, 120, 182, 210, 217, 220, 221, 234
Emperor Ashoka · 234
enlightened anarchy · 116
enlightenment · 4, 23, 94, 97, 122, 134, 164, 197-198, 205, 262, 287, 293, 303, 304
Enlightenment · 1-3, 184, 209, 210, 214-224, 231-234, 252, 258, 259, 260, 268
Eternal Doctrine · 2, 210
ethical order · 7
ethical principles · 2, 5, 252
Ethical Religion · 5
exclusive ownership · 19
exploitation · 5, 19, 65, 67, 70, 71, 76, 81, 307

F

faith · 1, 4, 6, 12, 14, 18, 25, 30, 35, 40, 42, 49, 55, 69, 79, 80, 83, 95, 110, 111, 112, 120, 121, 145, 157, 173, 184, 185, 192, 196, 218, 252, 256, 261, 271

fatalism · ii, 104, 186, 187, 260
fear of death · 58, 65, 316
fearlessness · 11, 16, 58, 65
Fifth Impulsion · 294
Fifth Race · 313
Fifth Root Race · 282, 314
First Council · 234, 255
First Noble Truth · 222
First Race · 310
Four Noble Truths · 220, 222, 223, 224, 225, 228, 230, 234
Fourth Council · 234
Fourth Noble Truth · 223

G

Giordano Bruno · 294, 311
Gita · 22, 25, 27, 28, 29, 68, 96, 97, 101, 102, 103, 104, 106, 108, 118, 120, 150, 174, 176, 198, 255, 266, 268, 272, 275, 277
glasnost · 21
Gnana · 204
God is Love · 10
God is Truth · 10, 25
Golden Age · 66, 142, 234, 289, 312, 321
golden egg of Brahmâ · 207, 318
Golden Rule · 19
Great Order · 234
greatest good of the greatest number · 70
greed · 5, 71, 76, 77, 93, 94, 114, 117, 159, 165, 169, 307
grihastha ashrama · 100
Guru · 271, 291, 296, 297, 305, 322
guru-chela relationship · 234
Guruparampara · 234, 322

H

hate · ii, 150, 218
Heart Doctrine · 274, 291
Heart Sutra · 234

Helena Petrovna Blavatsky · 26, 294
Henry Drummond · 26, 27, 28
heroic ideal · 9, 191
heroism · 9, 11, 14
Heroism · 9
higher carelessness · 266, 269
higher patience · 269
Higher Self · 266, 269, 275, 284
Himalayan blunders · 22
himsa · 12, 117, 169, 174
Hinayana · 106, 225, 234
Hiranyagarbha · 207, 318
Hitler · 14
hostility · 4, 13, 55, 218
human dignity · 3, 9, 78, 98, 175, 294
human interdependence · 88, 145
human perfectibility · 3, 25, 40, 46, 55
humility · 9, 10, 11, 24, 101, 120, 180, 189, 192

I

I-Ching · 318
ideal community · 90
Indian National Congress · 48
individuation · 7, 93, 126, 129, 167, 180, 234, 288
injustice · 12, 31, 45, 49, 55, 59, 61, 103
inner voice · 9, 25, 111, 112
intellect · 1, 4, 12, 29, 98, 145, 279
Ishvara · 96, 100, 107

J

Jacob · 18, 19, 20, 21, 23, 294
Jacob's ladder · 19
Jataka · 212, 256
Jivanmukta · 29, 287, 288
jnana · 101, 107, 234
Jnana Yoga · 104

justice · 49, 56, 71, 116, 157, 196, 296, 314, 322

K

Kala · 206
Kali Yuga · 25, 26, 99, 106, 108, 144, 297, 321
kamaraga · 218
Kant · 11, 173, 187
karana sharira · 96, 98, 312, 313, 314, 319
karma · 1, 9, 20, 22, 26, 107, 111, 117, 213, 230, 234, 260, 261, 262, 272, 275, 281, 282, 285, 286, 287, 290, 300, 301, 308
Karma · 30, 44, 92, 97, 101, 115, 220, 225, 226, 259, 260, 266, 269, 273, 300
Karma Yoga · 287
karma yogin · ii, 1, 20, 22, 26, 111
karuna · 213
Khandakala · 206
Khuddaka Nikaya · 256
Kingdom of God · 25, 187
Krishna · 27, 28, 29, 95, 96, 97, 99, 101, 103, 105, 106, 107, 108, 146, 198, 213, 268, 271, 272, 273, 274, 275, 276, 277, 297, 300, 301, 303
kshanti · 234
Kumarajiva · 264
Kurukshetra · 29

L

Lankavatara Sutra · 234
liberation · 6
Light of the Logos · 100, 102, 107, 108, 308
limits to growth · 82
linga sharira · 98, 102, 103
Logos · 20, 106, 107, 108, 144, 145, 150, 204, 271, 273, 274, 277, 301, 304, 309
Logos in the Cosmos · 304
lokadhatu · 234
lokasangraha · 6, 28
Love · 1, 10, 18, 26, 137, 145, 148, 149, 150, 156
lunar *Pitris* · 310

M

Madhyamika · 204, 234
*Madhyamika*s · 204, 234
Magic · 312
Magus-Teachers · 312
Maha Parinibbana Sutta · 234
Maha Pralaya · 202
Mahabharata · 103, 260, 276
Mahamaya · 106
Maha-Prajnaparamita · 264
Mahasanghika · 234
Mahasanghikas · 234
Mahat · 102, 129, 199, 202, 203, 204, 206, 207, 265, 299, 318
Mahatma · 1, 3, 1, 14, 18, 24, 28, 30, 31, 32, 38, 41, 42, 44, 45, 55, 57, 60, 65, 75, 85, 89, 94, 110, 111, 112, 115, 121, 183, 265, 272, 286, 287, 320
Mahatma Gandhi · 1, 3, 1, 14, 18, 24, 30, 31, 32, 38, 41, 44, 45, 55, 57, 60, 65, 75, 85, 89, 94, 111, 115, 121, 183, 272, 286, 320
Mahatmas · 95, 96, 108, 126, 283, 288, 293, 294, 295, 311, 322
Mahayana school · 23, 106, 204, 234, 252, 264
Maitreya · 234
mana · 218
Manas · 99, 123, 126, 127, 129, 136, 137, 147, 148, 149, 234, 279, 280, 286, 287, 291, 293, 306, 310, 318, 320
Manasaputras · 310
Manichaean · 1
Manjushri · 234
manovijnana · 234
Mara · 216, 217
Marx · 34, 37, 38, 45, 46, 72
Masters of Wisdom · 267
Maudgalyayana · 228, 229, 230
maya · 96, 139, 197, 198, 200, 205, 211, 221, 233, 254, 296
meditation · 1, 22, 24, 96, 104, 113, 128, 133, 197, 199, 202, 203, 205, 206, 207, 208, 214, 216, 217, 222, 224, 234, 252, 258, 261, 265, 271, 272, 273, 274, 275, 288, 290, 291, 304, 305, 307, 308, 318, 319
metaphysics · 120, 128, 132, 190, 201, 205, 234, 291, 321
microcosm of the macrocosm · 46, 135
Middle Way · 215, 223, 234, 257

Mikhail Gorbachev · 21, 22
Mohandas Karamchand Gandhi · 22, 24, 110
moksha · 5, 6, 65, 113, 128, 182
Monad · 124, 302, 306, 308, 312
moral asceticism · 87
moral authority · 59, 62, 72
moral conduct · 20
moral confusion · 56
moral courage · 15, 58, 77, 299
moral growth · 3, 175
moral heroism · 86
Moral Law · 115
moral stature · 7, 11, 83
moral welfare · 114
Mulaprakriti · 122, 124, 125, 128, 131, 199, 200, 201, 202, 203, 204, 206

N

Nagarjuna · 234, 264
namarupa · 128, 227, 234
namtar · 210
nation-state · 64
nevasanna nasannayatana · 215
New Jerusalem · 29
1975 Cycle · 298, 311, 317, 321
nirguna · 202
Nirguna Brahman · 202, 203, 204
Nirmanakaya · 234
nirodha · 223
Nirvana · 220, 223, 226, 231, 234, 262, 266, 269
nischaya · 98
Noble Eightfold Path · 223, 230, 234, 254, 256, 259
non-compliance · 61
non-possession · 16, 47, 50, 71, 72, 86, 87, 178
non-resistance · 41, 59
non-retaliation · 59, 193
non-violence · 6, 10, 11, 12, 13, 15, 37, 38, 50, 51, 52, 62, 67, 68, 77, 79, 83, 120, 121, 171, 174, 175, 178, 179, 180, 181, 193, 223
non-violent army · 15

non-violent non-cooperation · 82
non-violent resistance · 31, 32, 34, 55, 56, 57, 59
non-violent social reformation · 54
non-violent socialism · 72
non-violent socialist State · 81

O

obligations · 27, 70, 71, 100, 104, 266, 282, 288, 305
optimism · 5, 173
original sin · 83, 155, 164

P

pada · 154, 253
Padhana Sutta · 216
panchayats · 68
Pandavas · 29
Parabrahm · 124, 125, 199, 201, 204, 206, 208
Paramartha · 136, 137, 204
paramita Path · 234
paramitas · 216, 234, 252
paravritti · 234
Parinirvana · 211, 221, 225, 232, 233, 234, 255
parivrajakas · 100
patigha · 218
perestroika · 21
perfectibility · 38, 83, 90
perfection · ii, iii, 3, 105, 119, 142, 197, 234, 280, 284, 285, 302
Perfection of Transcendental Wisdom · 264
personal deity · 10
pitris · 277
Plato · 2, 10, 133, 135, 153, 162, 168, 171-174, 178, 284, 297, 310, 314, 315, 321
Platonic Academy · 316
possessiveness · 76, 94
poverty · 21, 68, 70, 71, 82, 83, 99, 115, 117, 165
power of a vow · 8, 106
prajna · 213, 224, 234

Prajnaparamita Sutras · 234
Prakriti · 199, 204
Pralaya · 122, 199, 206, 207
pranidhana · 234
Pratyeka Buddha · 234
praxis · 20, 209, 234
pre-cosmic Ideation · 201, 203
primordial unity · 2
Pudgalavadins · 234
pure joy · 221
pure subjectivity · 201
purification · 4, 11, 12, 13, 16, 62, 65, 67, 106, 210, 234, 269, 280
Pythagorean Academy · 314

Q

quadrivium · 317

R

Rajchandra · 22, 27
Ramarajya · 25, 26, 66, 69
Renaissance · 151, 161, 165, 311, 316
renunciation · 12, 16, 48, 75, 76, 90, 93, 113, 190, 191, 192, 212, 214, 261
restlessness · 46, 149, 167, 176, 218
Reverence for Buddha · 260
revolution · 33, 34, 35, 40, 52, 54, 229, 294, 299, 302, 305
Right action · 223
Right effort · 224
Right livelihood · 223
Right meditation · 224
Right speech · 223
Right thought · 223
rights · 3, 19, 31, 70, 76, 119, 153, 185
Rishis · 95, 96, 108, 310
Rita · 19, 71, 234
rupa · 133, 225, 234
ruparaga · 218

S

sacrifice · 7, 11, 19, 28, 32, 35, 39, 40, 48, 72, 93, 94, 101, 105, 120, 123, 149, 214, 234, 273, 309
sacrificial action · 72, 94, 113
samadhi · 224
Sambhogakaya · 234
samma sambuddha · 222
Sammitiyas · 234
Samsara · iii, 217, 226, 227, 234, 257, 266
Sanatana Dharma · 210
Sangha · 2, 23, 224, 227, 228, 229, 231, 233, 234, 255, 258, 259, 260, 262
sangiti · 233, 234
sanjna · 225
sannyasa · 26
sanskara · 225
Sanskrit · 8, 153, 154, 158, 159, 160, 234, 253, 264, 275, 279, 313, 317
Sanyutta Nikaya · 234, 252
Sarvastivadins · 234
sarvodaya · 19, 28, 31, 41, 45, 55, 69, 70, 71, 72, 73, 180
Sarvodaya · 1, 38, 69, 70, 71, 72, 73
sat · 3, 10, 56, 216, 272
Sat · 1, 42, 122, 131, 137, 174, 179, 259
SAT · 1, 18, 25, 122, 133, 135, 136, 137, 140, 143, 197
Sattva · 1, 122, 124, 125, 129, 131
satya · 1, 3, 15, 31, 45, 55, 56, 57, 66, 67, 68, 69, 113, 135, 140, 153, 174, 175, 182
Satya · 2, 122, 137, 140, 182
satyagraha · 31, 35, 41, 45, 49, 55, 57, 58, 60, 61, 62, 63, 69, 113, 116
Satyagraha · 1, 55, 56, 57, 58, 59
satyagrahi · 49, 56, 57, 58, 59, 60, 65, 68, 116, 180
satyayugakari · 26
Second Council · 234
Second Impulsion · 294
Second Noble Truth · 222
seed of enlightenment · 198
self-attenuation · 103
self-chosen vows · 113
self-conquest · 6, 28, 110

self-correction · 5, 69, 122, 173, 286, 291, 305
Self-discipline · 7
self-examination · 5, 11, 23, 69, 86, 262
self-governed Sage · 22, 28
self-government · 64, 166
self-honesty · 87
self-hood · 16, 125, 131, 268, 280-283, 285-290, 291
self-indulgence · 3, 215, 223, 261
self-initiation · 210
selfless service · 4, 26, 28, 68, 113
self-purification · 67, 234
self-realization · 6, 65, 114, 199, 265
self-reform · 8
self-regeneration · 18, 28, 117, 122, 199, 305
self-reliance · 2, 16, 39, 65, 66, 67, 170, 179
self-restraint · 7, 65
self-rule · 30, 57, 62, 63, 64, 65, 67
self-sacrifice · 7, 122, 182
self-transcendence · 1, 8, 77, 78, 94, 106, 175
self-transformation · 48, 68, 175, 209, 261
Seven Century Plan · 293, 294, 296, 297
Shankaracharya · 173, 208, 272, 293
Shantideva · 234, 261
Shariputra · 228, 229, 230
shila · 224, 234
shunyata · 23, 220, 234
Siddhartha · 25, 211, 212, 213, 228, 229, 234
Silabbataparamasa · 218
Sixth Impulsion · 294
skandhas · 99, 225, 226, 234
social conscience · 9
social order · 3, 45, 54, 72, 79, 80, 82, 185, 229
social reform · 27, 33, 34, 36, 37, 38, 39, 52, 54, 55, 56, 63
social revolution · 34, 52, 75
social transformation · 37, 38, 40, 56, 63, 69, 78, 110
socialism · 19, 25, 27, 28, 36, 44, 45, 48, 49, 50, 52, 69, 72, 75
Socialism · 1
socialists · 30, 33, 34, 36, 38, 40, 41, 48, 51, 81, 83
solidarity · 10, 19, 26, 30, 78, 94, 120, 302

Solomon's Temple · 26
soul-education · 104
soul-force · 11, 13, 58, 116
soul-growth · 114
soulless system · 114
speech control · 88
spinning wheel · 68
spiritual dignity · 11
spiritual heart · 98, 100, 103, 319
spiritual rebirth · 67
spiritual regeneration · 114
spiritual resolve · 8
Stanzas of Dzyan · 202, 279
state socialism · 82
stateless society · 73
stewardship · 39
Sthaviras · 234
sthula sharira · 98, 102
suffering · 1, ii, 4, 7, 22, 23, 24, 28, 56-60, 70, 95, 146, 182, 192, 193, 213, 216, 221-223, 227, 232, 234, 257, 262, 285, 293
supreme bliss · 221
sushupti · 98, 131
sutras · 234, 254, 305
svadharma · ii, 1, 27, 72, 94, 97, 101, 104-108
svasamvedana · 23
swadeshi · 16, 41, 65, 66, 67, 68, 179
swaraj · 1, 30, 42, 57, 63-69, 115, 179, 182

T

tanha · 12, 198, 223, 225, 227, 257, 262
tapas · 1, 4, 7, 9, 16, 22, 23, 29, 87, 105, 182
tapascharya · 9, 113, 118
tapasya · 182
Tathagata · 210, 226, 231, 234, 258, 267, 268
Tathagatagarbha · 226, 234, 260
tejas · 102, 103
Tenzin Gyatso · 293
The Key to Theosophy · 26, 139, 142, 145

The Light of Asia · 209, 217
The Secret Doctrine · 2, 122, 135-148, 197, 199, 204, 279, 283, 295, 310
The Voice of the Silence · 2, 143, 149, 217, 221, 233, 263, 264
The Way of Virtue · 253
Theophilanthropists · 42
theoria · 20, 209, 234
Theosophia · 204, 313
therapeia · 209
Therapeutae · 28
Theravada · 234
Theravadin · 234, 252
Third Council · 234
Third Eye · 314
Third Noble Truth · 223
Third Race · 310
Third Root Race · 280, 312, 321
thoughtlessness · 8
Tibetan view of religion · 189
total renunciation · 87
Tree of Life · 21
trikaya · 234, 260
triple criteria of holistic socialism · 52
Triple Gem · 224, 227, 261, 262
triratna · 224
trishna · 223, 227, 234
Trishna · 234
trivium · 317
trusteeship · 19, 28, 32, 39, 54, 71, 76, 77, 79, 81, 82, 84, 85, 86, 87, 89, 90, 91, 92, 94, 178
truth · 1, 2, 3, 5, 6, 10, 11, 13, 15, 16, 22, 45, 49, 55, 58, 60, 62, 64, 67, 68, 70, 71, 73, 78, 95, 101, 106, 113, 114, 118, 120, 135, 136, 137, 138, 139, 140, 141, 142, 144, 153, 157, 171, 174, 175, 179, 180, 184, 190, 193, 196, 197, 202, 211, 214, 215, 216, 223, 234, 256, 259, 264, 267, 286, 298, 300, 314, 315, 320
Truth · 1, 3, 4, 6, 9, 10, 13, 18, 25, 26, 42, 112, 113, 116, 117, 118, 119, 135, 136, 137, 138, 139, 140, 141, 142, 150, 171, 174, 182, 190, 192, 193, 197, 220, 234, 266, 268, 302, 309
truth and non-violence · 1, 2, 45, 55, 62, 70, 71, 118, 175, 176, 286
Truth is God · 10, 113
truth-force · 11, 55, 64, 73

U

U.L.T. · 296
Udanavarga · 2, 234, 252, 253, 254, 255, 263
uddhachcha · 218
ultimate values · 6
unconditioned Consciousness · 199
United Lodge of Theosophists · 296
universal interdependence · 19
universal self-consciousness · 23, 129, 202, 204, 205
universal welfare · 55, 73, 82, 94, 180, 303
University of Oxford · 316
unqualified resolve · 87
unshakeable resolution · 234
unsullied by ageing · 221
untouched by death · 221
Upali · 233, 234
Upanishads · 204, 323
upaya · 234

V

vairagya · 28, 106, 119
Vajrachchedika · 234
Vajrachedika · 264
Vajrayana · 234
varnashankar · 99
vedana · 225, 227
Vedanta · 203, 205
vichikichcha · 217
vijnana · 225, 227
vijnanas · 234
vinaya · 229, 232, 233, 234
violence · 11, 12, 13, 14, 15, 19, 24, 33, 45, 46, 47, 48, 50, 57, 59, 60, 61, 72, 73, 76, 77, 78, 79, 83, 84, 115, 117, 119, 139, 144, 152, 161, 164, 166, 168, 171, 172, 174, 175, 176, 177, 178, 180, 181, 190, 259, 260, 314
virya · 179, 234
viveka · 28

voluntary sacrifice · 94
vows · 7, 8, 9, 16, 50, 87, 108, 119, 120, 128
vrata · 8

W

war and peace · 14
wholeheartedness · 87
Wilfulness · 8
William Quan Judge · 272, 295
William Salter · 5, 26
willingness to kill · 12
Wisdom-Religion · 203, 208, 293, 295

Y

yajna · 11, 19, 28, 39, 72, 94
yama · 8
yoga · 9, 28, 96, 97, 102, 105, 118, 265
Yogachara · 204, 234